ITALY
TRAVELBOOK™

THIRD EDITION

AAA

President & CEO: Robert Darbelnet
*Executive Vice President, Publishing &
   Administration:* Rick Rinner
Managing Director, Travel Information: Bob
   Hopkins

Director, Product Development: Bill Wood
Director, Sales & Marketing: John Coerper
Director, Purchasing & Corporate Services:
   Becky Barrett
Director, Business Development: Gary Sisco
*Director, Tourism Information Development
   (TID):* Michael Petrone
Director, Travel Information: Jeff
   Zimmerman
Director, Publishing Operations: Susan Sears
Director, GIS/Cartography: Jan Coyne
*Director, Publishing/GIS Systems &
   Development:* Ramin Kalhor

Marketing Manager: Bart Peluso
Managing Editor, Product Development:
   Margaret Cavanaugh
Development Editor: Suzanne Lemon

AAA Travel Store & e-store Manager: Sharon
   Edwards

Manager, Product Support: Linda Indolfi
Manager, Electronic Media Design: Mike
   McCrary

Published by AAA Publishing, 1000 AAA
Drive, Heathrow, Florida 32746

The *AAA Italy TravelBook* was created and
produced for AAA Publishing by
Automobile Association Developments
Limited, Fanum House, Basing View,
Basingstoke, Hampshire, RG21 4EA,
England.

Written by Sally Roy
Managing Editor: Sheila Hawkins
Third edition verified by Tim Jepson
Page make-up by Keenes

Cover photos
Main photo: Sicily, Italy
© Sime/eStock Photo
Spine: Liguria, Italy
© Sime/eStock Photo

ISBN-13: 978-1-59508 104-9
ISBN-10: 1-59508 104-6

Cataloging-in-Publication Data is on file
with the Library of Congress.

Color separations by Leo Reprographic
Ltd., Hong Kong

Printed in Dubai by Oriental Press

A02491

Carnival time in Venice

FOREWORD

Welcome to the AAA Italy TravelBook!

If you're planning an Italian vacation, this book will help you discover the real Italy. We've selected not only the great cities, but the best of the towns and stunning countryside that will give a true taste of the diversity of this beautiful nation. You'll experience historic city centers packed with world-class sights and museums, and some of Europe's most beguiling small towns and villages. Discover the glories of Rome, Italy's capital; enjoy the unsurpassed artistic treasures of Florence; and delight in the unique beauty of Venice, a city built on water. You'll find there's more to dynamic Milan than industry and designer-name shopping, while the vibrant southern cities of Naples and Sicily's capital, Palermo, offer an intriguing contrast to the well-ordered northern centers.

Outside the cities there's a varied and welcoming country, the beauty of its landscape offering the perfect backdrop for urbanity and culture. Northern Italy butts up to the ragged peaks of the Alps; the glorious Italian lakes give way to the dramatic scenery of the Dolomites; and the Apennines – Italy's "backbone" – extend southward almost the entire length of the peninsula. You'll find bustling ports like Genoa, cities of art such as Siena, and sun-and-sand resorts like Rimini. We've also included some of Italy's prettiest small towns and villages, enabling you to put together a varied as well as a memorable trip, while suggested walks and drives will help you get the most out of your Italian experience.

Dip into this book to get your initial taste from the informative text and evocative photographs, then use it for more solid planning. There's practical information to smooth your way, from tips on getting around to suggestions on where to stay. We've included maps to help you find your way, ideas for eating, drinking and shopping, and descriptions of what to see. The insider advice offered by our specialist author will help you get the most out of enchanting Italy.

ITALY TRAVELBOOK™

CONTENTS

Contents

One of the graceful statues that
adorn Piazza della Signoria in
Florence

INTRODUCTION TO ITALY

"A COUNTRY whose beauty and art are more than matched by its people's charm and style is rich and blessed indeed."

Fishing boats drawn up at Sorrento, on the lovely coast south of Naples

Introduction to Italy

HUNGARY

CROATIA

BOSNIA
HERZEGOVINA

SERBIA & MONTENEGRO

SEA

argano • Vieste
San Severo
E55
Foggia Barletta
E842 Molfetta
Bari
Melfi Altamura Ostuni
lerno
Potenza Matera Brindisi
3 E45 Táranto Lecce
Lido di
Lagonegro Metaponto Gallipoli
Golfo
di Táranto
Castrovillari Marina
di Leuca
Rossano
Cosenza Crotone
Niacastró Catanzaro
Palmi A3
Messina IONIAN
0 SEA
A18 Réggio di Calábria
Taormina

Catánia **ITALY** N↑

Siracusa
0 50 100 150 200 km
Noto
0 50 100 miles

ALBANIA

A14

ITALY

Beautiful Italy (*bell' Italia*) has much to offer – varied and lovely scenery, a treasure trove of art, history and culture, and a population that truly understands the value of enjoying life. An Italian vacation means different things to different people, and therein lies its magic. Whether you're looking for heady days in the great outdoors, beaches to laze on, stunning art and culture, stylish cities, prosperous towns or picturesque villages, you'll find it here. You'll also find warm and sincere people, delicious food, splendid wine and a relaxed way of life that will enchant you. Whether you're here by chance or design, whether this is your first visit or your fiftieth, Italy will live up to your expectations and leave you ready for more.

Introduction to Italy

Italians have a great sense of style

Above: Clear waters lap a cove on the Monte Argentario peninsula

Right: Tuscany's tiny Renaissance town of Pienza

The Shape of the Land

From top to toe, Italy is scenically heart-stopping, with contrasting landscapes of varied beauty. The great Alpine massifs of the north, snow-capped even in summer, give way to mist-laden plains and to a rolling, fertile heartland, the classic landscape of grape and olive, and the dry and desolate beauty of the sun-baked south.

Italy's long coastline snakes around the country, encompassing everything from misty lagoons to pine-clad white cliffs to curving golden sands, all fringed with azure and turquoise waters. The country is predominantly mountainous, with the northern Alps and Dolomites (Dolomiti) forming a natural barrier with Italy's neighbors.

The long spine of the Apennines (Appennini) runs almost the whole way down the country, in some areas stretching virtually from coast to coast. Throughout Italy, much of this upland area is wooded, with huge tracts of natural forest and great stands of beech, oak and chestnut, which once played a vital part in the economy. The northern plains of the Po river valley are immensely fertile and intensively farmed, as is the rolling, serene countryside of central Italy.

Farther south, there are more mountains. Here the land is harsher, the country less fertile, the climate truly southern Mediterranean. Italy's coastal waters are dotted with islands, ranging in size from true land masses like Sicily and Sardinia to tiny and sometimes uninhabited outcrops.

Climate

Italy's long narrow shape jutting deep into the Mediterranean encourages the perception of a country bathed in perpetual sunshine. However, this

couldn't be further from the truth. The orientation of the peninsula and the fact that it is largely mountainous makes for a variety of climatic conditions and temperature differences between the north and south.

Winter brings cold and snow to north and central Italy, but in the south, it's confined to the mountaintops. Sun and showers punctuate spring, until gradually the heat intensifies, the showers dry up and glorious early summer arrives with warm days and cool, restful nights. July and August can usher in stiflingly hot, humid weather and mosquitoes, but the heat is sometimes broken by thunderstorms, accompanied by huge hailstones. This is the time to head for the coast or the mountains, where the sea is cooling, and the air is fresh and clear.

September heralds a mini-spring, with fresh growth and a flush of autumn flowers. In October temperatures drop, more rain falls, and chilling fog floats in the plains and valleys. By November, in the north, the first snow starts to fall.

The State of the Nation

Italy has a long history, but it's only been a united country since 1870, making it far younger than the United States. The country has been a republic since 1946; the 21 regions enjoy a large degree of self-government, with some, such as Sicily and Sardinia, being semi-autonomous. Since World War II, Italy has lurched politically through more than 50 governments. The great scandals of the 1980s and 1990s, when the real depths of corruption came into the open, still

Sunflowers add a splash of extra sunshine to fertile countryside

cause repercussions at every level. Surprisingly, this turmoil seems to have had little effect on the economy, one of the most successful in Europe. It's sometimes easy to forget how much has been achieved in just 50 years, as Italy has moved from being a peasant-based, largely agricultural country to one of the world's leading industrial nations. Early entry into the European Union aided economic development.

There is a very real economic and cultural division in the country. The north is richer, more advanced and more successful than the arid and impoverished south, from where the majority of American Italians emigrated. For the north, foreign markets are closer, the climate is better for agriculture and energy sources, and raw materials are near at hand. Vast sums have been poured into the south during recent years, but the gap remains, with southerners still traveling north to look for work, and northerners still resenting what they see as a drain on their hard work and effort.

Towns and Villages

Italy's history and culture have left a superb legacy. Towns and villages are packed with fine churches, civic buildings and works of art. Every settlement, no matter how large or small, retains its central piazza, with churches and municipal buildings grouped around it. Italians have a strong tradition of living in villages and towns. Even in rural areas, the tradition has been to go out from the village to work in the fields. Nevertheless, there's a huge – and historically rooted – gulf between the urban and rural population, with many farmers still working the land in traditional ways.

The middle class was a late arrival in Italy, only emerging in the decades following World War II, and still growing fast in some areas as the economic boom continues. Increasing affluence has led to much development in urban areas. You'll see spreads of unattractive industrial zones and dismal apartment blocks on the outskirts of countless towns.

Milan's Gothic-style church of Santa Maria delle Grazie

The Italian emphasis on family, sociability and *bella figura* is always present in small-town life

The People

Italy's complex history, more a story of a collection of separate states than the history of a nation, has left an indelible mark. Italian statesman Camillo Cavour's famous statement after the 1870 unification, "We have made Italy, now we must make Italians," still holds true. There is no such thing as "an Italian." Ask an Italian where he's from and the answer will never be "from Italy." Italians see themselves as primarily Roman, Sicilian, Tuscan or whatever. Everything about them stems from their native region and its history. So the work-driven Milanese fail to understand the turbulent Neapolitans, and the rational and conservative Tuscans have little in common with the abrasive Romans.

It is precisely these differences that give Italy its appealing diversity, which was strengthened until well into the 20th century by the huge number of regional dialects. With widespread literacy and the growth of television, the Italian language has come to prominence. Modern Italian derives from Tuscan, a medieval dialect used by Dante and Petrarch and firmly based on Latin. It's a beautiful, elegant, musical and expressive language, a joy to listen to whether you understand it or not.

Italian Style

Figuring out what makes Italians tick will add to the pleasure of your trip. You're bound to have your own ideas on what is typical – peasant farmer, Latin lover, pasta-cooking mamma – but

everyday Italian life. The tradition of the evening *passeggiata*, when everyone's out on the streets in their smart clothes, combines many of these elements; here is the *bella figura*, the chance to be with other people doing the same thing, enjoying one of life's simple pleasures. Watch Italian TV, and you'll see how many truly dreadful game shows there are. The content may be bad, but they're perfect for showing off.

Italians mean well and want to be well thought of; they'll go out of their way to solve small problems, and outbursts of anger are quickly over and forgotten. They make a good deal of noise, but voices are rarely ill-tempered or harsh.

Family Life

Family values are still important – to see them in action, have lunch in any restaurant on a Sunday to observe the 20-strong family groups catching up on the news. Despite having one of the lowest national birth rates in the world, family ties are still very close, with the mother's role being of paramount importance. It's said that the reason behind Italian men's constant philandering is a desperate search for a woman who will live up to the perfections of *mamma*.

Parents provide lavishly for their children, who reward them by living at home well into their 30s, then expecting *mamma* and *babbo* to provide the first marital home. Such largesse makes you look good – *bella figura* in action. There's genuine thoughtfulness in the treatment of the very young and very old. Italy is still a country where people value the experiences of older adults. There are few other countries where the coolest teenage boy will go out of his way to admire a baby. Transparent and simple on many levels, Italians are fundamentally lovable people.

beware of stereotypes. For every one that conforms, there's another that proves the exception. But a few points may hold true. Italians are social animals who abhor solitude and are happiest doing what everyone else is doing.

Bella figura – looking good – means a lot, whether it applies to clothes, cars or homes. Italians have an innate sense of style and are expert at putting themselves together to the best advantage. Their outlook on life is balanced, with an aptitude for hard work going hand-in-hand with natural spontaneity and a sensuous enjoyment of life's pleasures. Natural kindliness is tempered with a certain detachment; many seemingly deep emotions are fairly superficial. As you travel around, you'll observe these characteristics in

Pleasures and Pastimes

Italians enjoy all the same things that people in developed countries worldwide appreciate, though often with a distinctly Italian twist. Talking, eating and drinking – activities that allow for maximum attention to appearance and involve a group of people – are high on the list. Shopping is very popular for men and women, as everyone likes to have the newest styles as fast as possible. Italian men are real "peacocks," and you'll notice that men's stores often outnumber women's stores in the smartest areas of town. Both sexes visit their hair stylist regularly; it's an ideal opportunity for more talk.

On the whole, Italians are not big on the great outdoors. Skiing, hiking and sailing are as much about showing off designer outfits as exercising. The top two sports in Italy are soccer and cycling, with the Sunday sports schedules devoted to these two. Around 4 p.m. on Sunday, you'll notice men everywhere with tiny radios glued to their ears; they're tuning out the gossip and into their team's match.

Despite 97 percent of the population being baptized Catholic, only about 10 percent attend church regularly, with the attendance figures among young people falling disproportionately. Movies, music and nightclubs attract this age group.

With their innate sense of style, Italians stage excellent exhibitions of every type, so keep an eye open for one that might be of interest.

A Major Pleasure

Food is a major Italian pleasure. Cooking is immensely varied, with each region, province, town and village having its own specialties and recipes. Dishes are simple and rely on the superb quality of ingredients. Frozen food is available, but menus are still dictated by the seasons, with a rich procession of dishes punctuating the calendar. This makes for great variety, especially if your trip covers several regions. One of Italy's pleasures is the arrival of the "first" – the first Sicilian citrus in the fall, the first *cavolo nero* (black cabbage) from Tuscany and the first raspberries from the cool north.

If you're food shopping, look for the label *nostrano* on fruits and vegetables, proudly proclaiming they are grown locally. Different regions serve up

Below: Peaceful Tuscany is popular with anglers
Right: Hands are as important as voice in many Italian conversations

Introduction to Italy

The peaceful spa town of Bagni di Lucca in northern Tuscany – Italians enjoy taking a water cure

different types of food, and each thinks its own is best. Northerners fill up on *polenta* (cornmeal) and rice, while southerners couldn't imagine life without the daily mound of pasta. Tuscans eat beans and plain meat. Sicilians love pepper, chili and odd sweet-and-sour Arab-influenced flavor combinations. Rich cheese and cream appear in mountain recipes, truffles in those from Piedmont (Piemonte) and Umbria. Vegetable sauces, not meat, dominate the *cucina povera* (poor cuisine) of the south. Enjoy it all and emulate the Italians, who think nothing about driving to the coast to eat fish or lobster. Why plan your trip solely around great pictures and historic towns when you could plan it around white truffles, artichokes and red wine?

Getting Around

Traveling in Italy is easy. The excellent toll *autostrada* (freeway) network covers the whole country, with the option of driving on good highways if you're not pressed for time. Side roads, particularly in the mountains, can be twisting and steep, and country roads are not always very well surfaced.

If you're using public transportation, the train system is cheap, punctual and efficient. All towns have a railroad station, but cross-country routes can be slow and complicated. It makes sense to stick to more direct inter-city or Eurostar (ES) services when traveling by train. If you want to get off the beaten track, you'll find even the tiniest places are served by buses. Driving will be different from back home, but once you're accustomed to the style, you should have no problems. Bear in mind

Above: The good things of life on view in a Milan shopping center

Left: An appreciative eye from the *carabinieri*

the speed limits are higher than in the United States, and that Italians tend to drive fast and aggressively but safely.

All major cities have an airport, with frequent flights between cities. Hotel standards vary throughout the country, but all hotels are inspected and rated annually by regional authorities, and, whatever the price range, will be spotlessly clean. Air-conditioning is becoming more widespread but is by no means universal. Buildings can be stifling during summer. By law, heating in hotels and public places is not turned on until November 1.

Tourism is a major industry, so English is widely spoken in hotels and

Locals gather in Piazza del Popolo, the heart of Áscoli Piceno in the Marche region

and you'll get more from your vacation if you do a bit of homework. Think about what you'd like to see and do, read a few recipes, watch a few movies. Consider writing ahead to tourist boards in the areas you'll be visiting for information on attractions and sights.

restaurants in major tourist areas, though hardly at all off the beaten path. Tourist offices and the level of information they provide vary hugely, ranging from excellent, with up-to-the-minute books and maps in English, to very poor. Do try to speak a few words of Italian; the effect it has is well worth the effort, and it will add a whole new dimension to your visit. Above all, be flexible. Don't be surprised to find transportation schedules that mysteriously change, museums closed when they should be open and major attractions shrouded in scaffolding overnight – this is Italy.

Before You Go

Planning and researching your trip should be fun. There's a wealth of literature on every aspect of Italian life,

The Internet

Much information is available on the Internet, but the quality of data varies, and some sites are only in Italian. But it's fun to browse before you go. Following are some informative sites:

Official Italian State Tourist Board *www.enit.it*
New York office of the Italian State Tourist Board *www.italiantourism.com*
General information *www.travel.it*; *www.emmeti.it*; or *www.initaly.com*

You also can access regional sites that have visitor information (although not always in English) by visiting *www.regione.*(name of region in Italian).*it*. For example: *www.regione.lombardia.it*

TIMELINE

3000–1800 BC	First traces of migratory tribes appear in the peninsula.
700–300 BC	Etruscan federation, centered on present-day Tuscany and Lazio, exists alongside emerging Roman republic.
509 BC	Roman republic established; Etruscan power gradually diminishes.
264–146 BC	Punic Wars against Carthage; Rome emerges as master of the Mediterranean.
44 BC	Julius Caesar assassinated.
AD 200–400	Decline of the Roman Empire.
550–770	Peninsula fragmented, with different areas under Byzantine, Papal, Lombard and Frankish influence.
800	Charlemagne crowned Holy Roman Emperor. Northern Italy is torn between Pope and emperor for the next 400 years.
1000s	Norman invasions in south; Palermo becomes capital of Norman kingdom.
1300–1400	Emergence of the city-states in the north; prosperity is founded on trade and commerce. First stirrings of the Renaissance era.
1442	South unified under Spain and remains in Spanish hands until the 18th century.
1494	French invade the north.
1500–1848	Peninsula is again fragmented under foreign domination.
1848–61	Struggle for unification, led by Giuseppe Mazzini, Camillo Cavour and Giuseppe Garibaldi, with brief republic established in 1848; kingdom of Italy proclaimed in 1861.
1870	Unification completed by the annexation of Rome.
1915–18	Italy sides with Allies during World War I.
1921–25	Rise of Benito Mussolini amid postwar social and economic chaos. Mussolini comes to power as dictator.
1929	Mussolini signs Concordat with Vatican, which establishes the Vatican as an autonomous church-state within Italy.
1940	Italy enters World War II on the Axis side.
1943	Fall of Mussolini and armistice with Allies; Germany reinstates him as head of a puppet republic. Allies invade from the south and struggle north.
1944	Rome is liberated.
1945	Mussolini shot and killed near Milan.

1946	The Italian Republic is established.
1950	Establishment of Cassa del Mezzogiorno, an agency to fund the development of southern Italy.
1957	Treaty of Rome; Italy becomes founding member of the European Community.
1960–85	Period of social and political confusion, inflation and terrorism. Despite this, the population prospers.
1985	Economy steadies, although political confusion and scandal continue. Corruption is rife, but Italy flourishes while a desire for political and institutional reform grows.
1990s	Government drive, led by technocrat Giuliano Amato, against the Mafia following the murders of anti-Mafia judges Giovanni Falcone and Paolo Borsellino.
1992–96	Tangentopoli crisis; thousands of political figures are implicated and arrested for bribery and corruption. Public swings against established political parties.
1997	Giulio Andreotti, former prime minister, brought to trial for alleged Mafia connections.
1999	Italy becomes one of the first European Union entrants to adopt a single European currency (the euro).
2001	Silvio Berlusconi, prime minister for nine months in 1994, is re-elected in May.
2002	The euro becomes the official currency of Italy.
2006	Turin hosts the 2006 Winter Olympic Games.

THE NORMANS IN SICILY

In AD 827, the Arabs invaded and conquered the island of Sicily, heralding a period of economic growth and political stability. To help maintain their power, the Arabs used mercenaries, frequently Normans from France, who were quick to realize Sicily's rich potential. In 1061, Norman knight Roger Hauteville became the first Count of Sicily, when he seized Messina, and by 1072, Palermo had become the capital of the Norman Kingdom of Sicily. The kingdom lasted little more than a century, but in that time five kings left a legacy of incomparable art and architecture, while at the same time excelling in administration, religious tolerance and justice. Roger I and his son, Roger II, were among Europe's most successful medieval monarchs, expanding their kingdom to include southern Italy, Malta and parts of north Africa. They were followed by William I, William II and William III; the last was ousted by the Hohenstauffen emperor, Henry VI. The Normans' artistic influence can be seen all over Sicily and the south, while their genetic legacy lingers in redheaded and blonde Sicilians, with straight Norman noses and blue eyes. Even echoes of their language survive in the dialects of remote villages.

SURVIVAL GUIDE

- Inevitably, Italy's star attractions in Rome, Venice, Florence and other major centers become packed during the summer, as do many coastal resorts. Italians, too, are on vacation. Sightseeing can be exhausting in the heat, and big-city restaurants and shops are often closed while their owners take a break. It makes sense to visit in the spring, late fall or winter, when it's quieter and cooler. May and September are the most popular months in terms of international visitors.

- One of the chief pleasures of Italy is the *passeggiata* (early evening parade), when the streets are crowded with strolling and chatting locals. It occurs the length and breadth of Italy, in big cities and tiny villages, so be prepared for the streets to become packed for a couple of hours beginning at 6. By 8:30, they'll be deserted.

- Remember that opening hours, particularly for tourist offices, do fluctuate in Italy. Schedules often depend on the tourist flow; if in doubt phone before planning your day. Much of Italy closes down from around 12:30 until 4:30 or 5 while people eat lunch and have a siesta. You'll enjoy your sightseeing more if you do as the locals do and take a midday rest; shops stay open until 8 or 9 in towns and later at beach resorts.

- Generally, museums and art galleries throughout Italy are closed on Mondays. So if sightseeing is your main aim, plan to do your traveling on that day so you don't waste valuable time.

- Italians spend much time and effort on their appearance, always showering and changing their outfits for the evening *passeggiata*. They will appreciate it if tourists also make the effort, so try and look appropriately smart. Shorts are not acceptable city wear in Italy, and you will not be allowed into churches if too much arm or leg is showing – it's considered disrespectful.

- Mealtimes are different from those in the United States; it is unusual to eat dinner before 7:30 or 8; lunch is served starting at 12:30. Some restaurants offer fixed-price menus, but you may want to choose some of the local specialties. Vegetarianism is considered odd, but there are plenty of pasta and side dishes that are suitable for non-meat eaters. Check with the waiter on the ingredients; Italians sometimes think salami, prosciutto and meat stock don't count as meat. Children are welcome in many restaurants.

- Italians enjoy wine, which they drink at all meals, but the concept of the cocktail hour is alien, as they associate alcohol with food. For this

Lunchtime at one of the upscale restaurants in Milan's elegant Galleria Vittorio Emanuele II

reason, if you order a pre-dinner drink in a bar it will always be served with potato chips, nuts or canapés. In Italy, inebriation is a serious social taboo.

- Bars are much more than the name suggests; open from dawn until midnight or later, they offer coffee, tea, soda, snacks, sandwiches and pastries as well as alcohol. They are brightly lit, immaculately clean and efficiently run for speedy service. Italians rarely sit down, and you will be charged extra if you do, as it involves waiter service. All bars have public telephones, restrooms and newspapers, which are useful for weather maps on the back pages.
- Smoking is banned in many public places.
- One of the joys of Italy is shopping in little local stores, with their wonderful personal service, and at the colorful street markets. Italy has very few department stores except in the cities, and even these bear little

resemblance to what you're used to back home. There are virtually no shopping malls. Shop and market prices are fixed.

- If you buy goods to take home, remember to inquire about tax-free shopping. Many stores and outlets offer this, particularly those catering to tourists. If a purchase is a gift, tell the sales person. It will usually be beautifully and artistically wrapped and ribboned.
- In summer, be sure to drink enough water. With high temperatures, dry heat and little air conditioning, it's important to keep fluid levels high. Caffeinated and alcoholic beverages will further dehydrate you. Drinks in Italy are rarely served with ice; Italians think too much ice is bad for the stomach.
- Facilities for people with disabilities are improving, but are still not as good as those back home. If you need help, check ahead with local tourist offices.

THE NORTHWEST AND EMILIA-ROMAGNA

*"T*HE Northwest's Alpine peaks, coastline and dynamic cities are an interesting contrast to the wide flat plains, intensive agriculture and historic small cities of Emilia-Romagna.*"*

Colorful houses are reflected in the tranquil waters of Portofino's tiny harbor

THE NORTHWEST AND EMILIA-ROMAGNA

The huge swath of the northwest and Emilia-Romagna sweeps from coast to coast across the top of Italy, a region packed with major cities, historic towns and pretty villages. Its fine landscape encompasses the Alps, sparkling lakes, stunning coastal scenery, and the intensive agriculture of the great Po river valley. Prosperous and forward-looking, the entire area gives a taste of the true diversity of modern Italy, where the past has shaped the present against the background of a traditional way of life, and tourism is only a segment of the whole picture.

The Shape of the Land

Much of the northwest is either hilly or mountainous, with the major exception of the Po river valley, a huge, flat and intensively cultivated plain that stretches almost two-thirds of the way across Italy from west of Milan to the Adriatic. The Po valley lies in Lombardy and Emilia-Romagna, Italy's two richest regions.

Lombardy (Lombardia) also boasts the Italian Lakes, celebrated for centuries for their great natural beauty and entrancing mix of water, mountains, woodlands and charming villages. Emilia-Romagna is mainly flat, its fertile farmland giving way to a long stretch of sandy coast on the Adriatic, a favorite holiday destination for families from all over Europe.

In the west lie the regions of Piedmont, Valle d'Aosta and Liguria, where you'll find some of Italy's most beautiful coastline and glorious mountain scenery. Piedmont is bordered on three sides by the Alps; to the west and south the Maritime Alps straddle the border with France, and to the north is the Monte Bianco massif. The Western Alps continue south through the Valle d'Aosta and Piedmont.

Aosta is splendid, with deep-cut valleys, rushing torrents and soaring peaks. It has true wilderness country in some parts. Liguria, too, has mountains,

which run behind the coast from the French border as far as the north of Tuscany. The shelter they provide has created a microclimate along this stretch, where subtropical vegetation flourishes and cold weather is rare.

The Past

The history of this part of Italy is, as all over the country, one of fragmentation until the 19th-century process of unification. During the Middle Ages, the developing cities were largely independent, Milan being particularly important, while the Renaissance saw ruling families establish influential courts at their power bases in cities such as Mantua and Ferrara. On the west coast, Genoa was one of Europe's great maritime republics, while in Emilia-Romagna, Bologna became home to one of the Continent's oldest and most prestigious universities.

After the French invasions at the end of the 15th century, political power lay for centuries in the hands of outsiders; at various times the Spanish, the French and the Austrians all held Milan, Turin and other major centers. The House of Savoy, which ruled Piedmont, came to be a firm backer of the cause of unification; Victor Emanuel II of Savoy became the first king of a united Italy, and Turin was the capital for a short time. This background has produced the common Italian tendency to make local rather than regional or national loyalties the

The Northwest and Emilia-Romagna

The Castello di Sarre in the scenic Valle d'Aosta is backed by majestic mountains

strongest. People are passionately proud of their city, town or village, but not necessarily of Italy as a whole.

Modern Prosperity

The northwest, while scenically beautiful, is also work-driven and extremely prosperous, with a much faster pace of life than that in central or southern Italy. Milan is a major industrial and technological center, and has more in common with northern Europe than southern Italy. Turin is a major automobile manufacturing city, the home of Fiat and Lancia. Italy's industrial revolution began in Genoa, which is still Italy's largest port, while Bologna's present-day wealth comes from its computer-associated industries.

The lesser towns, too, have solidly based and thriving industries. Agriculture is still important, with rice, corn and tobacco thriving in the fertile Po river valley, and extensive vineyards in the hillier areas. Development has brought much new construction in its wake, and you'll find this part of Italy pretty built-up, with many lovely old towns surrounded by ugly modern industrial zones and stretches of new housing. The region has rarely been poor or isolated, and this long-established sense of security is evident in the open friendliness and politeness of most of the people.

Exploring the Region

If you're interested in a combination of great scenery, vibrant cities and historic towns, head for the Northwest's western section, where there's the bonus of a beautiful coastline. From the foothills of Piedmont there's easy access into the Alpine valleys, and you can hike or drive in clear mountain air surrounded by spectacular views. Lombardy, in the center, has a bit of everything, from the frenetic pace of Milan to the delights of lovely old Bergamo, while the beauties of Lakes Maggiore, Lugano and Como lie within easy reach to the north.

Farther east, in Emilia-Romagna, the flat plains are liberally sprinkled with such historic towns as Cremona, Ravenna and Ferrara, all packed with artistic treasures. Independent travel is easy in this thoroughly modern region, which has an excellent infrastructure and good roads. A rental car makes sense for your explorations, but if you're spending time in Milan, Turin or Bologna, arrange to pick up your car either before or after your visit; driving and parking can be difficult in each of these cities. It is

Sunflowers are grown for oil all over Italy

possible to explore using public transportation, an option that works well if you're concentrating on towns. If you're planning to spend time in the mountains, however, a rental car gives you the chance to go as you please.

When To Go

Spring, early summer and fall, before or after the hordes of European vacationers, are the best times to come. Summer in the Alps is lovely, but you'll be sharing the mountains and hotels with what will seem like half of Europe. September and October, with the spectacular autumn foliage at its best, are the perfect months. While winter brings its own charms, and an influx of skiing enthusiasts. Winter can be long and harsh in the mountains, city pollution is often at its worst, and the plains can be shrouded for days in penetratingly cold mist and fog. The only area to escape to is the western coastal strip, but the delightful villages here are primarily summer resorts, and winter facilities for visitors are few.

The Northwest and Emilia-Romagna

MILAN

Noisy, dynamic Milan (Milano) is like no other Italian city. One of the driving forces behind northern Italy's booming economy, it lacks the easy-going charm and relaxed pace you find elsewhere. The atmosphere has far more in common with the countries north of the Alps than with the Italian peninsula. Don't expect a beguiling city, but sample Milan as a vital element in modern Italy.

Seeing the City

Milan is well-endowed with museums, churches and galleries. In addition to the big sights, there's a host of smaller museums and historic churches, a couple of large parks and fantastic shopping at every price level. Don't neglect areas like Navigli and Ticinese to the south; these are arty and attractive districts with interesting shops, good bars, clubs and restaurants. They provide fine antidotes to the frenetic city center. Buy a copy of *Milan is Milano* (€2.50) from the tourist office; it's packed with general information and listings that will help you make the most of your stay.

Getting Around

Milan is a big and sprawling city, its main streets radiating from the Piazza del Duomo and crossed by three concentric roads. Most of what you'll want to see lies in a relatively small central area, and you should be able to walk for much of the time. Streets can be packed, so you may want to take the subway to a central point near several main sights, then proceed on foot. Or you could take a city tour; these run daily Tuesday through Sunday, last about three hours and have an English commentary.

Eating

Milan restaurants can be very expensive. But there are more fast-food eateries than in any other Italian city, and plenty of good, moderately priced places. Milan has its own specialties, too; the best-known is probably *cotoletta alla milanese* (wiener schnitzel) and *risotto alla milanese*, the simplest and most delicious risotto. Carbohydrates may also come in the form of *polenta*, a type of cornmeal-based porridge popular throughout Europe. Wine lists in restaurants are often extensive.

Shopping

Fashion and design are Milanese obsessions, so it's hardly surprising that shopping here is taken very seriously. The area to head for is the Golden Quadrangle (Quadrilatero d'Oro). Here, high-fashion boutiques line the elegant streets, and the customers are as eye-catching as the shops.

Other expensive shops cluster in the Galleria Vittorio Emanuele II, while nearby La Rinascente, on the Piazza del Duomo, is a slightly cheaper alternative, a major department store that's a Milan institution. For interesting smaller shops and antiques, head for the Navigli district. Milan also has a number of discount stores selling high-fashion designer clothes.

Entertainment

Opera fans will want to attend a performance at Milan's famous opera house, La Scala. There are other places to enjoy classical music around the city, as well as live theater and movies in English. Milan is known as Italy's hippest nightlife center, with a plethora of every type of club as well as jazz and rock concerts.

MILAN

The Northwest and Emilia-Romagna

ESSENTIAL INFORMATION

 TOURIST INFORMATION
•Via Marconi 1, ☎ 02 7252 4301;
www.milanoinfotourist.com
•Stazione Centrale ☎ 02 7252 4360
•City tours ☎ 02 8645 0433

URBAN TRANSPORTATION
Milan's public transportation system is a
well-integrated and efficient
combination of trams, buses and subway. The
subway is fastest, easiest and the most useful,
and consists of three lines, the red (MM1), the
green (MM2) and the yellow (MM3), which
converge at four main hub stations. You can pick
up a map at the information offices at either the
Duomo or Stazione Centrale subway stations.
Tickets are valid throughout the different systems;
buy them at bars, tobacco shops or subway

stations, either singly or in books of 10; 24- and
48-hour tourist tickets also are available. They
are valid for 75 minutes from the journey's start
and may be used for one subway ride plus an
unlimited number of tram and bus rides. Taxis are
available at key points throughout the city, or
☎ 02 4040, 8585.

AIRPORT INFORMATION
Milan has two airports:
Linate (☎ 02 7485 2200; www.
sea-aeroportimilano.it), 4 miles east of the city
center, and Malpensa (☎ 02 7485 2200;
www.sea-aeroportimilano.it), 28 miles northwest
of the city center. Each airport handles
both domestic and international flights, and
each has bus service to Milan and to the
other airport.

CLIMATE – Average highs and lows

JAN.	FEB.	MAR.	APR.	MAY	JUN.	JUL.	AUG.	SEP.	OCT.	NOV.	DEC.
6°C	8°C	13°C	16°C	21°C	25°C	28°C	27°C	24°C	18°C	11°C	7°C
43°F	46°F	55°F	61°F	70°F	77°F	82°F	81°F	75°F	64°F	52°F	45°F
-4°C	-2°C	-1°C	4°C	10°C	13°C	15°C	15°C	12°C	6°C	0°C	-4°C
26°F	27°F	34°F	40°F	50°F	55°F	59°F	59°F	54°F	43°F	32°F	25°F

The Northwest and Emilia-Romagna

MILAN SIGHTS

Key to symbols

⊞ map coordinates refer to the Milan map on page 33; sights below are highlighted in yellow on the map

⊠ address or location ☎ telephone number

⊙ opening times ⑪ restaurant on site or nearby

Ⓜ subway station 🚌 nearest bus or tram route

💵 admission charge: $$$ more than €6, $$ €3 to €6 , $ less than €3 ⓘ information

ACCADEMIA BRERA

By far the most prestigious of Milan's art galleries, the Accademia Brera (Brera Academy) houses a huge collection. It may be best to concentrate on the highlights or your own particular interests. The gallery's emphasis is firmly on Italian painting, with the core dating from the Renaissance. You'll be struck by the incredible perspective of Mantegna's *Cristo Morto* – a foreshortened view of Christ's dead body from the pierced soles of his feet. It's a fine contrast to the almost contemporary *St. Mark Preaching* by Gentile Bellini, filled with turbaned men and eastern animals – there's even a camel and a giraffe. Venetian art is represented by Veronese's action-packed *Supper in the House of Simon* and Carpaccio's lovely *Presentation of the Virgin*. The enigmatic Florentine Piero della Francesca is represented by the Brera's most outstanding work, the austere, balanced and compelling *Madonna with Angels, Saints and Federico da Montefeltro*, all grays and subdued tones with shafts of intense color.

⊞ B3 ⊠ Via Brera 28 ☎ 02 722 631 ⊙ Tue.–Fri. 8:30–7 Ⓜ M2 Lanza, M3 Montenapoleone 💵 $$$

CASTELLO SFORZESCO

The huge redbrick structure of the Castello Sforzesco (Sforza Castle) is one of Milan's most striking landmarks, rising above the chaotic traffic whirling around the Foro Buonaparte. The first version of the castle was built by the then-ruling family, the Viscontis, destroyed in 1447 by rebels, and rebuilt by the Visconti successors, the Sforzas. It became one of Europe's most glittering courts, powerful

and cultured – Leonardo da Vinci was among the artists patronized by the family. Milan fell to the French in 1499, and the castle was used as barracks until the late 19th century. Today it houses a series of museums, among them the Museo d'Arte Antica (Ancient Art Museum), where you can see Michelangelo's last unfinished *Pietà*, and the Pinacoteca del Castello (Castle Art Gallery). The most striking painting here has to be the bizarre *Primavera* by Arcimboldo, a portrait of a woman entirely composed of flowers – 16th-century surrealism at its best.

⊞ A3 ⊠ Piazza del Castello ☎ 02 8846 3701 ⊙ Tue.–Sun. 9:30–5:30 Ⓜ M1 Cairoli, M2 Lanza 💵 Free

DUOMO

The Duomo (Cathedral), Italy's biggest Gothic building and the third largest church in Europe (after St. Peter's in Rome and Seville Cathedral), should be at the top of your sightseeing list. Work started in 1386 and finally finished in 1813, when the last details were added to the riot of stone carving and tracery on the facade. The best place to appreciate the incredible complexity of the spires, sculptures and turrets is by strolling around the roof – where you'll have the bonus of wonderful city views. Inside, dim light filters in through stained-glass windows to illuminate the soaring marble columns and the crucifix suspended above the high altar, which contains the cathedral's most precious relic, a nail allegedly from Christ's cross.

⊞ B2 ⊠ Piazza del Duomo ☎ 02 8646 3456 ⊙ Museo del Duomo: Daily 10–1:15 and 3–6; Crypt: 9–noon and 2:30–6; Baptistery: 10–11:45 and 3–5; Roof: 9–5:45, Mar.–Oct.; 9–4:15, rest of year; Treasury: Mon.–Sat. 9–noon and 2:30–6, Sun. 2:30–6 ⑪ Bistrot Duomo, see page 199 Ⓜ M1, M3 Duomo 💵 Museo del Duomo $$$, Roof $$

GALLERIA VITTORIO EMANUELE II

Emerging from the cathedral, head across the Piazza del Duomo to the Galleria Vittorio Emanuele II, a splendidly opulent, 19th-century covered shopping gallery. The lofty cruciform structure was designed in 1865 by Giuseppe Mengoni, who was killed in a fall from the roof before the gallery opened. It is constantly busy with shoppers and patrons heading for the smart — and expensive — restaurants and cafés.

✚ B2 ✉ Galleria Vittorio Emanuele II 🍴 Savini, see page 200 🚇 M1, M3 Duomo

LA SCALA

Walk through the Galleria Vittorio Emanuele and you emerge on the Piazza della Scala, the site of Milan's world-famous opera house, La Scala. First opened in 1778, it recently has been extensively restored. La Scala's museum collection of opera memorabilia has been moved temporarily to the Palazzo Busca at Collegio San Carlo Corso, Magenta 71. From the square, Via Manzoni, one of Milan's most fashionable streets, runs toward the high-class shopping area known as the Quadrilatero d'Oro (Golden Quadrangle). It's the site of the Museo Poldi-Pezzoli, a varied assortment of paintings and jewelry assembled by a 19th-century collector.

✚ B2 ✉ Piazza Scala ☎ Opera bookings: 02 861 778 🍴 Savini, see page 200 🚇 M1, M3 Duomo
Museo Teatrale alla Scala ✉ Palazzo Busca, Collegio San Carlo, Corso Magenta 71 ☎ 02 469 1244 🕐 Tue.–Sun. 9–6 💲 $$
Museo Poldi-Pezzoli ✚ B2 ✉ Via Manzoni 12 ☎ 02 796 334 🕐 Tue.–Sun. 10–6 🚇 M3 Montenapoleone 💲 $$$

SANT'AMBROGIO

Milan is rich in churches, and there's none lovelier than Sant'Ambrogio, founded in the fourth century and dedicated to St. Ambrose, the city's patron saint. Today's structure, a superb Romanesque basilica reached through the colonnaded quadrangle, dates from the 11th century. The glittering apse mosaics are contemporary, as is the fine pulpit, intricately carved with ferocious wild animals. St. Ambrose's remains lie buried in the crypt; his fifth-century portrait is in the chapel near the sacristy. There is a

The glass-domed Galleria Vittorio Emanuele II

small museum in the church.

✚ A2 ✉ Piazza Sant'Ambrogio 15 ☎ 02 8645 0895 🕐 Daily 7–noon and 2:30–7 🚇 M2 Sant'Ambrogio

SANTA MARIA DELLE GRAZIE

The refectory attached to the church of Santa Maria delle Grazie draws more visitors than almost any other site in Milan, for here you can see Leonardo da Vinci's ghostly masterpiece, *The Last Supper*. Painted between 1495–97, this breathtaking composition captures the moment when Christ announces he will be betrayed by one of his disciples. Despite lengthy restorations, the fresco is in a bad and fragile state, its colors faded, much of its detail lost. This is chiefly due to da Vinci's technique; he scorned traditional wet-plaster methods and applied oil and tempera to dry plaster. Within five years the work had started to deteriorate. Matters were not helped by primitive restoration attempts and even whitewashing. Napoleonic troops used the painting as a target when they billeted here, and virtually the whole building around it was destroyed by a 1943 bomb.

✚ A2 ✉ Piazza Santa Maria delle Grazie 2 🕐 Tue.–Sun. 8:15–6:45. Reservations are required (☎ 02 8942 1146 or 02 498 7588) 🚇 M1, M2 Cadorna 🚊 Tram 24 💲 $$$

The flamboyant facade of Milan's huge cathedral dominates one of the city's busiest squares

WALK: THE TICINESE DISTRICT

Refer to route marked on city map on page 33.

This walk takes about three hours and leads you away from the most frequented sights and through the city to the Ticinese district – by day a peaceful area with attractive shops, by night the scene of some of Milan's best nightlife.

Take Via Torino out of Piazza del Duomo. At Piazza Santa Maria Beltrade, cross Via Torino and take Via delle Asole on the right to Piazza San Sepolcro.

Behind the church on the piazza, you'll find the Pinacoteca e Biblioteca Ambrosiana (Ambrosian Library and Art Gallery). Commissioned in 1607 by Cardinal Borromeo, this was one of Europe's first public libraries and contains more than 35,000 manuscripts, among them a copy of Virgil once belonging to Petrarch and the Atlantic Codex, a collection of notebooks and drawings by Leonardo da Vinci. The art gallery, too, has some real treasures; look out for a cartoon by Raphael for the *School of Athens* in the Vatican, and Caravaggio's tactile *Basket of Fruit*, the first Italian still life.

Take Via Zecca Vecchia, turn right onto Via San Maurilio, then left on Via Santa Marta. Follow Via Circo and Via Lanzone to Piazza Sant'Ambrogio, with its wonderful ninth-century church (see page 35). Leave Piazza Sant'Ambrogio on Via San Vittore, then branch left onto Via Olona and left again down Via Edmondo de Amicis. This leads to Corso di Porta Ticinese, where you'll find the entrance to the Basilica di San Lorenzo.

This is one of Milan's most important early churches, a central-plan basilica surrounded by three small octagonal chapels. Look for the row of columns outside; these are some of the few reminders of Roman Milan.

Turn right down the Corso di Porta Ticinese to the Piazza Sant'Eustorgio. After visiting this 12th- to 15th-century church, explore the canal-side areas of Ticinese and Navigli.

The canals and the basin known as the Darsena were part of Milan's port system from the 15th century up to the 1950s. The northern Italian plain was once networked with canals linking the river systems, giving inland cities easy trade access with each other and with the sea. The Corso di Porta Ticinese is packed with offbeat shops, and the surrounding streets are the scene of secondhand and antique markets on the last Sunday of the month. This is one of Milan's most desirable residential areas, and has some of the city's best restaurants.

The graceful exterior of La Scala opera house

The elegance of the Milanese

A DAY IN MILAN

Most Milanese have daily schedules similar to those of people in the United States and northern Europe – but with an Italian twist. The day starts early, with many workers commuting into the bustling city from the network of suburban subway stations. Many people drive, and the daily struggle to park lends a certain excitement to the day. As all over Italy, breakfast is often eaten in a bar; the time taken by the busy Milanese to drink a cup of coffee and eat a pastry is around five minutes maximum.

The Working Day

Office employees have the same schedules as those in London, Paris or New York. There is no stop for a long lunch and a siesta. People even go so far as to eat at their desks – which is largely unheard of in the rest of Italy. If people go out for lunch, it will be a quick sandwich from a bar or fast-food counter, unless they are entertaining clients. Most offices work until 6 or 7 p.m.

The Family Day

Many married Milanese women work outside the home; this is a city where equal rights really mean something, and women often hold down key positions.

But there are still plenty of old-fashioned wives and mothers who spend their mornings cleaning, shopping and preparing a traditional lunch to welcome the kids home from school at 2:30. Italian children have mounds of homework, and mothers often supervise them before chauffering the kids to sports events and other extracurricular activities. Dinner is around 8 or 9. Sunday lunch is the big family event.

The Sybaritic Day

There are many seriously rich people in Milan. They are the patrons of the smart art galleries, the exhibitions and the auctions. Women will spend hours at the hairdresser, and shopping is pursued with an obsessive attention to the finest details of personal appearance. Domestic help is common, so rich women need not worry about household chores.

The Evening

Milan has a wonderful nightlife, with great restaurants, bars and clubs, and a huge range of cultural events. Young people party during the week, but Friday and Saturday evenings are the traditional nights out.

REGIONAL SIGHTS

Key to symbols

⊞ map coordinates refer to the region map on page 28; sights below are highlighted in yellow on the map

✉ address or location ☎ telephone number

◷ opening times 🍴 restaurant on site or nearby

🚍 nearest bus or tram route

💶 admission charge: $$$ more than €6, $$ €3 to €6, $ less than €3 ℹ️ information

The Northwest and Emilia-Romagna

ALBA

Wine and food enthusiasts will love Alba, home of two of Italy's most splendid culinary treats: Barolo wine, "King of Italian Reds," and truffles, the world's most expensive food. You'll find both in the tempting local food stores – head for the bustling Via Vittorio Emanuele, Alba's main street. Wonderful shops burst with local products – wine, truffles, cheese, cakes, biscuits and mounds of aromatic fungi in autumn. The famous white truffles *(tartufo bianco)* are in season in November and December, but available in different preserved forms all year. Wine is everywhere, and many of the surrounding hill villages such as Barolo, Grinzane di Cavour and Annunziata have wineries offering tastings and *vendita diretta* (direct sale). The reds are mainly made from the Nebbiolo grape; the astonishing range of flavor and depth is dictated by the soil conditions in the different areas around Alba. Alba is a place for a lengthy lunch, and perhaps a peek at the lovely late-Gothic Duomo (Cathedral), which has fine inlaid Renaissance choir stalls.

⊞ B2

Tourist information ✉ Piazza Risorgimento 2 ☎ 0173 35 833 ◷ Mon.–Fri. 9–12:30 and 2:30–5:30, Sat.–Sun. 9–12:30 (closed Sun. Jan. and Feb.)

AOSTA

Heading into Italy through the Alps from France, the spectacularly scenic Valle d'Aosta leads to Piedmont. This is border country, with Alpine meadows and a chain of castles, where names are both French and Italian and the population is at home with both languages. Aosta, the

Snowcapped mountains form the perfect backdrop for Aosta's stone spires

capital of this beguiling region, is a historic and pleasant town with a wonderfully spacious central piazza and attractive streets. Founded by the Romans in AD 25 as a border camp, it makes an ideal base for exploring the Gran Paradiso (see pages 46–47) and the Monte Blanc areas. The fine Porta Pretoria dates from Roman times when it was the town's main gateway; there are other Roman remains in the shape of the Arco di Augusto (Augustus' Arch) and the Teatro Romano (Roman Theater). The Cattedrale (Cathedral) has a good Gothic interior behind its dull facade; be sure to see the presbytery floor mosaics and the carved choir stalls, a riot of saints, birds and beasts. Sant'Orso is another interesting church, with 10th-century frescoes hidden up near the roof and a tiny and charming Romanesque cloister.

⊞ A3

Tourist information ✉ Piazza Emilio Chanoux 8 ☎ 0165 236 627 ◷ Daily 9–1 and 3–8, Jun.–Sep.; Mon.–Sat. 9–1 and 3–8, Sun. 9–1, rest of year

Teatro Romano ✉ Off Via Porta Pretoria ◷ Daily 9–8, Apr.–Sep.; 9–6:30, rest of year 💶 Free

Cattedrale ✉ Piazza Giovanni XXIII ☎ 0165 40 413 or 0165 31 361 ◷ Daily 9–7 💶 Free; Museum $

Sant'Orso ✉ Via Sant'Anselmo ☎ 0165 262 026 ◷ Mon.–Fri. 9–6:30, Sat.–Sun. 9–noon and 2–5

One of the many fortified castles to be found at strategic points in the Valle d'Aosta

Bérgamo's lovely Cappella Colleoni, in the heart of the old town

ASTI

Asti's famous "bubbly," Asti Spumante, is enjoyed all over Europe and beyond, and this little town is the capital of Italy's sparkling wine industry.

In medieval times it rivaled Milan in importance; today it's a low-key and sedate town with fine towers, churches and palaces along or near its main street, the Corso Vittorio Alfieri. The 14th-century Duomo (Cathedral) has a checkered red-and-white façade, but the church of San Pietro in Consavia, with its little 12th-century circular baptistery, is far more alluring. San Secondo, behind Asti's pretty arcaded main Piazza Vittorio Alfieri, was founded in the second century; nothing that old remains, but the delicate crypt dates from the sixth century. Asti bursts into life in September, when its annual Palio is held. This bareback horse race around the Campo del Palio is similar to Siena's, although far less known.

➕ B2

Tourist information ✉ Piazza Vittorio Alfieri 29
☎ 0141 530 357 🕙 Mon.–Sat. 9–1 and 2–6:30, Sun.
10–1 🎌 Palio is held on the third Sun. in Sep.; details from the tourist office

San Pietro in Consavia ✉ Corso Vittorio Alfieri 2
🕙 Tue.–Sat. 9–noon and 3–6, Sun. 10–noon. Ring the bell for the *custode* (guardian) if not open

San Secondo ✉ Off Piazza Vittorio Alfieri ☎ 0141
530 066 🕙 Mon.–Sat. 7–noon and 3:30–7, Sun.
3:30–7 💺 $

BÉRGAMO

Lovely Bérgamo, clinging to the hills above the plain of Lombardy, is divided into two distinct parts, Bérgamo Bassa and Bérgamo Alta. Head straight for Bérgamo Alta, a beautiful old hill town with gated walls and architectural and artistic delights. The Venetians ruled Bérgamo for over 350 years until 1796, leaving a legacy of beautiful buildings and their lion symbol adorning walls and fountains everywhere. The old town centers around the Piazza Vecchia, a harmonious melange of architectural styles dominated by the medieval Palazzo dell Ragione (Palace of Reason), a Venetian-Gothic structure. Next to it looms the Torre della Civica (Civic Tower); its ancient bell still chimes a 180-peal curfew every night. Nearby on the Piazza del Duomo you'll find both the Duomo (Cathedral) and the glorious Santa Maria Maggiore, a Romanesque church with a gilded baroque interior. Flanking this is the Cappella Colleoni (Colleoni Chapel), a Lombard Renaissance gem designed for Bartolomeo Colleoni, who made his fortune as a Venetian mercenary. For views of the town, walk up the hill to the old military stronghold of the Cittadella. Leave time to visit the Accademia Carrara, one of northern Italy's least-known – yet most important – art galleries. The collection is outstanding, with luminous portraits by Botticelli, soulful virgins by Bellini, and Venetian canal scenes by Canaletto and Guardi.

➕ C3

Tourist information ✉ Via Aquila Nera 2 ☎ 035 242
226 🕙 Mon.–Sat. 9–12:30 and 3–5:30, Sun. 9–12:30
Torre della Civica ✉ Piazza Vecchia 🕙 Sun.–Thu.
10–8, Fri.–Sat. 10–10, May 1 to mid-Sep.; Mon.–Fri.
9:30–12:30 and 2–7, Sat.–Sun. 10–7, mid-Sep. to Oct.
31; Sat. 2–4, Sun. 10:30–4, Nov.–Feb.; Wed.–Sat.
10:30–12:30 and 2–6, Sun. 10:30–6, rest of year 💺 $
Santa Maria Maggiore ✉ Piazza del Duomo ☎ 035
223 327 🕙 Daily 9–12:30 and 2:30–6:30, Apr.–Oct.;
Mon.–Sat. 9–12:30 and 2–5:30, Sun. 9 a.m.–11 a.m.

and 2:30–6, rest of year
Cappella Colleoni ✉ Piazza del Duomo 🕐 Daily
9–12:30 and 2–6:30, Apr.–Oct.; Tue.–Sun. 9–12:30, rest
of year
Accademia Carrara ✉ Piazza dell'Accademia 82/a
☎ 035 399 643 🕐 Tue.–Sun. 10–1 and 3–6:45 💶 $

BOLOGNA

Beautiful, historic and booming Bologna is
the capital of Emilia-Romagna. It's an old-
brick city known for its wealth, its ancient
university, its left-wing politics and its
cuisine. Surrounded by sprawling suburbs
housing the computer-associated and other
industries from which its modern
prosperity derives, the inner historic core is
compact, a series of stunning porticoed
streets radiating from two main squares,
Piazza Maggiore and Piazza del Nettuno.
The latter is named after the great
Neptune Fountain, sculpted by native-born
Giambologna in 1556. It's the focal point
of the square and its medieval civic
buildings, including the Palazzo Comunale
and the Palazzo Re Enzo.

The Neptune Fountain is the focal point of one of
Bologna's central squares

The nearby Piazza Maggiore is
dominated by the church of San Petronio,
a huge 14th-century Gothic church
originally intended to be double its
present size. It houses some lovely
paintings and a splendid astronomical
clock where a shaft of sunlight striking a
brass meridian line tells the time.

Bologna's other attractions cluster near
the two main squares. Head first to the
university district, taking in Via
Clavatura, with its mouthwatering food
shops and market stalls, en route. The
oldest university structure is the
Archiginnasio, built in 1565 when the
university itself was already several
hundred years old. In this quarter, too,
you'll find the Due Torri (Two Towers),
the only survivors of the hundreds the city
contained in the Middle Ages. You can
climb the Torre degli Asinelli; it's a good
way to get an overview of the city.

South from the Archiginnasio stands
San Domenico, built in 1251 to house the
relics of St. Dominic. These are enclosed
in the Arca di San Domenico, a superb
piece of 15th-century sculpture with figures
by Pisano and the young Michelangelo.

The Pinacoteca Nazionale (National
Art Gallery) has some excellent paintings,
while the Museo Civico Archeologico
(Archeological Museum) features Roman
and Etruscan antiquities. For something
different, visit the Museo di Anatomia
Umana, a bizarre and highly idiosyncratic
collection of anatomical waxworks used in
medical demonstrations at the university
until the 19th century. Above all, leave
time for wandering the city's arcaded
streets and squares, sitting in cafés,
window-shopping and enjoying a meal.
✚ D1
Tourist information ✉ Palazzo d'Accursio, Piazza
Maggiore 1 ☎ 051 246 541 🕐 Mon.–Sat. 9–7,
Sun. 9–2
San Petronio ✉ Piazza Maggiore 🕐 Daily 7:30–1
and 2:30–6 💶 Free
Torre degli Asinelli ✉ Piazza di Porta Ravegnana
🕐 Daily 9–6 💶 $
San Domenico ✉ Piazza San Domenico ☎ 051 640
0411 🕐 Tue.–Sat. 10–12:30 and 3–5, Sun. 3–5 💶 Free
Pinacoteca Nazionale ✉ Via Belle Arti 56 ☎ 051
243 211 🕐 Tue.–Sun. 9–6:30 💶 $$
Museo Civico Archeologico ✉ Via
dell'Archiginnasio 2 ☎ 051 233 849 🕐 Tue.–Sat.
9–6:30, Sun. 10–6:30 💶 $$
Museo di Anatomia Umana ✉ Via Irnerio 48
☎ 051 209 9360 🕐 Phone for opening times; closed
Sat.–Sun. 💶 Free

CINQUE TERRE

A string of idyllic coastal villages, crouching beneath precipitous hills running straight into the sea, spreads along the coast of Liguria just north of the port of La Spézia. These are the Cinque Terre, the Five Lands, one of the most alluring clusters of seaside settlements anywhere in the peninsula. Each village is little more than a picturesque jumble of pale-colored houses assembled around a tiny fishing harbor – although today the fishing boats share space with yachts and pleasure craft. Stony paths, crisscrossing through woods, mountains and coastlines, used to be the only link between the villages. The surrounding steep cliffs, carpeted with springtime flowers and planted with olives and grapes, plunge into the crystal-clear sea.

For centuries, the easiest route between the villages was by sea, and you can still take a boat trip; it's a wonderful way to admire the superb scenery. The railroad arrived in the 19th century and links all the villages; trains run frequently and it's only a few minutes between stops. From north to south, Monterosso is the biggest village, with a good-sized beach and more accommodations than elsewhere. South lies Vernazza, a huddle of houses with a tiny beach, and then Corniglia, the smallest of the five. Manarola is the pick of the bunch, the quintessential Mediterranean charmer, with a sliver of beach, pretty houses and a busy little harbor. Riomaggiore, the farthest south, is a little larger with an allure all its own.

All the villages have romantic waterfront restaurants where you can sample the white wine produced from the vines clinging to the hills behind. This coast is the perfect place to relax for a few days, but it's very popular with visitors in summer, so be sure to reserve ahead. You could base yourself in Lévanto, a small coastal town just to the north. It has a laid-back holiday atmosphere and plenty of accommodations. You can explore the Cinque Terre from there; it's only a few minutes away by train.

Lévanto ✚ C1

Tourist information ✉ Piazza Mazzini 1 ☎ 0187 808 125 🕐 Mon.–Sat. 9:30–1 and 3–6, Sun. 9:30–12:30, Apr.–Oct.; Mon.–Fri. 9:30–12:30 and 3:30–5:30, rest of year

A clifftop view of Vernazza, one of the main villages along the stunning coastline of the Cinque Terre

CREMONA

Stradivari and his violins draw visitors to Cremona, an unpretentious, prosperous provincial town that once was the home of the world's greatest violin maker. Here, in 1566, Andrea Amati established the world's first violin-making workshop, passing down his secrets to his son Nicolo and his pupils, Stradivari and Guarini. There are still more than 80 violin makers and an internationally famous school of violin-making in Cremona. The oddly shaped Piazza del Comune marks the town's center; it's surrounded by the pretty redbrick Loggia dei Miltia and the Palazzo del Comune. You can climb the 13th-century Romanesque Torrazzo in the plaza's northeast corner for great views before visiting the Duomo (Cathedral). Music lovers should first head upstairs in the Palazzo del Comune, where some of Cremona's most treasured violins are kept.

The cathedral overlooks the heart of Cremona

Time also is well spent in the Museo Stradivariano, a fascinating museum devoted to violin-making, with an enlightening English-language video to fill you in. Before you leave town, buy some of Cremona's famous *mostarda di frutta*, a deliciously piquant, mustard-enhanced, candied-fruit condiment.

➕ E2

Tourist information ✉ Piazza del Comune 5
☎ 0372 23 233 🕐 Mon.–Sat. 9–12:30 and 3–6, (also Sun. 9–12:30 Jul.–Aug.)

Palazzo del Comune ✉ Piazza del Comune 8
☎ 0372 407 250 🕐 Tue.–Sat. 8:30–6, Sun. 10–6
💵 $$ ℹ Guided tours only (in Italian)

Museo Stradivariano ✉ Via Ugolani Dati 4 ☎ 0372 407 777 🕐 Tue.–Sat. 9–6, Sun. 10–6 💵 $$$ (combined ticket with Pinacoteca and Palazzo del Comune)

FERRARA

Peaceful Ferrara, surrounded by fruit orchards, makes a good stopover if you're heading northeast from Bologna to Venice. This lovely and little-visited town was once a major player on the Renaissance political scene; its court was one of the most dynamic in Europe. The ruling dynasty was the d'Este family, whose palaces and monuments are scattered across the city and whose members married into Italy's most powerful ruling families. It was d'Este money that paid for the artistic treasures you see today. Their seat of power was the Castello d'Estense, a bulky, late 14th-century structure worth visiting for the decorated apartments and spooky dungeons. Another d'Este palace, the Palazzo Schifanoia, has delightful frescoes by Cosimo Tura in the Sala dei Mesi (Room of the Months), complete with lively court and hunting scenes. Try to visit the Palazzo Diamante, the home of the Pinacoteca Nazionale (Art Gallery) and the Duomo (Cathedral), which has a magnificent facade and a museum full of treasures. It is a pleasure to wander the medieval tangle of streets around Via delle Volte, which provide a rich contrast to the restrained elegance of the Renaissance palaces.

➕ E2

Tourist information ✉ Castello d'Estense ☎ 0532 209 370 🕐 Daily 9–1 and 2–6

Castello d'Estense ✉ Piazza Castello ☎ 0532 299 233 🕐 Tue.–Sun. 9:30–5 💵 $$$

Palazzo Schifanoia ✉ Via Scandiana 23 ☎ 0532 209 988 🕐 Tue.–Sun. 9–6 💵 $$

Pinacoteca Nazionale ✉ Corso Ercole d'Este 21 ☎ 0532 205 844 🕐 Tue.–Sat. 9–2 (also Wed. and Fri.–Sat. 2–7), Sun. 9–1 💵 $$

Duomo and Museo del Duomo ✉ Piazza Cattedrale 🕐 Tue.–Sat. 9–1 and 3–6 💵 $$

The Northwest and Emilia-Romagna

GÉNOVA

Génova's (Genoa) greatest days were the Middle Ages, when the city was one of Italy's five maritime republics and had territories stretching from Syria to North Africa. Christopher Columbus was born here, but the bankers wouldn't back him and he had to turn to Spain to fund his voyages. Italy's industrial revolution, based on steel and shipbuilding, began in Genoa, and despite the decline of its industry and docks, it's still the country's main maritime city. The port lies at the heart of the city and is backed by an eclectic quarter of medieval streets.

This confusing city will require perseverance as it sprawls over the coastal hills, with different levels linked by elevators and cog railroads. Don't miss a stroll down Via Garibaldi, an imposing stretch of Renaissance palaces built by rich bankers in the 16th century. Two now house galleries, the Palazzo Bianco and the Palazzo Rosso. The Palazzo Bianco displays Flemish masterpieces, including the sensuous *Mars and Venus* by Rubens. The Palazzo Rosso has a sumptuous interior that houses some fine paintings.

South from here is Genoa's cathedral, San Lorenzo; its black-and-white Gothic facade was constructed by French workmen. There is some fabulous precious metalwork in its treasury. Just up the street lies Piazza Matteotti, the medieval heart of the city. The huge striped building is the Palazzo Ducale, the last in a line of buildings erected for Genoa's ruling Doges from 1384 to 1515. Streets lead down to the revitalized waterfront, a pleasant place to spend time and perhaps take the elevator up the Grande Bigo (a cylindrical container suspended more than 600 feet in the air), architect Renzo Piano's visual centerpiece of the port's Expo 1992 revitalization. The views of the city are superb. Also on the waterfront is the Aquarium, a major crowd-pleaser with sea creatures from all the world's major habitats. Boat trips around the harbor also leave from here.

✛ B1

Tourist information ✉ Palazzina Santa Maria, Via al Porto Antico ☎ 010 248 711 🕐 Daily 9:30–1 and 2–6
Palazzo Bianco ✉ Via Garibaldi 11 ☎ 010 557 2013 🕐 Tue.–Fri. 9–7, Sat.–Sun. 10–7 ✋ $$
Palazzo Rosso ✉ Via Garibaldi 18 ☎ 010 557 2013 🕐 Tue.–Fri. 9–7, Sat.–Sun. 10–7 ✋ $$
Cattedrale di San Lorenzo ✉ Via San Lorenzo 🕐 Guided tours only Mon.–Sat. 9–11 and 3–5:30 ✋ Free
Grande Bigo ✉ Molo Vecchio 🕐 Tue.–Sat. 11–1 and 3–6, Sat.–Sun. 11–1 and 2–8 ✋ $
Aquarium ✉ Ponte Spinola ☎ 010 248 1205 🕐 Mon.–Wed. and Fri. 9:30–7:30, Thu. 9:30 a.m.–10 p.m., Sat.–Sun. 9:30–8:30 ✋ $$$

LAGO DI GARDA

The largest of all the Italian lakes, Lago di Garda (Lake Garda) has become a popular year-round destination for visitors from all over Europe. People are attracted by its range of scenic beauty and lovely climate. The southern end is fringed by gentle hills; the central area is lush with olives, grapes and citrus; and the north is squeezed by craggy mountains.

Northern Riva del Garda is the liveliest resort; it's packed throughout the season. Head down the lake's west side to escape the crowds, perhaps detouring onto the scenic backroads in the hills

The harbor of the great and historic port of Génova

Idyllic Sirmione and its castle jut into the southern end of Lago di Garda

behind Limone sul Garda before a stop at elegant Gardone Riviera. Heading along the lake's south side you'll come to exquisite Sirmione, where there is a beautifully sited castle. To the northeast lies Punta di San Vigilio, with its cypress-filled gardens and white beaches. Farther on, pleasing Malcésine gives access via cable car to the summit of Monte Baldo. In the mountains, there's superb hiking amid carpets of wildflowers. If you've got kids, head for Gardaland, Italy's biggest theme park.

✚ D2

Riva del Garda tourist information ✉ Giardini di Porta Orientale 8 ☎ 0464 554 444 ◷ Mon.–Sat. 9–noon and 3–6:30, Apr.–Sep.; 9–noon and 2:30–5, rest of year

Gardone Riviera tourist information ✉ Via della Repubblica 37 ☎ 0365 20 347 ◷ Mon.–Sat. 9–12:30 and 3–6 (closed Thu. afternoon), Sun. 10–noon, mid-Jun. to mid-Sep.; Mon.–Sat. 9–12:30 and 3–6, rest of year

Sirmione tourist information ✉ Viale Marconi 8 ☎ 030 916 114 ◷ Daily 9–12:30 and 3:30–6, Apr.–Oct.; Mon.–Fri. 9–12:30 and 3–6, rest of year

Malcésine tourist information ✉ Via Capitanato del Porto 6–8 ☎ 045 740 0044 ◷ Daily 9–1 and 3–6:30

Monte Baldo Cable Car ☎ 045 740 0206 ◷ Every half-hour 8–4, Apr.–Oct.; 8–4:45, rest of year ▯ $$$ ❶ Expect long lines in summer

Gardaland ✉ Castelnuovo del Garda ☎ 045 644

9777 ◷ Daily 9 a.m.–midnight, mid-Jun. to mid-Sep.; 10–6, Apr. 1 to mid-Jun. and last 2 weeks of Sep.; Sat.–Sun. 9–6, Oct. ▯ $$$

LAGO MAGGIORE

When exploring Lago Maggiore (Lake Maggiore) be selective, as some parts are marred by factories and industry. Stresa is an elegant lakeside town with good transportation links along the lake. From here you can take a boat to the Isole Borromee (Borromean Islands), an exquisite archipelago famed for the baroque gardens on the Ìsola Bella. Ferries run on to the Ìsola dei Pescatori (Fishermen's Island), a favorite of Ernest Hemingway. Back on the western shore, garden lovers shouldn't miss the many plant species in the gardens at Villa Táranto, created in the 1930s. Cannobio is a charming village that combines a lakeside position with a tangle of stepped alleys.

✚ B3

Stresa tourist information ✉ Via Canonica 8 ☎ 0323 30 150 ◷ Daily 10–12:30 and 3–6:30, mid-Mar. to Oct. 31; Mon.–Fri. 10–12:30 and 3–6:30, Sat. 10–12:30, rest of year

Ìsola Bella tourist information ☎ 0323 30 556 ◷ Daily 9–noon and 1:30–5:30, mid-Mar. to Sep. 30

Villa Táranto ✉ Via Vittorio Veneto 111, Pallanza ◷ Daily 8:30–7:30, Apr.–Oct. ▯ $

A glimpse of the cathedral from the colonnade of Mántova's vast Palazzo Ducale

MÁNTOVA

You'll have to penetrate some pretty grim outskirts to reach Mántova's (Mantua's) stunning medieval core, circled by three tranquil lakes, but it's well worth it. The Gonzaga family, another of the great Renaissance dynasties, built the astounding Palazzo Ducale, a huge complex with 500 rooms that was once the largest palace in Europe. You can take a tour here that includes the Camera degli Sposi, a room that contains masterful, intimate and tender frescoes by the 15th-century artist Mantegna, showing the Gonzaga Marquis Ludovico with his family and much-loved dog.

Across town lies the family's summer residence, the lavish Palazzo Te, one of the finest Mannerist ensembles anywhere, frescoed throughout by Giulio Romano. This palazzo is a must-see, from the portraits of the Gonzaga's favorite horses to the excesses of the topsy-turvy world of the Sala dei Giganti (Room of the Giants). Elsewhere in town, take a look at Alberti's facade for the church of Sant'Andrea before spending time in the cobbled central Piazza dell'Erbe.

🔒 D2

Tourist information ✉ Piazza A Mantegna 6
☎ 0376 328 253 🕐 Mon.–Sat. 8:30–12:30 and 3–6, Sun. 9:30–12:30
Palazzo Ducale ✉ Piazza Sordello 40 ☎ 0376 320 283 🕐 Tue.–Sun. 9–6:30 🖐 $$$ 🛈 Guided tours only (in Italian but occasionally in English) lasting around 90 minutes
Palazzo Te ✉ Viale Te 19 ☎ 0376 323 266 🕐 Tue.–Sun. 9–6, Mon. 1–6 🖐 $$
Sant'Andrea ✉ Piazza Mantegna 🕐 Daily 8–1 and 3–6 🖐 Free

MÓDENA

Módena is a quintessential northern town – quietly prosperous, its medieval core a delight, its industrial outskirts thriving. Ferrari and Maserati build their cars nearby, and its most famous contemporary citizen is the great tenor Luciano Pavarotti. The historic center is a ring of tight medieval streets around the Piazza Grande; sprinkled with shops and fine restaurants, this area is a delight. The town's main artistic sight is the 12th-century Duomo (Cathedral), a Romanesque masterpiece with a lurching campanile, the Torre Ghirlandina. The west facade, its portal supported by stately lions, and the south side have impressive stone relief work, while the serene and lofty interior has more fine wall sculpture. Módena's museums are housed in the Palazzo dei Musei, a five-minute walk from the cathedral along Via Emilia. The best of these is the Galleria Estense, a pleasing collection amassed by the d'Este family, who left Ferrara (see page 43) for Módena in 1598.

🔒 D2

Tourist information ✉ Piazza Grande 17 ☎ 059 206 660 🕐 Mon.–Sat. 8:30–1 and 3–7, Sun. 9–12:30
Duomo ✉ Piazza Grande 🕐 Daily 7–12:30 and 3:30–7 🖐 Free
Galleria Estense ✉ Piazzale Sant'Agostino 5 ☎ 059 439 5711 🕐 Tue.–Sun. 8:30–7:30 🖐 $$

PARCO NAZIONALE DEL GRAN PARADISO

The Parco Nazionale del Gran Paradiso (Gran Paradiso National Park) is a spectacular reserve around the Gran Paradiso massif, the only peak over 13,000 feet solely in Italy. You can explore it by

The majestic icy splendor of the Parco Nazionale del Gran Paradiso

driving up any of the three valleys west of the Valle d'Aosta, perhaps combining your drive with cable-car rides and hiking. The park was once a royal hunting zone where the Savoys pursued game; in 1920 they bequeathed it to the state to become Italy's first national park. The variety of scenery is stupendous, ranging from glaciers and snowy mountains to forests and Alpine meadows.

The little town of Cogne makes a good base for great walks, while the high tops are served by cable car. Nearby, at Valnontey, you'll find the Giardino Alpino Paradisia, at its best in June when there are splendid spreads of native Alpine flora. But for the true experience, take to the hills to see chamois, ibex and birds in their natural environment.

✚ A2

Cogne tourist information ✉ Piazza Emilio Chanoux 36, Cogne ☎ 016 574 040 🕐 Mon.–Sat. 9–12:30 and 3–6, Sun. 9–12:30

Giardino Alpino Paradisia ✉ Above Valnontey 🕐 0165 905 808 🕐 Daily 9–noon and 2:30–6, mid-Jun. to mid-Oct. 💶 $$

PARMA

There's much more to Parma than *prosciutto* (Parma ham) and *parmigiano* (parmesan cheese), as you'll soon discover on arrival in this affluent provincial town. Most sights lie east of the Parma river, although music lovers might want to visit Casa Natale di Toscanini (Toscanini's birthplace) and stroll in the lovely 18th-century gardens of the Parco Ducale across the river. In the old center you'll find the beautiful 11th-century Lombard-Romanesque Duomo (Cathedral); the interior has works by both Corregio and Parmigianino. The cathedral's 12th-century baptistery, four stories of sculpted pink marble, deserves more than a cursory glance before you head for the massive Palazzo della Pilotta. Built as a Farnese palace in the 16th century and restored after World War II bombing, it houses the Galleria, with a collection of massive Renaissance paintings. Parma also is noted for opera – the Teatro Regio has a reputation that rivals Milan's La Scala.

✚ D2

Tourist information ✉ Via Melloni 1/B ☎ 0521 218 889 🕐 Mon.–Sat. 9–7, Sun. 9–1

Casa Natale di Toscanini ✉ Borgo Tanzi 13 ☎ 0521 285 499 🕐 Tue.–Sun. 10–1 and 3–6 💶 Free

Duomo and Baptistery ✉ Piazza del Duomo ☎ 0521 235 886 💶 Free

Galleria Nazionale ✉ Palazzo della Pilotta 15 ☎ 0521 233 309 🕐 Tue.–Sun. 8:30–2 💶 $$$

Teatro Regio ✉ Via Garibaldi 16a ☎ 0521 218 678 ℹ Reserve in advance for good seats at the opera

DRIVE: MOUNTAINS AND LAKES

Duration: 3½ to 4 hours

This drive takes you around Lago di Como (Lake Como), the most beautiful of the Italian lakes, a dream of water, mountain peaks, lush vegetation and gracious buildings.

The route is straightforward, although for some stretches you'll have the option to take either the older, more scenic route along the lakeshore, or the faster route higher up the slopes through numerous tunnels. En route you'll have a chance to explore some of the lakeside towns and villages, enjoy some breathtakingly lovely gardens, take steamers up or down the lake, or spend time at one of the beaches along the water's edge. Lake Como's proximity to Milan means huge crowds on weekends and in July and August, so bear this in mind when planning your trip.

The drive starts in Como, the main town at the lake's southern end.

Como's main industry is silk manufacture, and the revamped old town center has plenty of outlets where you can buy locally made scarves and fabrics. The town's locale is lovely, but it's always crowded with visitors and the industrial outskirts don't add to its

The red-roofed houses of Menággio

charm, so don't linger – although the cathedral is certainly worth more than a glance.

Take the SS340 up the west shore of the lake, heading for Argegno.

En route you'll pass Cernobbio, a pleasant lakeside village that is the starting point for a 130-kilometer (80-mile) hiking trail through the mountains, the Via dei Monti Lariani. Argegno is a medley of old houses with wooden eaves, steep and narrow streets, and an appealing array of lakeside cafés. Boats run from here to the Isola Comacina, Como's only island, a wild little place that's the home of a small artists' colony.

Continue along the SS340 to Tremezzo.

Look for signs to Mezzegra; the Villa Belmonte there was the scene in 1944 of the execution of Mussolini and his mistress Clara Petacci by partisan leader Walter Audisio.

Elegant Tremezzo, with its villas and hotels, has a distinctly fin-de-siècle air. It's worth stopping here to visit the Villa Carlotta, a lavish neoclassic pink-and-white villa built by a Prussian princess and now filled with 18th-century statuary. Its main attractions are the gardens, 14 acres of beautifully tended grounds renowned for camellias, azaleas and rhododendrons. These shrubs flower between January and July and are a glowing range of reds, pinks, whites and yellows. They're at their peak around Easter.

Continue along the lake, passing through bustling and lively Menággio, to

Lovely villas and fertile gardens border the Lago di Como at Bellágio, the jewel of the lakeside towns

Gravedona, an old lakeside town.
At the northern tip of the lake, cross the River Mera, then head down the east fork on the SS36. If time is short, you have the option of taking this higher, faster road or sticking to the old scenic route along the water's edge. Both roads are extremely busy on weekends.

Varenna makes a good stopping point along this shore, a pretty place with two more outstanding gardens, Villa Cipressi and the Villa Monastero. South from here you'll be heading down Como's east fork, a fjord-like stretch with huge granite ridges rising behind the water.

At Lecco pick up the SS583 to Bellágio.
Standing on the tip of land separating Como's two forks, Bellágio has to be one of northern Italy's loveliest towns. Its oleander-planted waterfront, cobbled streets and gracious hotels and villas make it a great place for a stopover. There are more horticultural treats at the Villa Serbelloni, or you might simply want to relax by taking a steamer trip down the lake.

From Bellágio take the SS583, which runs along the lake's eastern shore back to Como.

Como tourist information
✉ Piazza Cavour 17 ☎ 031 330 0111 🕐 Mon.–Sat. 9–12:30 and 2:30–6
Bellágio tourist information
✉ Piazza della Chiesa 14 ☎ 031 950 204 🕐 Mon.–Fri. 9–noon and 3–6

PAVIA

Only half an hour by train from Milan, Pavia makes a nice excursion. It's one of those small and enjoyable northern towns where you can take a leisurely stroll through narrow streets past towers and piazzas. Its zenith was more than a thousand years ago when it was capital of the kingdom of the Lombards; two major churches, San Pietro in Ciel d'Oro and San Michele, both date from the 11th to 12th centuries. There's a 14th-century fortress, the Castello Visconteo, which houses the local museum, and a big, cobbled central square adjacent to the cathedral. Pleasant enough, but for a real treat drive the 10 kilometers (6 miles) to the Certosa di Pavia (Carthusian Monastery), one of Europe's most impressive monasteries. It was built for the Milan Viscontis in the 15th century as a mausoleum and is dazzlingly rich in Renaissance and baroque art. You can tour the church, cloisters and refectory, then stop off and purchase some chartreuse at the monastery shop, still made by Carthusian monks who live here.

➕ C2

Tourist information ✉ Via Fabio Filzi 2 ☎ 0382 22 156 🕐 Mon.–Sat. 8:30–12:30 and 2–6

Castello Visconteo and Museo Civico ✉ Viale XI Febbraio ☎ 0382 33 853 🕐 Tue.–Fri. 9–1:30, Sat.–Sun. 10–7, Sep.–Nov. and Mar.–Jun.; Tue.–Sat. 9–1:30, Sun. 9–1, rest of year 👋 $$

Certosa di Pavia ✉ Certosa di Pavia ☎ 0382 925 613 🕐 Tue.–Sun. 9–11:30 and 2:30–5, Mar.–Oct.; 9:30–12:30 and 2:30–4:30, rest of year 🚩 Guided tours only, led by a monk and almost always in Italian

PIACENZA

If you enjoy low-key, prosperous small towns, Piacenza, near the Lombardy border, merits a stop. The Roman town marked the end of the Via Emilia, one of the big consular roads, and Piacenza's street plan still adheres to the old Roman grid pattern. The main square, Piazza dei Cavalli, gets its name from the splendid bronze equestrian statues on either side – they're the work of a pupil of Giambologna and were cast in the 17th century. The redbrick Palazzo del

Comune dates from 1280, the same period as the nearby church of San Francesco. The cathedral is a grand Lombard Romanesque structure dating from the 1220s, much altered over the centuries – the interior is particularly lovely. Piacenza's Musei di palazzo Farmese (Civic Museum) houses the odd bronze known as the *fegato di Piacenza* (Piacenza liver). This liver-shaped object, covered with inscriptions, dates from Etruscan times and was used to divine the future. The museums' building itself was built in the 16th century.

➕ C2

Tourist information ✉ Piazzetta dei Mercanti 7 ☎ 0523 329 324 🕐 Tue.–Sat. 9:30–12:30 and 3–6; closed Thu. afternoon

Musei di Palazzo Farmese ✉ Piazza della Cittadella 29 ☎ 0523 328 270 🕐 Tue.–Sat. 9–1 (also Fri.–Sat. 3–6), Sun. 9:30–1 and 3–6, Apr.–Oct.; Tue.–Sat. 8:45–1 (also Fri.–Sat. 3–6), Sun. 9:30–1 and 3–6, rest of year 👋 $$

RAVENNA

The finest Byzantine mosaics in the world (other than Istanbul's) are found in Ravenna, an appealing small town near the Adriatic coast. In AD 402, the Emperor Honorius moved the capital of the rapidly declining Roman Empire to Ravenna, an easily defensible marshland town near the important Roman port of Classis. Until it fell to the Goths in AD 476, it was the imperial capital and continued to thrive under first barbarian and then Byzantine rule.

We owe the wondrous sixth-century churches and their mosaics to the last Romans and the Byzantine rulers, notably Theodoric and Justinian. San Vitale, a typical Byzantine-style basilica richly decorated with glowing mosaics, was begun in AD 525. The mosaics show biblical scenes, while the walls portray the Emperor Justinian and his wife, Theodora, an unattractive character who was a prostitute and circus performer. In the basilica grounds you'll find the tiny and jewel-like Mausoleo di Galla Placidia (Tomb of Galla Placidia), whose interior walls glitter with lustrous blue-and-gold mosaics. Nearby there's Ravenna's Museo

The plain exterior of Ravenna's Basilica di San Vitale hides some of Europe's finest Byzantine mosaics

Nazionale (National Museum), worth a quick look. From there head across town to Sant'Apollinare Nuovo, another mosaic-rich sixth-century church. The mosaics here run along each side of the nave, with stately processions of martyrs bearing gifts for Christ and the Blessed Virgin.

On the way to Sant'Apollinare you'll pass through the main Piazza del Popolo, a pretty 15th-century square. Also en route is Dante's Tomb, a small 18th-century building housing the great poet's remains; he died in Ravenna in 1321 after having been exiled from his native Florence. Ravenna's other Byzantine masterpiece, the great church of Sant'Apollinare in Classe, lies just outside the city near the remains of Roman Classis. Perhaps the most evocative of all Ravenna's churches, Sant'Apollinare's interior is spacious and beautifully proportioned, with glittering gold mosaics. ✚ E1

Tourist information ✉ Via Salara 8/12 ☎ 0544 35 404 🕐 Mon.–Sat. 8:30–7, Sun. 10–4
San Vitale ✉ Via Benedetto Fiandrini ☎ 0544 215 193 🕐 Daily 9–7, Apr.–Oct.; 9–5:30, rest of year 🎟 $$$
Mausoleo di Galla Placidia ✉ Via Benedetto Fiandrini 🕐 Daily 9–7, Apr.–Oct.; 9–5:30, rest of year 🎟 $$
Museo Nazionale ✉ Via Benedetto Fiandrini ☎ 0544 34 424 🕐 Tue.–Sun. 8:30–7:30 🎟 $$

Sant'Apollinare Nuovo ✉ Via Roma ☎ 0544 219 938 🕐 Daily 9–7, Apr.–Oct.; 9–5:30, rest of year 🎟 Free
Tomba di Dante ✉ Via D Alighieri 9 ☎ 0544 30 252 🕐 Daily 9–7 🎟 Free
Sant'Apollinare in Classe ✉ Via Romea Sud ☎ 0544 473 569 🕐 Mon.–Sat. 8:30–7:30, Sun. 1–7:30 🎟 $$

RIMINI

Big, brash and glitzy, with miles of sandy beaches and baking summer sun, Rimini is the archetypal seaside town, a successful combination of family resort and a buzzing center for the best of European nightclubs. It can be noisy and sleazy, but it's never dull. If you're looking for an Italian taste of the European club scene, this is the place to come. The downside is Rimini's reputation for an active prostitution scene involving all lifestyles.

Rimini, with its satellite resorts, stretches for 20 kilometers (12 miles) along the coast. The other face of Rimini can be seen inland; here you'll find the old town. The high spot is the Tempio Malatestiana, designed by the famous Renaissance architect Alberti in 1450 to honor Rimini's ruler, Sigismondo Malatesta. It's a bizarre and pleasing building, with an interior housing a Giotto crucifix and a fresco portrait of Sigismondo by Piero della Francesca.

The Northwest and Emilia-Romagna

Summer swimmers frequent one of the Riviera di Levante's picturesque villages

✚ E1

Tourist information ✉ Piazzale Federico Fellini 3
☎ 0541 56 598 🕐 Daily 8:30–7, Jun.–Sep.; Mon.–Sat.
9:30–12:30 and 3:30–6:30, rest of year 🚌 The Blue
Line bus runs nightly (11 p.m.–4 or 5 a.m.) during the
summer between Rimini's clubs
Tempio Malastestiano ✉ Via IV Novembre 35
☎ 0541 51 130 🕐 Mon.–Sat. 8–noon and 3:30–7, Sun.
9–1 and 3:30–7 💳 Free

RIVIERA DI LEVANTE

The stretch of coast southeast of Genoa
(see page 44) is known as the Riviera di
Levante, a chain of fishing villages and
resorts backed by mountains and cliffs
with pines and aromatic maquis. The
finest section is the Cinque Terre (see
page 42), but if you're looking for an
alternative there are serveral choices.
Down the coast from Genoa is Camogli;
quieter than some villages, its steep streets
are lined with colorful houses clustered
around a tiny harbor. Rapallo makes a
good contrast. Built in gentle Edwardian
times, it's a pleasing mix of elegance and
fun, with a lively cultural season in
summer. Beautiful and picturesque
Portofino to the west is synonymous
with sophisticated *dolce vita*, a classy and
exclusive resort frequented by the rich

and famous, with prices to match. For
much the same type of village and
atmosphere, but less expense, you can
head down the coast to Portovenere, just
south of the Cinque Terre. You can
explore the coast from here, or take a trip
to the lovely and relatively unspoiled
island of Palmária just off the coast.

✚ C1

Camogli tourist information ✉ Via XX Settembre 33
☎ 0185 771 066 🕐 Mon.–Sat. 9–noon and 3:30–6,
Sun. 9–1
Rapallo tourist information ✉ Via Daz 9
☎ 0185 230 346 🕐 Mon.–Sat. 9:30–12:30 and 3–7:30,
Sun. 9:30–12:30 and 4:40–7:30, mid-Apr. to Oct. 31;
Mon.–Sat. 9:30–12:30 and 2:30–5:30, rest of year
Portofino tourist information ✉ Via Roma 35
☎ 0185 269 024 🕐 Daily 10:30–1:30 and 2:30–7:30,
mid-Apr. to Oct. 31; Tue.–Sun. 10:30–1:30 and
2:30–5:30, rest of year
Portovenere tourist information ✉ Piazza Bastreri 1
☎ 0187 790 961 🕐 Mon.–Sat. 9–noon and 3–7, Sun.
9–noon

TORINO

A fitting capital of Piedmont, Italy's
second-richest region, Torino (Turin)
stands on the banks of the Po river. Turin
is a sprawling industrial city with an
elegant baroque heart. Its still-discernible
French flavor arrived with the ruling
house of Savoy in 1574; three centuries
later the house teamed up with the
Risorgimento's liberal politician, Camillo
Cavour, to lend credibility to the
unification movement.

In 1860 Turin was the first capital of
Italy, and 10 years later its Savoy
monarch, Vittorio Emanuele II, became
king of the united country. During the
20th century Turin was the headquarters
of Fiat, whose owners, the immensely
powerful Agnelli family, are an
undisputed force throughout Italy.

The elegant Via Roma, all designer
stores and classy cafés, bisects the city-
center grid plan, and most of what you'll
want to see is around here. First stop
should be Turin's two main museums, the
superb Museo Egizio (Egyptian
Museum) and the Galleria Sabauda
(Sabauda Gallery), housed in the same
building. The Sabauda's artistic base is the

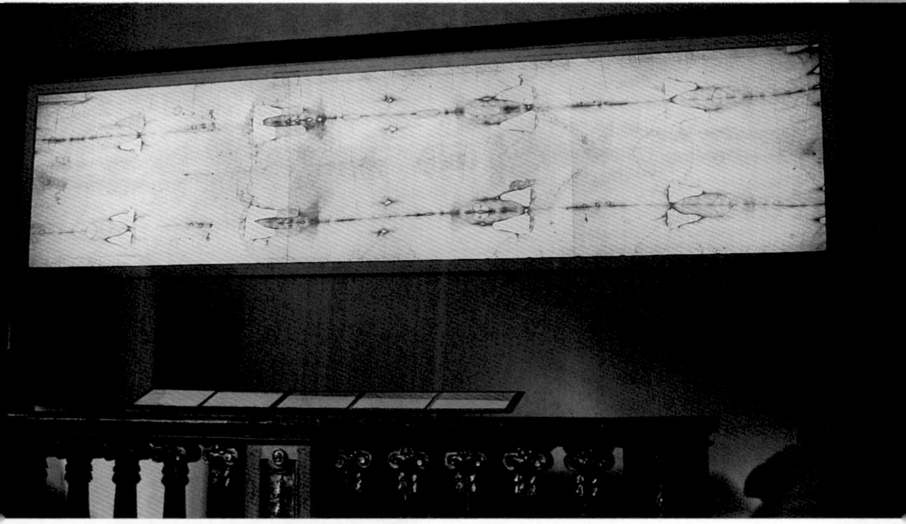

A replica of the Holy Shroud is exhibited in the cathedral in Torino

Savoy private collections, particularly strong on Dutch and Flemish schools, although you should not miss Pollaiuolo's wonderful *Tobias and the Angel*, a taut and colorful 15th-century masterpiece.

Nearby, visit the Museo Nazionale del Risorgimento, devoted to Turin's role in unification, with a fascinating section on Garibaldi. Piazza Castello is home to the incredibly opulent Palazzo Reale (Royal Palace), the more restrained Palazzo Madama and the Armeria Reale (Royal Armory), one of the world's great museums of arms and armor. Off Piazza Castello is the Duomo (Cathedral); its best-known treasure is the Holy Shroud (Sindone). This length of linen contains what many Christians believe to be the imprint of the face and body of Christ. Many people contend the shroud was used to wrap Jesus' body after the crucifixion.

From the cathedral, head toward the river and walk the three miles down to the Parco del Valentino. Here you can visit the Borgo Medioevale, an attractive synthesis of Piedmont's best medieval buildings, constructed in 1884. Farther along the river, is the Museo dell'Automobile (Automobile Museum).

A2

Tourist information Atrium Torino, Piazza Solferino 011 535 181; www.turismotorino.org

Daily 9:30–7

Museo Egizio Via Accademia delle Scienze 6 011 561 7776 Tue.–Sun. 8:30–7:30 $$$

Galleria Sabauda Via Accademia delle Scienze 6 011 547 440 Tue. and Fri.–Sun. 8:30–2, Wed.–Thu. 2–7:30 (also Wed.–Thu. 10–2, Oct.–May) $$

Museo del Risorgimento Via Accademia delle Scienze 5 011 562 1147 Tue.–Sun. 9–7 $$

Armeria Reale Piazza Castello 191 011 543 889 Closed for restoration $$

Duomo Via XX Settembre Daily 7–6 Free

Borgo Medioevale Parco del Valentino 011 443 1701 Daily 9–7 Free

Museo dell'Automobile Corso Unità d'Italia 40 011 677 666 Tue.–Sun. 10–6:30 (also Sun. 6:30–8:30) $$

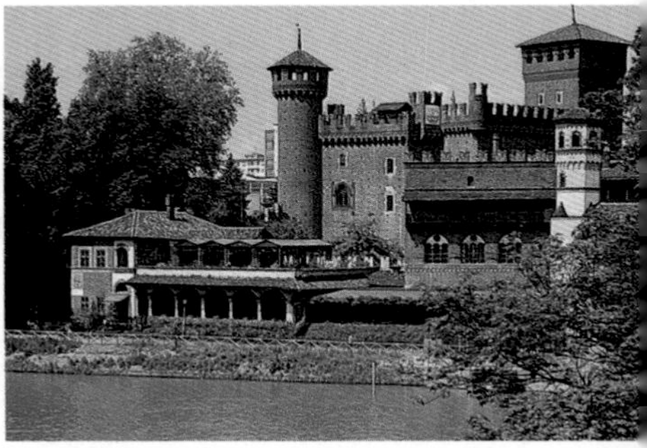

The Po river cuts through the heart of Torino

A TASTE OF THE NORTH

The Northwest and Emilia-Romagna

In the prosperous regions of northern Italy, you'll find some of the country's best cooking. It features a rich cuisine based on superb-quality fresh ingredients and a range of local specialties. Many of these are either imported or imitated in the United States, but make a point of sampling them on their home ground, where cheese is made from unpasteurized milk and hams, wild mushrooms and wine have had to travel only a few miles from their point of origin. You'll taste the difference.

Valle d'Aosta and Piedmont

These regions display close links with France, so it's not surprising that there are French overtones in local food. Butter, cream and cheese are freely used, and you should try *fonduta*, a melted cheese dish similar to fondue. Piedmont's prize food is the white truffle, in season in the fall from the hills around Alba (see page 39). With an intensity of flavor impossible to describe, this is one extravagance you should indulge in for a once-in-a-lifetime experience. Wild mushrooms are less expensive and another culinary treat; the best variety are *porcini*, a meaty-textured and robustly flavored woodland giant often served grilled. The full-bodied wines from the region, such as the fabulous Barolo and Barbaresco, could have been invented as an accompaniment. They go equally well with roasted sweet chestnuts. Much sparkling wine is made in Asti (see page 40), while worldwide favorite vermouths like Martini and Cinzano are made near Turin.

Lombardy

Piedmont's neighbor, Lombardy, has its own gifts. This is a region where the staple is either rice or *polenta*, as well as pasta. *Polenta* is cornmeal, stirred and boiled for 40 minutes or so, then served as it comes or cooled and used to accompany different meats and sauces. Rice (mainly the firm and plump-grained *arborio*, ideal for risotto) is grown in the Ticino area. The classic risotto is the seemingly simple *risotto alla Milanese*, which uses

veal juices, saffron and butter. Milan was the birthplace, too, of *osso buco*, a slow-cooked dish of veal shanks; it is rich and deep-flavored.

Lombardy, one of Italy's biggest cheese-making regions, is the home of *gorgonzola*, *mascarpone* and *Bel Paese*.

If you've enjoyed a light, vanilla-scented *panettone* cake at Christmas, remember that this also originates in Milan.

Liguria

With Liguria's long shoreline, fish is inevitably a treat, and you'll find it on menus everywhere. The most wonderful local ingredient has to be basil, and you may be lucky enough to see – and smell – a whole field of this heavenly herb as you travel in Liguria. It's used to make the ubiquitous *pesto* and many other dishes – even as a flavoring for ice cream. The aroma is comple-mented by wines from the Cinque Terre (see page 42). Dry and clean-tasting, the wines have a light and flinty bouquet that goes well with the local pizza variant, *focaccia*.

Left: Ingredients for Liguria's famous pesto sauce
Below: Rice, the basis for intensely flavored risotto

Emilia-Romagna

Across the country in Emilia-Romagna there's more rich, smooth cooking. Many Italians freely admit that you eat better here than almost anywhere else in Italy (except their own region, of course). Parma, the home of *prosciutto di Parma* (Parma ham) and *parmigianino* (parmesan cheese), is in this region. Much local produce is of a quality and flavor to live up to these two culinary superstars. Balsamic vinegar is produced here; buy a precious bottle to bring life to your cooking, as just a few drops will go a long way. Pasta, usually made with eggs and stuffed with meat, cheese and herb combinations, is enjoyed here.

Lambrusco is the great local wine. Be sure to try a DOC (Denominazione di Origine Controllata) variety, which guarantees the origin and quality; even the most critical wine connoisseurs will be impressed by its dark, deep nose.

THE NORTHEAST

The Northeast

"THE beauty of Venice, the grandeur of the Dolomites and the quiet serenity of the hinterland and its splendid towns draw countless visitors to the northeast."

The Grand Canal, lined with superb buildings, is Venice's main highway

THE NORTHEAST

Many visitors to the northeast never discover the immense variety of this diverse region. Made up of the Veneto, Trentino-Alto Adige and Friuli-Venezia Giulia, the area encompasses some of Europe's finest mountain scenery and a clutch of Italy's most alluring towns. Add to this the economic prosperity brought by the region's industry and a long tradition of agriculture and wine-making, and the attractions of this tucked-away corner of Italy become clear.

Shaping of the Northeast

The region of the Veneto forms this area's core; this was the heartland of independent Venice, the mainland territories ruled by the Venetian Republic from the 14th to the 18th centuries. Historically settled and prosperous, the Veneto is very much a part of mainstream Italy.

North of the Veneto, the situation changes in Trentino-Alto Adige, a multicultured hybrid of a region made up of Italian-speaking, mainly rural Trentino, and the German-speaking Alto Adige, also known as Sudtirol.

The Northeast

The Alto Adige was ceded to Italy at the end of World War I, having previously been part of the Austro-Hungarian Empire. Ethnic differences here have caused tension and an undercurrent of terrorism over the years, but a large measure of autonomy has, on the whole, kept the lid on nationalist ambitions.

Friuli-Venezia Giulia borders Austria and Slovenia. This area has quite a mixture of cultures, languages and allegiances. It straddles the hazy bridge between the Mediterranean world and that of Teutonic and Slavic central Europe. Becoming part of Italy after World War I, its final border disputes with Yugoslavia were not settled until the 1970s.

The Northeast Today

Although industrialization has marred some of the region's scenic beauty, it has also brought prosperity. The flat coastal plains are scattered with light industry and modern housing. The vast industrial complex around Marghera is best avoided. But agriculture is still vital, with arable farming in the lowlands and extensive wine-producing areas in the lower hills. Tourism is important throughout this region; apart from Venice itself, Verona and Padua draw the crowds, while the mountain splendor of the Dolomites lures skiing and hiking enthusiasts year-round.

On the whole, vacationers here are Italian, and outside Venice you won't encounter the vast numbers of visitors found in other regions. You'll notice more than a touch of Teutonic efficiency in some parts, while the general affluence is striking. Well-dressed people, smart shops and expensive cars catch the eye. There's a good balance between traditional ways and the 21st century, making this corner a real Italian microcosm.

European Influences

Throughout the Veneto, people are polite, friendly, efficient and hard-working, but without the relentless drive of their neighbors nearer Milan. Like all Italians, they live life to the fullest in a less dramatic and passionate way to that so evident farther south. Accustomed to dealing with international visitors, they know what people expect in the way of facilities. In the service industries, you'll find English widely spoken. In the main towns and cities, the siesta is not as important, which means longer hours for museums and churches.

In Trentino-Alto Adige, you'll immediately notice the Teutonic influences. Trentino is mostly Italian

Mellow sunlight warms a peaceful corner of Treviso

speaking, but Alto Adige is bilingual, with German the dominant language in many places. Teutonic efficiency reigns and mixes delightfully with typical Italian pleasures. Cuisine pays homage to its northern roots, with dumplings and sauerkraut, wiener schnitzel and apple strudel often on the menu.

Similar culinary links exist in Friuli-Venezia Giulia, but here the accent is middle European with a strong café culture, cream cakes, goulash and more dumplings. Friuli-Venezia is more ethnically jumbled, comprising a cocktail of Italian, Slavic and middle European cultures. You'll see evidence of this in the bilingual street signs throughout the region; the dialect here is *friulano*.

Appreciating the Northeast

Venice is one of the world's most enticing cities, but there's much more to the area. If you make the trip this far north, take time to explore. You should see Verona, as beautiful now as when Shakespeare set *Romeo and Juliet* there, while Vicenza, with its tight-knit center and Palladian architecture, should also be high on your list. Padua, although less immediately appealing, has unrivaled artistic treasures. These three can be tackled individually as day trips from Venice, but each deserves an overnight stay to be appreciated fully.

In Trentino-Alto Adige, Bolzano and Merano have great charm, but the real attraction is the Dolomites. These magnificent mountains can be enjoyed

Scenic grandeur surrounds many of the upland villages in Italy's northeast corner

by rail or car, but to appreciate them at their best you should try to fit in some skiing or hiking. Farther east, the scenery of Friuli-Venezia Giulia offers immense variety, from the Alps and the limestone plateau known as the Carso to alluvial plains and stretches of varied coastline.

Trieste has an atmosphere all of its own, while the charms of Cividale dei Friuli and Aquiléia are on a par with much better-known areas. Getting around is easy, with good roads, public transportation and plenty of accommodations. To get the most out of a Dolomite trip, rent a car (if you're a nervous driver, however, avoid the dramatic mountain roads).

When To Go

If you enjoy winter sports, you could combine skiing with a Venice trip; December and January, when the city is virtually empty of tourists, are the best times to visit. The weather then can be sparkling clear and bitterly cold or romantically mist-shrouded. If seeing Venice in sunshine is your goal, wait until late spring; May and June are the optimum months. This also is a splendid time for the mountains, when the snows are retreating and the Alpine meadows spread with wildflowers. It's best to avoid the cities in the peak summer months (July and August), when the crowds and the heat can make sightseeing rather unpleasant.

VENICE

The city built over water, Venice
(Venézia) never fails to enchant.
Familiar from a thousand pictures, the
magical blend of stone and water, with
all of its accompanying sounds and
scents, will be a highlight of your
Italian experience. It may be crowded
and expensive, crumbling and shabby,
but this treasure-packed city will win
your heart. It's a dream waiting to
come true.

Picturesque Surroundings

If money is no object, the optimum

place to stay is one of the luxury hotels
along the Grand Canal, but there are
many other options, often in quieter but
just as picturesque surroundings. The
sestieri (city areas) of Dorsoduro, San
Marco, Castello and San Polo are
perhaps the nicest parts. Avoid the area
around the railroad station where it is
less pleasant, although there are plenty
of accommodations here for late
arrivals. Don't stay in Mestre, a polluted
industrial sprawl across the causeway.

Take time daily to work out your
itinerary; Venice can be slow to move
around in, and shortcuts through the
maze of streets will save valuable time.
You'll be doing a huge amount of

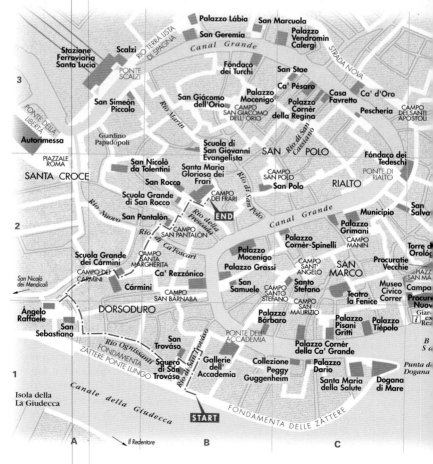

walking as you negotiate the bridges; come prepared with comfortable, well broken-in shoes. Main through-city routes are designated by yellow signs above head height. The tourist office publishes a bilingual monthly guide to Venice, *Un Ospite di Venezia* (Venetian Guest), which has everything you'll need to know.

Try to allow three to four days at least to see Venice; there are enough sights to keep you busy for months. Start by getting a feel for the place before venturing into the crowded visitor areas. A good way to ease yourself in is by taking a *vaporetto* boat; numbers 1 or 82 down the Grand

Gondolas

The elegant gondola is a shallow-draft vessel propelled by a single oarsman standing at the back of the boat. Their shape and depth make them ideal for penetrating even the narrowest and shallowest canals. A ride in a shiny-black gondola is an essential experience for many visitors, but they are very expensive and normally follow a set route.

The Northeast

Canal or 51 or 52 around the northern part of the city are all good bets. Take a boat trip to some of the lagoon islands; public transportation is more fun than a tour. Or simply wander.

Dining Out

It's worth paying a little extra to enjoy typical Venetian dishes. Starters include delicate plates of mixed seafood and *sarde in saor*, sardines cooked with vinegar, and pasta dishes range from *spaghettie alle vongole* (with clams) to various rice dishes. Venetians eat a lot of fish but some can be expensive, and you often pay for the weight of your portion. Liver and onions *(fegato alla veneziana)* is another local dish.

Tiramisù, now found everywhere, is a Venetian dessert. Made from coffee-soaked spongecake and sweetened *mascarpone* cheese, its name means "pick-me-up." Most wine comes from the Veneto region on the mainland; wines to look out for include Soave, Valpolicella, Bardolino and the excellent Bianco di Custoza. Be sure to try a glass of dry sparkling *prosecco* as an apéritif; mixed with fresh peach juice, it becomes a Bellini. An essential city experience is relaxing over a drink at Florian or Quadri, Venice's smartest cafés, situated on either side of Piazza San Marco.

Venetian Craftware

The main stores are clustered along the Calle dei Fabbri, the Frezzeria and the so-called Merceria, a network of streets connecting Piazza San Mark's with the Rialto. Here the best of the Murano glass manufacturers have their showrooms. Artisan shops selling imaginative craftware are found in the oddest corners, while another temptation comes in the shape of stunning silk and velvet fabrics. Marbled paper and exotic papier-maché masks are other good souvenirs. You can even buy a gondolier's shirt or hat – try Emilio Ceccato, near the Rialto.

Entertainment

Carnival, when thousands of people wearing costumes and elaborate masks parade the city streets, lasts for 10 days before the start of Lent. The main summer festival is the feast of *La Sensa*, when the mayor and his entourage sail out in the state barge and enact a symbolic marriage to the waters. This is followed in July by the *Festa del Redentore*, a festival of thanksgiving for deliverance from a plague. A pontoon bridge is built across the Giudecca canal to the great Redentore church, and the feast culminates in a spectacular fireworks display. During the *Regata Storica* in September, there are races of decorated craft manned by crews in period dress. Year-round entertainment includes classical concerts, theater, football games and the casino. *Un Ospite di Venezia* carries full listings of what's going on.

ESSENTIAL INFORMATION

TOURIST INFORMATION
•San Marco 71/f ☎ 041 529 8711 (for all tourist offices); www.turismovenezia.it
•Palazzina del Santi, Giardini ex Reali
•Stazione Santa Lucia
•Viale Santa Maria Elisabetta, Lido di Venezia (summer only)

URBAN TRANSPORTATION
If you arrive by car, you must leave the vehicle in one of the parking lots on the outskirts. Venice's public transportation system is operated by ACTV (☎ 041 528 7886) and uses two types of boats, *vaporetti* (bigger and slower) and *motoscafi* (smaller and faster). All boats are numbered and follow set routes that frequently change. *Vaporetti* leave from docks that are clearly marked with the service numbers. As the same numbers sometimes go in two directions, ascertain which way you're heading before boarding. Tickets can be bought at the dock or at shops showing the ACTV sticker. You can save money by buying a 12-, 24- or 72-hour pass. All tickets must be validated at the machine on the dock before boarding. ACTV publishes two booklets, one showing routes, the other timetables. Water taxis are fast and expensive. They can be hailed on various canals, but it is easier to phone; ☎ 041 522 2303, 041 522 1265 or 041 523 0575. Gondolas are a fun way to travel but they are very expensive. The seven *traghetti* (ferries) crossing the Grand Canal at various points also are useful. Pay as you board.

AIRPORT INFORMATION
Venice's Marco Polo Airport (☎ 041 260 9260; www.veniceairport.it), on the northern edge of the lagoon, handles domestic and international flights. For city connections take a bus or taxi from outside the terminal to Piazzale Roma at the edge of the city and then connect with your hotel by *vaporetto* (water bus). The transfer takes around 20 minutes. Purchase tickets from the office inside the terminal before boarding. Alilaguna runs a boat service from the airport to the city center. It leaves from outside the terminal and calls at Murano, the Lido, Arsenale, San Marco and the Záttere. The fastest way to the city is by water taxi; these leave from outside the terminal and take around 20 minutes to the center.

CLIMATE – Average highs and lows

JAN.	FEB.	MAR.	APR.	MAY	JUN.	JUL.	AUG.	SEP.	OCT.	NOV.	DEC.
5°C	8°C	12°C	17°C	21°C	24°C	27°C	26°C	23°C	18°C	12°C	8°C
41°F	46°F	54°F	63°F	70°F	75°F	81°F	79°F	73°F	64°F	54°F	46°F
0°C	2°C	5°C	9°C	13°C	17°C	19°C	18°C	16°C	12°C	7°C	3°C
32°F	36°F	41°F	48°F	55°F	63°F	66°F	64°F	61°F	54°F	45°F	37°F

VENICE SIGHTS

Key to symbols

➕ map coordinates refer to the Venice map on page 62; sights below are highlighted in yellow on the map
✉ address or location ☎ telephone number
🕐 opening times 🍴 restaurant on site or nearby
🚢 nearest boat or ferry stop 💶 admission charge:
$$$ more than €6, $$ €3 to €6, $ less than €3
ℹ information

BASILICA DI SAN MARCO

Venice's cathedral, the Basilica di San Marco (St. Mark's Basilica), was built in 1094 on the site of the ninth-century basilica that reputedly houses the body of St. Mark, Venice's patron saint. Its profusion of domes and sculptures, mosaics and marbles, and a superb fusion of Byzantine, Islamic and Western art and architecture, make it one of Europe's most exotic cathedrals. Allow time to study the thousands of mosaics high above the undulating marble pavements, and to admire the Romanesque carvings around the main door. Don't miss the great gold altar panel, the Pala d'Oro, encrusted with jewels and precious enamels, or the four gilded bronze horses possibly dating from the fourth century BC and stolen by the Venetians from Constantinople in 1204.
➕ D2 ✉ Piazza San Marco 1 ☎ 041 522 5697 or 041 522 5205 🕐 Mon.–Sat. 9:45–4 (also Mon.–Sat. 4–4:30, Oct.–Apr.), Sun. 2–4 🚢 1, 42, 52, 82 (San Zaccaria) 💶 Free; Pala d'Oro $

CA' D'ORO

The beautiful 15th-century Venetian-Gothic Ca' d'Oro (Golden House) got its name from the gilding that once covered its elaborate waterfront facade. Behind the facade it houses a small art gallery set around the palazzo's central *portego*, or inner courtyard. Showpieces include Andrea Mantegna's *Saint Sebastian* and Vivarini's polyptych of *The Passion*. There also are lesser works by Titian, Giorgione and Tintoretto, and some lovely sculpture fragments, bronzes and tapestries.
➕ C3 ✉ Calle di Ca' d'Oro, off Strada Nova ☎ 041 523 8790 🕐 Mon. 8:15–2, Tue.–Sun. 8:15–7:15 🚢 1 (Ca' d'Oro) 💶 $$

Appreciate the sites by taking a boat on the Canal

CAMPANILE

Venice's original campanile was reputedly built in AD 902; this graceful edifice collapsed in 1902, killing no one and leaving St. Mark's untouched. The Venetians vowed to rebuild it, *"Dov'era e com'era"* – "Where it was and like it was" – and 10 years later a perfect replica was complete. It's worth the elevator ride to the top for superb views of the city and as far away as the Alps. Take a look at the instruments that record temperature, tides, wind, moon phases and much more.
➕ D2 ✉ Piazza San Marco ☎ 041 522 4064 🕐 Daily 9–9, Jul.–Aug.; 9–7 Apr.–Jun. and Sep.–Oct.; 9:30–4:15, rest of year 🚢 82 (San Marco) 💶 $$$

CANAL GRANDE

The Canal Grande (Grand Canal), an enchanting stretch of water crossed by three bridges and lined with a magical parade of palaces, divides Venice. By day it's traversed by *vaporetti*, tugboats and gondolas and photographed by multitudes of visitors. The pearly morning light imbues it with magic, while darkness adds its own enchantment. For the trip of a lifetime, take a number 1 or 82 boat from the train station, sit back and enjoy.
➕ B2, C1, C2, C3, D2, D3 🚢 1, 82

The Scala d'Oro (Golden Staircase) leads to the sumptuous upper floor of the Palazzo Ducale

COLLEZIONE PEGGY GUGGENHEIM

An 18th-century palace on the Grand Canal is home to the modern art collection amassed by American millionaire Peggy Guggenheim. There are exciting works by Magritte and Picasso, while Jackson Pollock and Joseph Cornell represent American artists. The lovely garden is the perfect backdrop for Marino Marini's disturbing *Angel of the Citadel* and some striking sculpture by Henry Moore.

➕ C1 ✉ Palazzo Venier dei Leoni, Calle San Cristoforo, Dorsoduro 701 ☎ 041 240 5411 🕐 Wed.–Mon. 10–6 🚤 1 (Salute) 💲 \$\$\$

GALLERIE DELL'ACCADEMIA

The Gallerie dell'Accademia (Academy Galleries) is Venice's greatest art gallery, a true must-see. Arranged chronologically, the gallery's 24 rooms will introduce you to Bellini's luminescent *Virgins*, Giorgione's enigmatic *Tempest* and the dizzying perspective of Tintoretto's *Translation of the Body of St. Mark*. Don't miss Veronese's sumptuous *Feast in the House of Levi* or the two lively and colorful narrative painting cycles by Carpaccio and

other artists, the *Miracle of the True Cross* and the *Life of St. Ursula*. Don't waste time looking for works by Canaletto; there's only one in the whole gallery.

➕ B1 ✉ Campo della Carità ☎ 041 522 2247; reservations 041 520 0345 🕐 Tue.–Sun. 8:15–7:15, Mon. 8:15–2 🚤 1 (Accademia) 💲 \$\$\$ ℹ An audio guide of the gallery's highlights is available in English

MUSEO CIVICO CORRER

The Museo Civico Correr (Correr Museum) is the place to go for a fascinating overview of the history of the republic of Venice, the Serenissima. A bit of background reading will enhance your enjoyment, but the museum is packed with documents, maps, pictures, regalia, coins and miscellaneous items relating to the city. It's housed in the Procuratie Nuove, which runs along the entire south side of St. Mark's Square. At the end, overlooking the piazzetta, you can visit the Libreria Sansoviniana, a 16th-century architectural gem designed by Jacopo Sansovina to house the state library.

➕ C2 ✉ Piazza San Marco, Ala Napoleonica ☎ 041 522 5625 🕐 Daily 9–7, Apr.–Oct.; 9–5, rest of year 🚤 1, 51, 52, 82 (San Marco) 💲 \$\$\$ Entry is by a combination ticket (the "Museum Card") to the Palazzo Ducale, Museo Civico Correr, Museo Archeologico, Biblioteca Marciana, Glass Museum on Murano, Lace Museum on Burano, Plazzo Mocenigo and Ca' Rezzonico

PALAZZO DUCALE

Tackle the huge Gothic complex of the Palazzo Ducale (Ducal Palace) when you're fresh, for this is triumphalism on the grandest scale. Each reception and council room outdoes the one before in size, scale and splendor. The palace was the seat of Venetian government, where the Doge lived and held state, the council met, ambassadors were received and prisoners incarcerated. The present building dates largely from the 15th century, with alterations made after two 16th-century fires. Follow the marked route through the building. It leads through overwhelmingly lavish rooms culminating in the sumptuous Sala del Maggior Consiglio (Great Council

Revel in the sights and sounds as you cross the Rialto bridge

Chamber), dominated by Tintoretto's *Paradiso*, the world's largest painting. Don't miss the prison building, reached by crossing over the famous Bridge of Sighs, which spans a canal to the right of the Palazzo's waterfront facade.
✚ D2 ✉ Piazzetta San Marco ☎ 041 522 4951 ◷ Daily 9–7 (last admission 5:30), Apr.–Oct.; 9–5 (last admission 3:30), rest of year. Guided tours morning only 🚤 1, 51, 52, 82 (San Zaccaria) 💰 $$$ 🛈 An audio guide in English is available from the front desk

PIAZZA SAN MARCO

Napoleon called the Piazza San Marco (St. Mark's Square) "Europe's largest drawing room," and this wonderful open space is crowded around the clock with chattering crowds. It's Venice's only piazza – the others are all officially *campi* – and is lined with a harmonious melange of fine buildings and arcades. The 15th-century Torre dell'Orologio (Clock Tower), with its zodiac clock, leads into the Merceria, an elegant shopping street that connects to the Rialto. Near the water, on the piazzetta, you'll see two columns topped by St. Mark's lion and St. Theodore's crocodile, both ancient symbols of the city.
✚ D2 ✉ Piazza San Marco 🚤 1, 3, 4, 82 (San Marco) or 1, 41, 42, 51, 52, 82 (San Zaccaria)

RIALTO

During the Middle Ages, the Rialto was Europe's financial and banking center, a sort of medieval Wall Street, where fortunes were made and lost. The Grand Canal is spanned here by a shop-lined bridge, which you should cross to wander in Venice's main market, one of the city's best sights. Stalls are bright with fruit and vegetables or glistening with fish and shellfish, while the surrounding streets are edged with enticing food stores and lined with cheerful souvenir stalls.
✚ C2 ✉ Rialto 🍴 Trattoria alla Madonna, see page 203 🚤 1 82, (Rialto)

SAN GIÓRGIO MAGGIORE

The architect Andrea Palladio bequeathed two great churches to Venice, the Redentore and San Giórgio Maggiore (St. George the Great). The harmonious structure of San Giórgio adds the finishing touch to the view of St. Mark's Basin; take a boat to get there. The church's graceful lines perfectly embody Palladio's strict neoclassic tenets, while the view from the campanile has to be one of Venice's best.
✚ D1 ✉ Campo San Giórgio, Isola San Giórgio ☎ 041 528 9900 ◷ Daily 9:30–12:30 and 2:30–6:30 🚤 82 (San Giórgio) 💰 Campanile $

Housed in the Scuola Grande di San Rocco,
Tintoretto's *Crucifixion* is one of Venice's most
powerful paintings

SANTA MARIA DELLA SALUTE

The great domed church of Santa Maria
della Salute (Our Lady of Health and
Salvation) dominates the entrance to the
Grand Canal. It was constructed in 1630
in thanksgiving for Venice's deliverance
from the plague, in which 45,000 people
died. Every November on the feast of *La
Salute*, Venetians cross a temporary bridge
to give thanks for their deliverance more
than 350 years ago. Not only is it one of
the city's outstanding landmark buildings,
the church's impressive interior contains
fine paintings and sculpture.
✚ C1 ✉ Campo della Salute ☎ 041 522 5558
🕒 Daily 9–noon and 3–6 🚤 1 (Salute) ✋ Free

SANTA MARIA GLORIOSA
DEI FRARI

Both Titian and the composer
Monteverdi are interred in the lofty
Franciscan Gothic church of the *frari*
(brothers). Built as a preaching church
around 1250, Santa Maria Gloriosa dei
Frari (Glorious Virgin Mary of the
Brothers) contains two superb Titians –
the great *Assumption*, prominently hung
over the high altar, and his *Madonna of
Ca' Pesaro*. Best of all, though, is Giovanni
Bellini's luminous *Madonna and Child
with Saints*. Considered one of the world's
greatest paintings, you'll find it tucked
away in the right transept.
✚ B2 ✉ Campo dei Frari ☎ 041 275 0462
🕒 Mon.–Sat. 9–6, Sun. 1–6 🚤 1 (San Tomà) ✋ $ or
$$ with multi-church "Chorus Pass" ticket

SANTI GIOVANNI E PÁOLO

Venice's largest church is dedicated to St.
John and St. Paul and was built by the
Dominicans in the 14th century. It's a
massive and imposing Gothic structure
that is the resting place of more than 25
doges. The monuments on their tombs
represent the best of Venetian medieval
sculpture. Inside, don't miss Giovanni
Bellini's polyptych of *St. Vincent Ferrer*.
Outside, the great equestrian statue of
mercenary Colleoni by Verocchio is
among the city's sculptural treasures.
✚ D3 ✉ Campo SS Giovanni e Páolo ☎ 041 523
5913 🕒 Daily 7:30–12:30 and 3:30–7:30; closed Sun.
morning 🚤 41, 42, 51, 52 (Ospedale or Fondamente
Nove) ✋ Free

SCUOLA DI SAN GIÓRGIO
DEGLI SCHIAVONI

From 1502 to 1508, Carpaccio painted
the modest headquarters of Venice's Slavic
(Schiavoni) community with a series of
paintings including scenes from the lives
of Dalmatia's patron saints, St. George,
St. Tryphon and St. Jerome. The
highlights are *St. George Slaying the
Dragon* and *St. Augustine in His Study*.
✚ E2 ✉ Calle dei Furlani 3259/A ☎ 041 522 8828
🕒 Tue.–Sat. 9:30–12:30 and 3:30–6:30, Sun.
9:30–12:30, Apr.–Oct.; Tue.–Sat. 10–12:30 and 3–6,
Sun. 10–12:30, rest of year 🍴 Corte Sconta, see
page 203 🚤 1, 52, 82 (San Zaccaria) ✋ $

SCUOLA GRANDE DI
SAN ROCCO

In 1564 Tintoretto won a competition to
decorate the walls of the headquarters of
the wealthy confraternity of St. Roche.
He spent the next 23 years working on
this stupendous cycle of wall paintings
and ceiling panels, more than 50 in all,
which illustrate Old and New Testament
scenes. Start your tour upstairs in the Sala
dell'Albergo, which spotlights the
magnificent and revolutionary *Crucifixion*,
then move into the upper hall before
viewing the 1587 ground-floor paintings.
✚ B2 ✉ Campo San Rocco ☎ 041 523 4864
🕒 Daily 9–5:30, Apr.–Oct.; 10–4, rest of year 🚤 1, 82
San Tomà ✋ $$ ℹ English audio guide available

WALK: QUIET STREETS AND SMALL CANALS

Refer to route marked on city map on page 62.

Venice is a city without traffic noise, a city where the only sounds on the streets are those of human feet and human voices. You'll walk a lot during a Venetian stay, and some of your most serendipitous discoveries will be made en route. This walk runs through the Dorsoduro and San Polo quarters of the city, and will take about an hour.

Start on the Fondamenta delle Záttere alongside the water. Head right, turn right before the first bridge and walk along the Rio di San Trováso. Cross the first bridge, then turn left and pass the church of San Trováso.

As you walk along Rio di San Trováso, look out for the gondola yard, or *squero,* on the other side of the canal. It was established in the 17th century and there are always gondolas under construction to be seen. The church of San Trováso was built between 1584 and 1657. The cool and spacious interior has two fine paintings by Tintoretto, the *Temptation of St. Anthony* and the *Last Supper.*

Keep bearing right until you come to another canal; this is the Rio Ognissanti. Walk beside it, crossing one canal and passing a total of five bridges on your left. Cross another canal, then walk straight ahead down Calle Chiesa until you meet a wider canal. Turn right. Keep the canal on your left and pass two bridges. When you come to another canal in front of you, turn right, keeping the water on your left once more. Continue straight along the Fondamenta del Soccorso beside the canal until you come to the Campo dei Cármini.

The Scuola Grande dei Cármini stands on one side of the square. Once the Venetian base of the Carmelite order, this 17th-century building's upstairs hall has an exuberant ceiling painted by Giambattista Tiepolo. All azure skies and spiraling perspectives, the panels show a crucial scene from the order's history, *Simon Stock Receiving the Scapular.*

The *squero,* one of the last traditional working gondola boatyards

The church itself is a mixture of styles from Gothic to baroque.

Veer left through the square and walk into Campo Santa Margherita.

One of the most appealing of all Venetian squares, Campo Santa Margherita has a genuine neighborhood feel. There are always fruit and vegetable stalls set up, and local stores and bars predominate. It's a good place to pause for a drink or ice cream at Causin, a long-established *gelateria.*

Go straight ahead through the long square and down the narrow street at the far end, Calle della Chiesa. Cross the bridge over the wide Rio di Ca' Foscari into Campo San Pantalòn. Bear right across the square, past the church, and turn left down Calle San Pantalòn.

San Pantalòn, otherwise San Pantaleone, was a healer. The church ceiling is wildly decorated with 60 panels depicting his life. The artist Fumiani never saw his work completed, falling off a scaffold at the end of his labors. Of more artistic merit is the fine *San Pantaleone Healing a Boy*, the last work completed by Veronese.

Cross the next street, turn right and then immediately left down another narrow street ending at a bridge over a canal, Rio della Frescada. Turn left, then directly right past the front of the Scuola Grande di San Rocco (see page 68). After visiting the Scuola, exit and turn left, then right down the Salizzada San Rocco and skirt around the church of Santa Maria Gloriosa dei Frari (see page 68) into the Campo dei Frari. From here, you can pick up the yellow signs that will lead you back to the Rialto district.

The Northeast

ISLANDS IN THE LAGOON

There's more to the Venetian lagoon than just the city. This fragile, landlocked sea is scattered with islands, some thriving and historic communities, others as remote and peaceful as if they were a hundred miles from the noise and glitter of St. Mark's. Try to explore a few; they fall handily into groups, and you could spend a marvelous day away from the crowds.

Graves and Glass

San Michele and Murano are very different. San Michele is the site of the city's main cemetery. Murano is home to Europe's oldest glass-making industry. It might seem odd to visit a cemetery, but stop

The 15th-century Barovier wedding cup

for half an hour on your way to Murano at this unique burial ground, surrounded by high walls and studded with cypresses. Among the well-tended graves and monuments bright with flowers are the last homes of Ezra Pound, Sergei Diaghilev and Igor Stravinsky.

Bustling Murano makes a good contrast. Glass has been made here since 1291, when the furnaces were moved away from the city as a fire precaution. Venetian craftsmen were Europe's most skillful glass-blowers, producing intricate and delicate work under secretive conditions. Today the skills are very much in place, and there are large numbers of workshops where you can see glass being blown. Sadly, most of the design is horrendous, although there are treasures. The fascinating Museo Vetrario (Glass Museum) has a huge collection; don't miss the Barovier wedding cup, an enamel-worked 15th-century piece. Murano's main church is Santi Maria e Donato, a superb 12th-century structure with a wonderful colonnade and equally fine mosaics and marble pavements within.

Four Islands to the North

You'll need a whole day to do justice to the four islands lying across the lagoon to the north of the city – Burano, Mazzorbo,

Torcello and San Francesco del Deserto. Burano, all brightly painted houses, drunkenly leaning campaniles, narrow canals and sun-splashed piazzas, is still a fishing community with a salty atmosphere and robust inhabitants. It's historically noted for the exquisite lace made by island women; the industry has practically died out, but you can admire local work in the the Museo dei Merletti (Lace-making Museum).

A bridge links Burano to pastoral Mazzorbo, which has a clutch of canal-side houses, complete with vegetable plots and grass. It's a lovely place to pass a short time, and you'll feel a sense of history here. Venice's age is at its strongest in timeless Torcello, just across the water. This dreamy island, with its overgrown canals and green fields, is one of the most evocative and magical places in Italy. Once the most important island in the lagoon, Torcello was pushed off history's map and left to gentle decay by 12th-century silt and malaria. Today, only the great basilica of Santa Maria Assunta and the neighboring church of Santa Fosca are reminders of its heyday. Santa Maria was first built in the seventh century; the pulpit dates from this time, but the rest of the church is 11th century. Its chief glories are two 12th-century mosaics completely covering the apse and the opposite wall. High above the altar, the apse mosaic shows a lovely Byzantine *Madonna and Child*, their poignant beauty highlighted by the simple gold background, while the graphic *Last Judgment* scenes at the west end make a dramatic contrast. Leave time to see smaller and more intimate Santa Fosca; its arcaded porch is full of wheeling swifts.

If time permits, ask a boatman to row you across to San Francesco del Deserto from Burano. This Franciscan monastery, with its serene old church and gardens, is one of the lagoon's loveliest corners.

The Northeast

San Lazzaro degli Armeni and San Servolo

The islands of San Lazzaro degli Armeni and San Servolo are each fascinating in their own way. Since the 18th century, San Lazzaro has been an Armenian monastery, a center of learning for this ancient branch of Christianity. Young Armenians still come here to study their culture and religion. One of the multilingual monks will show you the church and museum; look for the room where the poet Byron spent the winter of 1816 struggling with the intricacies of the Armenian language. The monastery has run a polyglot printing press for more than 200 years, and you can buy the items it produces.

San Servolo also was once a monastery island and Benedictine foundation that later became a hospital and asylum. Today it's a training center for a range of craft and conservation techniques needed for architectural restoration. Students from Italy and many other countries study here.

Murano 🚣 5, 13, 41, 42

Basilica dei Santi Maria e Donato ✉ Fondamenta Giustinian ☎ 041 739 056 ⏰ Mon.–Sat. 9–noon and 3:30–7, Sun. 3:30–7 ✋ Free

Museo Vetrario ✉ Fondamenta Giustinian 8 ☎ 041 739 586 ⏰ Thu.–Tue. 10–5, Nov.–Mar.; 10–4, rest of year ✋ $$

San Michele 🚣 41, 42 **Burano** 🚣 12

Museo del Merletto ✉ Piazza Baldassare Galuppi 187

Top: Burano's colorful houses reflected in a canal
Bottom: Lace of all types is sold in Burano

☎ 041 730 034 ⏰ Wed.–Mon. 10–5 ✋ $$

Mazzorbo 🚣 LN

Torcello 🚣 LN

Basilica di Santa Maria della Assunta
☎ 041 270 2464 ⏰ Daily 10–5:30 ✋ $$

Museo di Torcello ☎ 041 730 761
⏰ Tue.–Sun.10–12:30 and 2–5 ✋ $

Santa Fosca ⏰ Daily 10:30–12:30 and 2–5 ✋ Free

San Francesco del Deserto 🚣 12

Convento di San Francesco del Deserto
☎ 041 528 6863 ⏰ Tue.–Sun. 9–11 and 3–5
🚣 Access by *sándolo* (rowing boat) from Burano. Negotiate price with boatman on the dock near the church on Burano ✋ Free

San Lazzaro degli Armeni 🚣 20

Monastero Mekhitarista ☎ 041 526 0104 ⏰ Daily 3:30–5 ✋ $$$; guided tours only

San Servolo 🚣 20

REGIONAL SIGHTS

Key to symbols

⊞ map coordinates refer to the region map on page 58; sights below are highlighted in yellow on the map
✉ address or location ☎ telephone number
🕐 opening times 🍴 restaurant on site or nearby
💰 admission charge: $$$ more than €6, $$ €3 to €6, $ less than €3 ⓘ information

AQUILÉIA

The pancake-flat plains south of Udine, which feature acres of dull cornfields and characterless villages, leave you unprepared for the treasure of Aquiléia. The colony was established in 181 BC and by the fourth century had become a patriarchate, a region ruled by a prince-bishop or patriarch. The first patriarch was Theodore, who built a great basilica. Sacked by Attila and the Lombards, this early church was rebuilt several times, and today is a superb blend of Romanesque and Gothic elements. Its chief glory is the jewel-like mosaic pavement undulating along the nave like a multicolored carpet. Its Christian and pagan scenes are as fresh as when they were assembled around AD 320 during Theodore's patriarchate. Look for the mosaic bestiary around the base of the 11th-century campanile and the evocative 12th-century Byzantine frescoes in the shadowy crypt.

Sleepy Aquiléia also has two museums – the Archeological Museum has everything from fine Roman sculpture to a reconstructed galley, and a stroll along the River Natissa will take you to the Museo Paleochristiano (Paleocristiano Museum), a pithy collection of more local Roman finds.

⊞ C2
Tourist information ✉ Piazza del Capitolo 4 ☎ 0431 919 491 🕐 Mon.–Sat. 9–3 (hours may vary)
Basilica ✉ Piazza del Capitolo ☎ 0431 91 067 🕐 Daily 8:30–6:30, Apr.–Oct.; 9–12:30 and 2:30–5, rest of year 💰 Basilica free; Crypts $; Belltower $
Museo Archeologico ✉ Via Roma 1 ☎ 0431 91 016 🕐 Tue.–Sun. 9–7, Mon. 9–2 💰 $$
Museo Paleocristiano ✉ Piazza Pirano, Monastero delle Benedettine ☎ 0431 91 131 🕐 Tue.–Sun. 9–7, Mon. 9–2

ÁSOLO

Ásolo's charms gave the Italian language a new verb – *asolare*, meaning to pass the time in pleasant aimlessness. This medieval walled town, sprinkled with enchanting piazzas and pretty churches and set in the Dolomite foothills, is perhaps the loveliest in the Veneto. Its surrounding villa-studded countryside is stunning.

Famous figures have loved Ásolo, among them 15th-century Catarina Cornaro, one of the few women to have played an important part in Venetian history. Scion of a powerful family, she became, through marriage, queen of Cyprus, but was duped out of the island by the Venetian state, which gave her Ásolo as a consolation prize. The actress Eleanor Druse was born here in 1859. Famous as much for her love life as her acting, Druse often retreated home to escape gossip and scandal, and although she died in far-off Pittsburgh, she is buried here. There's plenty of information on her life in the Museo Civico, which also devotes space to the English poet Robert Browning, who lived here for some time.

⊞ B2
Tourist information ✉ Piazza Garibaldi ☎ 0423 529 046 🕐 Mon.–Sat. 10–noon and 4–7
Museo Civico ✉ Via Regina Cornaro 74 ☎ 0423 395 2312 🕐 Sat.–Sun. 10–12:30 and 3–7 💰 $

Roman remains at Aquiléia

The jagged peaks of the Dolomites contrast with fertile upland pastures

The Northeast

DRIVE: THE GREAT DOLOMITES ROAD

Duration: 3 to 4 hours

This drive follows the route known as La Grande Strada delle Dolomiti (The Great Dolomites Road), which was constructed in 1909 to link Bolzano and Cortina d'Ampezzo. It runs 110 kilometers (70 miles) through Europe's most breathtaking mountain scenery and offers frequent opportunities to take a scenic side road or a cable car up a mountain slope. The road is well-maintained but inevitably twisting in places, so bear this in mind if you suffer from vertigo or travel sickness.

From Bolzano (see page 76), take the SS241 along the Val d'Ega to the Lago di Carezza.

East of Bolzano, you leave the road over the Brenner Pass, one of the historic trans-Alpine routes, and head along the gorge of the Val d'Ega. This narrow corridor, edged with waterfalls, offers the first taste of the superb views along this route, with the Catinaccio and Latemar massifs rising on either side of the road. Make your first stop at the Lago di Carezza, a picture-postcard lake whose deep blue waters reflect mountain ridges sprinkled with dark fir trees and punctuated with white gravel slides. The road climbs from the lake to the Passo di Costalunga (5,750 feet), the first of the high passes along this route, which marks the boundary between the Alto Adige and Trentino regions.

Continue on the SS241 through the Passo di Costalunga to Vigo di Fassa.

Once over the pass, the road descends through the Val di Fassa, running beside the River Avisio to Vigo di Fassa, a mountain resort town with a pretty 15th-century Gothic church. Vigo makes a good starting point for

The Dolomites provide a splendid backdrop to Bolzano's central square

hikers wanting to explore the Catinaccio range. There are trails catering to all levels of fitness and experience, and a cable car takes away the worst of the initial hike. You also can hike south back to the Lago di Carezza.

About 1.5 kilometers (1 mile) outside Vigo, turn left onto the SS48 to Canazei. The road becomes increasingly dramatic, with views of wild countryside, soaring mountains and constantly changing vistas as it hairpins its way to Canazei. This is another mountain resort town, with good hotels and a range of restaurants catering to the winter skiers, summer climbers and walkers who make it their base. There's a choice of cable-car rides into the surrounding mountains.

Stay on the SS48, climbing steeply to the Passo Pordoi and on to Arabba. Twenty-seven hairpin turns over 12 kilometers (7 miles) of road mark the next section of driving, leading inexorably to the Passo Pordoi (7,400 feet), one of the highest passes on the route. Enjoy the superlative scenery until you arrive at the little village of Arabba, a cluster of family-run hotels set in peaceful mountain pastureland. The huge massif to the south is the Marmolada; you can take a cable car up to the Porto Vescovo for a closer look at its icy slopes.

If you want to make this drive a round trip, turn left onto the SS243 for the Passo di Gardena. At Plan de Gralba, turn right onto the SS242. Stay on this road through Ortisei (where it becomes the SS242d) and after 3.5 kilometers (6 miles) branch left to Ponte Gardena, where you can join the SS12 south to return to Bolzano. To continue to Cortina, stay on the SS48 through Arabba and Pocòl to Cortina d'Ampezzo.

Donatello's statue of the mercenary Gattamelata outside Pádova's Basilica di Sant' Antonio

You'll cross another pass on the way to Pocòl. This is the Passo di Falzarego (8,200 feet). Look for the relatively rare stone pines that dot the slopes of the high meadows around here. The descent to Cortina runs along the slopes of the Tofane massif to emerge into the stunning mountain bowl that encircles this chic resort.

Bolzano tourist information (see page 76)
Cortina d'Ampezzo tourist information ✉ Piazzetta San Francesco 8 ☎ 0436 3231 ⏰ Daily 9–12:30 and 3:30–6:30 (4–7, Jul.–Aug.)

Tourists and locals enjoying a moment's pause in the sun in central Bolzano

BOLZANO

Capital of the German-speaking Alto Adige region, mountain-hemmed Bolzano (Bozen) makes a good base for exploring the scenic splendors of the Dolomites (see page 74). This area ultimately became part of Italy at the end of World War I and retains a distinctly Teutonic flavor, which is manifested in its cuisine, language and efficiency. Head first for the café-fringed Piazza Walther, the central square, to visit the Gothic Duomo (Cathedral), with an eye-catching carved spire and yellow-and-green tiled roof. Its lovely Porta del Vino (Wine Door) is decorated with carvings of peasants working the vineyards, and was erected in 1387 when the church was granted a license to sell wine.

Nearby, the Chiesa dei Domenicani contains Bolzano's best frescoes; you'll find a 14th-century cycle in Cappella di San Giovanni (St. John's Chapel) and 15th-century scenes of life in the cloisters. North from here lies the Piazza dell'Erbe, scene of the colorful daily market, while across the Talvera river is the grandiose Piazza della Vittoria, with its monumental Fascist architecture and a triumphal arch built by Mussolini in 1928. To taste the glorious mountains,

you could take a cable car to Soprabolzano; from there a tiny tramway runs to the hamlet of Collalbo.

➕ A3

Tourist information ✉ Piazza Walther 8
☎ 0471 307 000 🕐 Mon.–Fri. 9–6:30, Sat. 9–12:30
ℹ For information on the Dolomites, visit the regional tourist office at Piazza Parrochia 11/12
☎ 0471 999 999 🕐 Mon.–Fri. 9–6
Duomo ✉ Piazza Parrochia 🕐 Mon.–Fri. 9:45–noon and 2–5, Sat. 9:45–noon ✋ Free
Chiesa dei Domenicani ✉ Piazza Domenicani
🕐 Mon.–Sat. 9:30–6 ✋ Free

CIVIDALE DEL FRIULI

Tucked up near the border with Slovenia, the lovely old town of Cividale is a beguiling tangle of medieval streets and interesting buildings. It lies on the Natisone river and is one of the few places in Italy with tangible reminders of the Lombards. This Teutonic warrior race invaded Italy in the sixth century, establishing three dukedoms and leaving a sparse legacy of superb carvings and sculpture. The finest example here is the Tempietto Longobardo (Lombard Temple); the eighth-century stucco arch features smiling saints, a peerless example of Lombard art. There's more to be seen in the Museo Cristiano (Christian

Museum), in the precincts of the 15th-century Duomo (Cathedral). Here you can admire the stunning Altar of Ratchis, a hauntingly lovely eighth-century masterpiece, and the octagonal Baptistery of Callisto, made from fifth-century stone and marble fragments. The cathedral's main draw is the silver *pala* (altar piece), a heavily embossed 12th-century work showing the Blessed Virgin, angels and saints.

➕ C2

Tourist information ✉ Corso Paolino d'Aquileia 10 ☎ 0432 731 461 🕐 Mon.–Fri. 9–1 and 3–6, May–Sep.; 9–1 and 3–5, rest of year

Tempietto Longobardo ✉ Piazza del Duomo ☎ 0432 700 867 🕐 Mon.–Sat. 9:30–12:30 and 3–6, Sun. 9:30–1 and 3–5:30 💲 $

Museo Cristiano ✉ Piazza del Duomo ☎ 0432 731 144 🕐 Mon.–Sat. 9:30–noon and 3–6 💲 Free

MERANO

Staid and placid Merano (Meran), with its mild climate and thermal springs, provides a splendid contrast to the dramatic mountain scenery that surrounds it. The town attracted wealthy central Europeans at the beginning of the 20th century. They came here to "take the cure" and to stroll in its parks and along its promenades. The most famous is the Passeggiata d'Inverno e d'Estate (Winter and Summer Path), which runs along the banks of the Passirio river. Higher up, you can enjoy the winding Passeggiata Tappeiner, which runs through vineyards and gardens overlooking the town.

The Via dei Portici marks Meran's historic center. The streets are a charming mix of local architecture, shops and fin-de-siécle elegance. The cathedral and castle are worth a visit. But for the true Meran experience, take a dip in the thermal baths. You can use the town as a base from which to explore the Texelgruppe mountains, about 10 kilometers (6 miles) away, or the far more dramatic Ortles range, an incredible area of rocks and glaciers.

➕ A3

Tourist information ✉ Corso Libertà 45 ☎ 0473 272 000 🕐 Mon.–Fri. 9–12:30 and 2–6:30, Sat. 9:30–12:30 ℹ Third week in Oct.: Grape Fest with processions, concerts, and wine and food tastings

Statues around Pádova's largest square, Prato della Valle, commemorate notable native citizens

PÁDOVA

The Veneto's most important economic center and a major university city, Pádova (Padua) was heavily bombed during World War II. The subsequent rebuilding makes first impressions less than immediately alluring. But there are some real gems here, chief among them the frescoes by Giotto in the Scrovegni Chapel. Painted in the early 1300s, the scenes of the life of Christ and his Blessed Mother are one of the turning points of Western art development, with a wholly innovative naturalism and fluency.

Also visit the Civic Museum next door before heading through the city center to visit the Basilica di Sant'Antonio, a many-domed church dedicated to Padua's own St. Anthony. Outside stands the fine equestrian statue of the mercenary Gattamelata (Honey Cat), sculpted by Donatello in 1453.

Down Via del Santo from the basilica, you'll find Padua's two main squares, the Piazza della Frutta and the Piazza delle Erbe. Morning is the best time to stroll here; the daily fruit and vegetable markets are in full swing. The extraordinary building between the two squares is the Palazzo della Ragione (also known as the

Hills rise behind the stately port city of Trieste

Salone), a vast 13th-century structure once used as the city council's assembly hall. It contains a huge wooden model of a horse, made for a joust in 1466. Other buildings include the university and the wonderful Café Pedrocchi, once the meeting point for the city's intellectuals.

🚩 B1

Tourist information ✉ Stazione Ferroviaria ☎ 049 875 2077 🕐 Mon.–Sat. 9–7, Sun. 9–noon ℹ You can take a cruise along the Brenta river from Padua to Venice and back again from March through early November, visiting some of the magnificent villas en route. Details from Padova Navigazione ☎ 049 526 909

Cappella degli Scrovegni and Musei Civici
✉ Piazza Eremitani 8 ☎ 049 201 0020 🕐 Museum: Tue.–Sun. 9–7, Feb.–Oct.; 9–8, rest of year. Chapel: Daily 9–7, Jan. and Feb.; 9 a.m.–10 p.m., rest of year (possible changes – check before visit) 💰 $$$

Basilica di Sant'Antonio ✉ Piazza del Santo ☎ 049 663 944 🕐 Daily 6:30 a.m.–7:45 p.m. 💰 Free

Palazzo della Ragione ✉ Piazza delle Erbe ☎ 049 820 5006 🕐 Tue.–Sun. 9–7, Mar.–Oct.; 9–6, rest of year 💰 $$$

Treviso

Home to the Benetton company, Treviso is an alluring and prosperous provincial town enclosed by 16th-century walls, with canals, long porticoes and frescoed facades. The main street is the

Calmaggiore. This leads right through the center, beautifully rebuilt and restored after heavy bombing in both world wars.

Treviso's cathedral is the Duomo San Pietro, where you'll find an atmospheric crypt with a thicket of 12th-century columns. Treviso is noted for the production of *radicchio*, the red-leaf salad vegetable. Wine lovers can use Treviso as the gateway to some of the Veneto's best wine areas; two wine trails head out from the town of Conegliano to the north.

🚩 B2

Tourist information ✉ Piazzetta Monte di Pietà 8 ☎ 0422 547 632 🕐 Mon.–Fri. 9–12:30 and 3–6, Sat.–Sun. 9:30–12:30 and 3:30–6

Duomo San Pietro ✉ Piazza del Duomo 🕐 Daily 7:30–noon and 3:30–7 💰 Free

Trieste

With its superb Piazza dell'Unità d'Italia opening to embrace the sea, Trieste rates as one of Italy's finest port cities. Founded in Roman times, Trieste's ownership over the centuries has swung between the different powers whose interests lay in this corner of the Adriatic. Thus Italian, Austro-Hungarian and Slavic influences have all shaped today's city, which finally became part of Italy in 1954.

The Northeast

Trieste is beautifully set on the slopes of a limestone plateau overlooking the sea and owes much of its appearance to the Empress Maria Teresa, who constructed the monumental 18th-century city center as a fitting background for its role as the main Hapsburg southern port. This central area has good shops and wide streets, well worth a visit before you climb through the remnants of Roman and medieval Trieste to the hilltop Castello (Castle), which houses a small museum, and Cattedrale di San Giusto (St. Just's Cathedral). The main museums in town are the Revoltella, the Museo di Storia e dell'Arte (History and Art Museum) and the Museo Morpurgo. Or you could follow the footsteps of James Joyce, the Irish author of *Ulysses*, who lived here for many years.

By far the nicest attraction is the idiosyncratic Castello di Miramare just outside town. It's a wonderfully situated castle overlooking the sea and standing in delightful gardens. It was built for the Archduke Ferdinand Maximilian in the 1860s; assassinated in 1867, Ferdinand was never able to enjoy it.

✚ C2

Tourist information ✉ Piazza dell'Unità d'Italia 4/B
☎ 040 347 8312 ◷ Daily 9–7

Castello ✉ Piazza della Cattedrale 3 ☎ 040 309 362
◷ Museum: Tue.–Sun. 9–1. Grounds: daily 9–6 🖐 $

Cattedrale di San Giusto ✉ Piazza della Cattedrale
☎ 040 309 666 ◷ Daily 8–6:30 🖐 Free

Revoltella ✉ Via Diaz 27 ☎ 040 300 938
◷ Wed.–Sun. 10–1 and 3–7 🍴 Terrace bar open
Jul.–Sep. 🖐 $$$

Museo di Storia e dell'Arte ✉ Via della Cattedrale
15 ☎ 040 310 500 ◷ Tue.–Sun. 9–1 (also Wed. 9–7)
🖐 $

Museo Morpurgo ✉ Via Imbriani 5 ☎ 040 636 969
◷ Tue.–Sun. 9–1 (also Wed. 9–7) 🖐 $$

Castello di Miramare ✉ Viale di Miramare ☎ 040
224 4143 ◷ Castle: daily 9–7, Apr.–Sep.; 9–5, Mar.
and Oct.; 9–4, rest of year. Gardens: daily 8–7,
Apr.–Sep.; 8–6, Mar. and Oct.; 8–5, rest of year 🖐 $$

VERONA

One of northern Italy's most captivating cities, overflowing with artistic delights and hedonistic pleasures, beautiful Verona lies on the banks of the Adige river. Start your tour in the sweeping Piazza Brà, the largest square. It's dominated by the first-century Arena, one of the world's largest surviving Roman amphitheaters and scene of Verona's famous summer opera festival. You can climb its tiers of seats to enjoy great views of the city. The pedestrian Via Mazzini, lined with swanky shops and cafés, leads to the heart of Verona, centered around the intimate Piazza dell'Erbe. Lined with loggias, town houses and Renaissance palaces, the piazza also has been the site of the market since medieval times. From here, head down Via Cappello for a glimpse of the Casa di Giulietta (Juliet's House), complete with balcony. Shakespeare based his tragedy on true families, the Cappelli and Montecchi, although Romeo and Juliet are fictional. This hasn't deterred thousands of modern lovers from leaving their initials on every available surface of the house's walls.

Behind the Piazza dell'Erbe lies the stunning ensemble of the Piazza dei Signori; its 12th-century buildings were once the focus of public life, and there are wide views from the top of the Torre dei Lamberti (Lamberti Tower). Don't miss the Arche Scaligeri (Scaligeri Monuments), the superb Gothic funerary monuments to Verona's medieval ruling family. The main figure is Cangrande (Big Dog), protector of Dante and a great artistic patron.

North from here lies the Duomo (Cathedral) and Santa Anastasia, Verona's largest church, built from 1290 to 1481. Nearby, you can see the Ponte Pietra (Stone Bridge), a first-century Roman bridge; the present one is a careful reconstruction of the original, which was bombed in World War II. Across the river stand the remains of the Roman theater. Head parallel with the river to the Castelvecchio, the medieval fortress seat of the Scaligeri. It houses the city's Museo Civico d'Arte (Civic Art Museum), but is especially fascinating as a building – a maze of passages, walkways and stairs around a serene courtyard. Another short walk will bring you to the church of San Zeno, a superb Romanesque basilica that's among the finest in northern Italy, built atop an earlier church in 1117. Its lovely bronze doors are enclosed by marble bas-reliefs and topped by a "Wheel of Fortune" rose window. Inside, don't miss Mantegna's hauntingly lovely *Madonna and Saints* over the high altar.

➕ A1

Tourist information ✉ Via degli Alpini 9 ☎ 045 806 8680 🕐 Tue.–Sat. 9–7, Sun. 9–3, Mon. 1–7
ℹ The VeronaCard ($$$) is valid for three days and covers admission to museums, churches, monuments and entrance to Gardaland (see page 45)
Arena ✉ Piazza Brà ☎ 045 800 3204; box office 045 800 5151 🕐 Tue.–Sun. 9–6; 9–3:30 during opera season (Jul.–Sep.) 🎫 $$ ℹ Reserve well in advance for opera
Casa di Giulietta ✉ Via Cappello 23 ☎ 045 803 4303 🕐 Tue.–Sun. 9–6:30 🎫 $$
Torre dei Lamberti ✉ Piazza dei Signori, Cortile Mercato Vecchio ☎ 045 803 2726 🕐 Tue.–Sun. 9–6 🎫 $
Duomo ✉ Piazza del Duomo 🕐 Mon.–Sat. 10–5:30, Sun. 1:30–5:30 🎫 $
Santa Anastasia ✉ Corso Santa Anastasia 🕐 Mon.–Sat. 9–6, Sun. 1–6 🎫 $
Castelvecchio and Museo Civico d'Arte ✉ Corso Castelvecchio 2 ☎ 045 806 2611 🕐 Mon. 1:45–7:30, Tue.–Sun. 8:30–7:30 🎫 $$
San Zeno ✉ Piazza San Zeno 🕐 Mon.–Sat. 8:30–6, Sun. 1–6 🎫 $

VICENZA

Vicenza grew rich in the second half of the 20th century on textiles, electronics and printing. Prosperity has given the city a gloss and polish without detracting from its historic charm. The center is a splendid amalgam of Gothic architecture from the days when Vicenza was a Venetian possession, as well as the classical buildings of the great 16th-century architect Andrea Palladio. Vicenza's main street, Corso Andrea Palladio, commemorates him and is lined with examples of his work. One of his palaces now houses the Museo Civico, a fairly pedestrian collection enlivened by some masterpieces by Tiepolo and Tintoretto.

The church of Santa Corona, a mid-13th-century Dominican building, houses two superb paintings, Giovanni Bellini's serene *Baptism of Christ* and the contrasting *Adoration of the Magi* by Paolo Veronese. Nearby is the Gallerie di

Palazzo Montanari (Montanari Palace Gallery), where a splendid baroque palace houses two collections, a range of intimate domestic paintings by Longhi, Guardi and other Venetian artists, and a huge collection of richly colored Russian icons. Across Piazza Matteotti you'll find Palladio's Teatro Olimpico (Olympic Theater), Europe's oldest indoor theater, which opened in 1585. Palladio died before it was completed; the astonishing backdrop of a classical city behind the stage was added by Scamozzi. Head south from here to the Piazza dei Signori, the heart of the *centro storico* (historic center), to visit the basilica, Palladio's first major project and the one that made his reputation. The harmonious structure solved a long-standing problem of how to buttress the 15th-century city hall. The building facing the basilica is the Loggia del Capitaniato, a late and unfinished Palladian structure built for the Venetian military commander.

Behind here, the Piazza dell'Erbe sells fruits and vegetables as it has since medieval times – a good place to shop or enjoy a drink at one of the cafés. Leave time to take in one of Palladio's famous villas. The Villa Capra (La Rotonda) was built as a pleasure pavilion, its balanced classical lines providing the inspiration for many public buildings in the United States.

➕ B2

Tourist information ✉ Piazza Matteotti 12 ☎ 0444 320 854 🕐 Mon.–Sat. 9–1 and 2:30–6, Sun. 9–1
Museo Civico ✉ Palazzo Chiericati 39 ☎ 0444 321 348 🕐 Tue.–Sun. 9–7, Jun.–Aug.; 9–5, rest of year 🎫 $$$
Santa Corona ✉ Contrà Santa Corona ☎ 0444 321 924 🕐 Tue.–Sun. 8:30–noon and 3–6 🎫 Free
Galleria di Palazzo Montanari ✉ Contrà Santa Corona 25 ☎ 800 578 875 🕐 Fri.–Sun. 10–6 🎫 $$
Teatro Olimpico ✉ Piazza Matteotti 11 ☎ 0444 222 800 🕐 Tue.–Sun. 9–7, Jun.–Aug.; 9–5, rest of year 🎫 $$
Basilica ✉ Corso San Felice Fortunato 219 ☎ 0444 547 246 🕐 Mon.–Sat. 9–11:30 and 3:30–6 🎫 Free
La Rotonda, Villa Capra ✉ Via Rotonda 29 ☎ 0444 321 793 🕐 Villa: Wed. 10–noon and 3–6, Mar.–Nov. Gardens: Tue.–Thu. 10–noon and 3–6, Mar.–Nov. 🎫 Villa: $$$. Gardens: $$

Skiers enjoy great views, snow and brilliant sunshine in the Dolomites

WINTER SPORTS

Italy's mountains offer a vast range of skiing, with good facilities and a relaxed atmosphere. Many northern Italians, with the Alps right on their doorstep, are keen skiers and head for the slopes most weekends during the season. The Valle d'Aosta area in the northwest gives access to Mont Blanc and the splendid Gran Paradiso, but Italy's favorite winter play area is the Dolomites in the northeast.

Where To Go

From Christmas through March, the Dolomites offer some of Europe's best skiing in fantastically beautiful mountain scenery. Although Italians are generally much more relaxed about skiing than the Swiss or French, their resorts are excellently run, with well-tended *pistes* (slopes) and plenty of access via cable cars, chairlifts and drags. The main resorts are Cortina d'Ampezzo, east of Bolzano (see page 76), and Madonna di Campiglio, on the fringe of the Dolomiti di Brenta. Both towns are among Europe's most stylish international winter sports centers, offering superb facilities and steep prices to match. If you're looking for good value for your money, head for the Val Gardena or the Val Badia; both are noted for good snow and good value.

Wherever you go, you'll find the full range of ski runs, schools, classes and personal guides, plus snowboarding, which is incredibly popular in Italy.

Cross-country skiers are catered to also, with miles of well-groomed tracks; two of the best centers are Ortisei and Dobbiaco in the Val Pusteria. Non-skiers will find lovely Alpine walks through silent woods, sleigh rides, bars and restaurants where you can enjoy lunch or a drink, and resort activities such as swimming, ice-skating and some of the most tempting window-shopping in Europe. Après ski offerings range from a quiet dinner in a wood-paneled restaurant to throbbing discos and smoky piano bars.

Accommodations

The best way to experience Italian winter sports is to book a package during the *settimane bianche* (white weeks). These generally fall during the quiet weeks of January and February and are a superb value. Contact the regional tourist boards for details.

Valle d'Aosta tourist information ✉ Piazza Emilio Chanoux 8 ☎ 0165 236 627

Trentino-Alto Adige tourist information ✉ Via Romagnosi II, Trento ☎ 0461 839 000

Tuscany, Umbria and the Marche

"Italy's Renaissance heartland is where modern prosperity and historic towns combine with some of the country's most beautiful landscapes."

Ancient olive groves are an integral part of the Tuscan landscape

TUSCANY, UMBRIA AND THE MARCHE

The political regions of Tuscany (Toscana), Umbria and the Marche cut right across north-central Italy. This is the Renaissance heartland, where the great 14th-century upsurge of culture and the arts truly began. Its timeless landscape epitomizes the visitor's dream of Italy. Prosperous cities, a sound infrastructure, an abundance of history, art and culture, and good food and wine make this area one of the most-visited in the whole peninsula. Bear this in mind when planning your trip; art-lovers will do best out of season when museums and galleries are less crowded, while the countryside looks its dazzling best in May and June.

Tuscan Towns and Villages

Florence is Tuscany's major city and the capital of this thriving region, with high-technology industry, a university and a rich agricultural community. It's also among Italy's most popular tourist spots. Visitors seem to outnumber locals in many parts of the city, but Florence has a life of its own that few visitors experience. Local life is more accessible in the region's lesser cities, many of which deserve a day's visit.

Medieval Siena is the perfect contrast to Florence, while Pisa contains one of Europe's most perfect

Portoferraio on Elba, one of Italy's holiday islands

architectural ensembles. Lucca, Cortona and Volterra have much to offer, and are all set in contrasting and beautiful landscapes. You also may appreciate San Gimignano, the best-known hill town, and Montalcino, Montepulciano and the city of Pienza in the south.

Traveling in Tuscany

To enjoy the beauty of Tuscany at its best, rent a car for the freedom it allows to explore off-the-beaten-track roads and villages. Tourists are important to the Tuscan economy, and facilities are excellent, with a wide range of accommodations and restaurants throughout the region. English is widely spoken, particularly in the main tourist centers, and levels of courtesy and service are generally high. You'll find that many Tuscans are reserved and rational people, not given to the dramatic outbursts found in other parts of Italy. Accustomed to an annual influx of international visitors, they are professional and reliable. In Tuscany, as everywhere in Italy, a few words of Italian will work wonders.

Tuscany, Umbria and the Marche

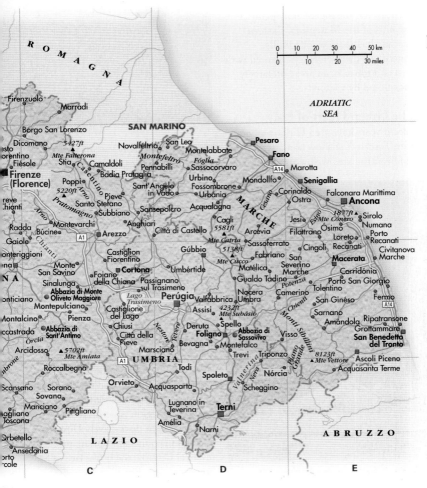

Tuscany, Umbria and the Marche

Rural Tuscany

For many people, Tuscany encapsulates Italian countryside. Rolling hills, vineyards, olive groves and glowing wheatfields punctuated by pencil-thin cypress trees are quintessentially Italian, and all can be found in Tuscany. There's more; head north to explore the Alpi Apuane, where you'll find dramatic mountains, their flanks glistening white with marble quarries. Or discover the scenic splendors of the Garfagnana, Tuscany's "Little Switzerland." South of Siena lie the rolling wheatlands and bare clay slopes of the *crete,* a strange, almost lunar landscape, while along the coast stretch the melancholy plains and low hills of the Maremma. Eastern Tuscany has more wooded hills, punctuated by river valleys planted with corn and tobacco, an area still largely unexplored by visitors.

The Green Heart of Italy

Recent years have seen Umbria emerge from Tuscany's shadow as a fascinating and beautiful area well worth visiting in its own right. Many visitors prefer its less crowded cities. This is a varied, tranquil and lovely region and is well-deserving of its title, *il cuore verde d'Italia* (the green heart of Italy). Historically poor and undeveloped, the region's infrastructure and economy have taken huge strides during the last 30 years. Growing prosperity blends with the traditional to attract growing numbers of visitors.

Part of Umbria'a charm is its largely untouched countryside, scattered with historic hill towns, each increasingly able to cater to visitors' needs. The landscape includes gentle hills, vineyards, woodland and the dramatic peaks of the Monti Sibillini to the east. The whole region is permeated by a hazy blue light distinctively Umbrian. The light is quite appropriate to mystical Umbria, the birthplace of St. Francis and St. Benedict.

An elderly Tuscan enjoying the tranquility

A traditional Tuscan farmhouse, in the lovely area between Volterra and San Gimignano

Umbrian People and Places

Courteous and friendly, the Umbrians are welcoming and kind. Outside the main towns, few people speak more than a few words of English, but they do have time for and patience with visitors. Many of the remote areas are inhabited by people whose way of life has seen little change for decades. But accommodations are very easy to find, restaurants are excellent and roads, towns and villages are still relatively quiet. The main attractions are Perúgia the capital; Assisi, with its Franciscan associations; and Orvieto, for its superb cathedral. Make sure to leave time for historic Spoleto and Gubbio, and don't neglect the smaller towns of Spello, Todi and hilltop Trevi. Lovers of unspoiled scenery will find some of the best in the wild uplands above Nórcia.

A Place Apart – the Marche

Daunted by the barrier of the Apennines, relatively few visitors penetrate the Marche, a wonderfully varied region with mountains, jumbled hills and valleys, fertile plains and a long coastline. The northern part of this area has the most to offer. Incomparable Urbino is one of Italy's most perfect Renaissance towns. San Leo is dramatically situated, San Marino is popular and Pesaro, with two miles of beach, draws sun-seekers from all over Europe.

To the south lies lovely Ascoli Piceno in the Tronto valley, possibly the most logical route to the Marche from Umbria. Hotels and restaurants, particularly on the coast, are more than adequate, but the road system away from the coast still lags behind those of many other Italian regions.

FLORENCE

Florence (Firenze) is the capital of Tuscany and one of the world's great artistic shrines. But with a resident population of fewer than 400,000 and around 7 million annual visitors, Florence can be overwhelming for the wrong reasons: the heat, crowds and traffic mar many people's enjoyment. At first sight the city can seem architecturally dour, with narrow streets and overpowering buildings. Open and relaxed spaces are few and far between. It's the contents of the buildings that tourists come to see, so be prepared to spend much of your time inside and plan ahead. The churches, musems and galleries contain a plethora of treasures within a surprisingly small area.

Background

The Roman city of Florentia re-emerged as an independent city-state, its prosperity based on wool, banking and commerce, in the 12th century.

The Medici Balls

On buildings and statues all over Florence you'll notice the Medici emblem, a cluster of red balls *(palle)* on a black background. This is the coat-of-arms of the city's ruling family, with which they adorned every building owned by or connected to them. The number of balls varied throughout the centuries, so you'll notice any number between five and 12. Their original meaning is obscure, but most historians agree they derive from either medicinal pills (family members were once apothecaries) or coins, a reference to the Medici interests in banking and money-lending.

Between the early 14th and late 15th centuries, the Medici were the pre-eminent family; they ruled Florence and later Tuscany until the 18th century. During World War II, Florence was occupied by the Germans; because of its artistic importance, they declared it an open city. Huge damage was caused to the city and its treasures by the floods of 1966 when the Arno river burst its banks.

Plan Ahead

Choose the time of your visit carefully; although the city is less crowded in the winter months, there is no longer any time of year when Florence is empty. Winter temperatures are better for sightseeing, as few museums and public buildings in Florence are air-conditioned. Above all, don't do too much. See what you want to see, not what you feel you should see. Be prepared to walk a fair amount; many of the major attractions, however, are in the city center.

Venture off the tourist circuit and explore the quieter back streets and hidden piazzas, where you'll find neighborhood stores, artisans' workshops and atmospheric corners. To avoid the worst crowds, arrive at opening time or late in the day at the big museums. Enjoy a relaxing lunch or you'll be wilting by mid-afternoon.

The City

Florence's highlights lie close together on the north bank of the Arno river. You should see the Piazza della Signoria, which contains the Palazzo Vecchio, the Piazza del Duomo with the cathedral and baptistery, and the Uffizi and Bargello galleries. Many superb works of art are found in the city's churches; Santa Maria della Carmine for Masaccio, Santa Croce for Giotto, San Marco for Fra Angelico and San Lorenzo for Michelangelo top the list. Be sure to take in the Ponte Vecchio bridge, the elegant stores on and around the Via de'Tornabuoni and the markets.

Friendly Eating

Florence is overflowing with restaurants of every type. Many are specifically aimed at tourists, with prominently displayed fixed-price menus. It's a good idea to check how many Italians are eating in a restaurant. As a general rule, you'll find the cheaper restaurants near the railroad station, chic places in the city center, and small and friendly eating houses on the south side of the Arno river.

The graceful curve of the dome of Florence's cathedral, with the city beyond

Lunch is served any time after 12:30 and dinner beginning around 7:30. For a simple lunch, try a slice of freshly baked pizza-to-go or a quick snack in a bar or traditional wine shop, a

fiaschetteria. The food markets are particularly tempting, and you could

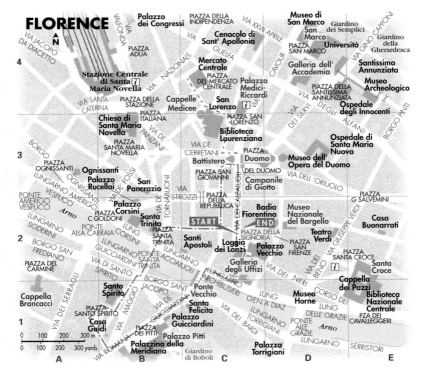

put together a picnic. Tuscan food is simple and excellent, with plenty of soups, superb pork products, grilled meats and vegetables. Bean dishes are especially popular – other Italians nickname Tuscans *mangiafagioli*, bean-eaters. The most famous wine is Chianti, but also look for Brunello di Montalcino. Vino Nobile is a superb wine that comes from Montepulciano.

Shopping

Florence is home to some of Italy's finest shops and most intriguing boutiques. Leather goods such as shoes, bags and accessories are famous, as are fine china, exquisite bed and table linen, and gold jewelry. Designer-label fans can visit Pucci and Gucci on their home ground, and brilliantly glazed majolica pottery, marbled paper, prints and antiques make tempting souvenirs.

Via Tornabuoni and the surrounding streets house the most elegant stores; less expensive fashion can be found around Piazza della Repubblica and

Via dei Calzaiuoli, while jewelers line the Ponte Vecchio. There are many factory leather outlets near Santa Croce. The main street market is the huge Mercato San Lorenzo, which has the added bonus of its proximity to the Mercato Centrale, Florence's central food market. Most stores will ship direct to the United States.

Entertainment

Many tourists are content to round off the day with a leisurely dinner and evening stroll, but Florence also offers a good range of theaters, concerts, opera, ballet, movie theaters, clubs and discos. Summer visitors can catch one of the two big cultural festivals, the *Estate Fiesolana* or the *Maggio Musicale Fiorentino*. Concerts, opera and ballet are often performed outdoors in a historic setting. Look out for the free monthly tourist magazine *Florence Concierge* (Concierge Tourist Information); it has full listings and lots of other helpful information.

ESSENTIAL INFORMATION

TOURIST INFORMATION
•Piazza della Stazione 4/A ☎ 055 212 245; www.firenzturismo.it
•Via Cavour 1r ☎ 055 290 832/3
•Borgo Santa Croce 29r ☎ 055 234 0444
•Perètola Airport ☎ 055 315 874

schedule from the ATAF office (Piazza del Duomo 57r). Stamp tickets as you get on; look for the orange box on the bus. Taxis can be hailed at various locations or ordered from Radio Taxi Cotafi (☎ 055 4390) or Radio Taxi Socata (☎ 055 4242).

URBAN TRANSPORTATION
Buses, both regular and electric, run from Sta. Maria Novella station all over town. Tickets must be purchased from machines and tobacco shops before boarding. They are valid for unlimited journeys over a period of 70 or 120 minutes, and 24-hour passes also are available. You can pick up a map and

AIRPORT INFORMATION
Most visitors arrive and leave from Pisa's Aeroporto Galileo Galilei (☎ 050 849 300 for flight information), connected to Florence's Sta. Maria Novella railroad station by hourly trains (journey time 1 hour). Florence's own airport is at Perètola (☎ 055 306 1702 for 24-hour information) 4 miles from the city and easily reached by bus or taxi.

CLIMATE – Average highs and lows

JAN.	FEB.	MAR.	APR.	MAY	JUN.	JUL.	AUG.	SEP.	OCT.	NOV.	DEC.
4°C	8°C	13°C	18°C	23°C	26°C	28°C	27°C	23°C	17°C	10°C	6°C
39°F	46°F	55°F	64°F	73°F	79°F	82°F	81°F	73°F	63°F	50°F	43°F
0°C	2°C	5°C	9°C	13°C	17°C	20°C	19°C	16°C	11°C	5°C	2°C
32°F	36°F	41°F	48°F	55°F	63°F	68°F	66°F	61°F	52°F	41°F	36°F

FLORENCE SIGHTS

Key to symbols

✚ map coordinates refer to the Florence map on page 89; sights below are highlighted in yellow on the map

✉ address or location ☎ telephone number

🕐 opening times 🍴 restaurant on site or nearby

🚌 nearest bus or tram route

🎫 admission charge: $$$ more than €6, $$ €3 to €6, $ less than €3 ℹ️ information

CAPPELLA BRANCACCI

Comprehensively and sensitively restored in the 1980s, the Cappella Branacci frescoes represent a pivotal point in art development. Commissioned in 1424 by Felice Brancacci, a wealthy merchant, the cycle illustrates the life of St. Peter. It was painted by Masolino, his dazzling pupil Masaccio, and Filippino Lippi, who completed the work 60 years later. Masaccio's radiant work, with its superb handling of light and space, drama and realism, was an inspiration for many other Renaissance artists. Highlights are the *Tribute Money*, with its weighty figures, the heart-rending *Expulsion from Paradise* and *St. Peter Healing the Sick*.

✚ A1 ✉ Santa Maria del Carmine, Piazza del Carmine (enter through cloisters) ☎ 055 238 2195 🕐 Mon. and Wed.–Sat. 10–5, Sun. 1–5 🚌 B 🎫 $$

CAPPELLE MEDICEE

Set behind San Lorenzo is Florentine architect Filippo Brunelleschi's serene 1419 structure that served as the Medici parish church. The Cappelle Medicee (Medici Chapels) were built as the mausoleum for Florence's most powerful family. Family members were interred in the crypt, the Sagrestia Nuova, (New Sacristy) and Buontalenti's grandiose domed *Chapel of the Princes*. The Sagrestia Nuova was built by Michelangelo between 1520 and 1534 and contains some of his most powerful sculpture. Reclining figures representing *Night*, *Day*, *Dawn* and *Dusk* decorate the tombs of Lorenzo, duke of Urbino, and Giuliano, duke of Nemours. The chapel also contains the artist's lovely *Madonna and Child*, as well as charcoal

The Baptistery rises serenely over the city's crowds

drawings thought to be by the master.

✚ C4 ✉ Via Madonna degli Aldobrandini ☎ 055 238 8602 🕐 Daily 8:15–5 (except alternating Sun. and Mon., when it's closed) 🚌 In pedestrian zone 🎫 $$$

DUOMO, BATTISTERO AND CAMPANILE DI GIOTTO

The richly marbled Gothic Duomo (Cathedral) of Santa Maria del Fiore, the first domed structure erected in Europe since Roman times, was built between 1296 and 1436 on the site of a seventh-century church. Pass through the cathedral's austere interior, with its fine Uccello fresco, to climb the 463 steps to the top of Brunelleschi's dome, its herringbone brickwork copied from the Pantheon in Rome. The chief draw of the marble Battistero (Baptistery), probably built between the fifth and seventh centuries and marble-covered in the 11th and 13th centuries, is the three sets of bronze doors with their Old Testament scenes. Pisano cast the south pair in 1326, and they inspired Ghiberti to design the north and east doors in the 1400s; the originals are in the Museo dell'Opera del Duomo. The graceful campanile was designed by Giotto and built by Pisano and Talenti between 1334 and 1359. Its pink, green and white marble walls are decorated with copies of the original superb relief sculptures, also displayed in the Museo dell'Opera.

✚ C3 ✉ Piazza del Duomo ☎ 055 230 2885 🕔 Cathedral: Mon.–Wed. and Fri. 10–5, Thu. and Sat. 10–3:30, Sun. 1:30–4:45. Baptistery: Mon.–Sat. noon–7, Sun. 8:30–3. Museo dell'Opera: Mon.–Sat 9–7:30, Sun. 9–1:40. Campanile: daily 8:30–7:30 🚌 1, 6, 7, 11, 14 ♿ Cathedral free; Baptistery $$; Museo dell'Opera $$$; Campanile $$$

GALLERIA DEGLI UFFIZI

Arguably the world's greatest collection of Renaissance paintings, the Galleria degli Uffizi (Office Gallery) is an elegant arcaded building designed by Giorgio Vasari as administrative offices. Here, in chronological order, are paintings representative of the greatest names in art from the 13th through 18th centuries. You can trace the technical development of painting through masterpieces of perspective such as Uccello's *Battle of San Romano* (1456), while Renaissance neo-Platonic philosophy is expressed in the iconography underlying Botticelli's beautiful *Birth of Venus* and *Primavera*. Don't miss Piero della Francesca's austere double portrait of Federico da Montefeltro and his wife, Battista Sforza, Leonardo da Vinci's sublime *Adoration of the Magi* and Titian's *Venus of Urbino*. Come early or late to avoid the lines; it also is possible to reserve your visit in advance.

✚ C2 ✉ Loggiato degli Uffizi 6 ☎ 055 238 8651 🕔 Tue.–Sun. 8:15–6:50 (occassional late opening in summer) 🚌 In pedestrian zone ♿ $$$

GALLERIA DELL'ACCADEMIA

Founded as an art school in 1784, the Academy Gallery today houses the world's most important collection of Michelangelo sculptures. The main attraction is his *David*, possibly the most famous in the history of sculpture. Other sculptures by the artist include the four *Prisoners*, the figures struggling to escape the stone. The gallery also has work by other Renaissance artists.

✚ D4 ✉ Via Ricasoli 58–60 ☎ 055 238 8609 🕔 Tue.–Sun. 8:15–6:50 🚌 San Marco ♿ $$$

GIARDINO DI BOBOLI

Florence's green lung is a revelation of geometric garden design. Laid out for the Medici in 1550 and open to the public since 1766, the Giardino di Boboli (Boboli Gardens) are truly Renaissance in spirit, an amalgam of nature and artifice. Fountains, crumbling statues, aromatic bosky shrubs, trees and pools combine to create a garden very different from the Anglo-Saxon ideal. Highlights include the offbeat statue of Bacchus astride a tortoise and the 1785 *Limonaia*, where citrus trees were once stored to protect them from winter frosts.

✚ C1 ✉ Piazza dei Pitti ☎ 055 265 1816 🕔 Daily 8:15–one hour before sunset. Closed first and last Mon. of month 🍴 Refreshment kiosk in gardens 🚌 B, C, 11, 36, 37 ♿ $

MUSEO DI SAN MARCO

Rebuilt in 1437 and decorated by Fra Angelico, the convent attached to the church of San Marco is one of Florence's loveliest treasures. It's a peaceful religious house where each of the 44 cells is adorned with a tiny fresco to aid prayer. Designed by Michelozzo in 1437, it was funded by Cosimo il Vecchio, the first truly prominent Medici, who used to spend time in the monastery. The pilgrims' hall contains many paintings by Angelico and his school, and more are found in the cloisters and on the stairs, notably the radiant *Annunciation*. The great Dominican reformer Savanarola was prior here at the end of the 15th century.

✚ D4 ✉ Piazza San Marco ☎ 055 238 8608 🕔 Mon.–Fri. 8:15–1:50, Sat. 8:15–6:50, Sun. 8:15–7; closed alternate Sun. and Mon. 🚌 1, 6, 7, 10, 11, 17, 20, 25, 31, 32, 33 ♿ $$

MUSEO NAZIONALE DEL BARGELLO

The Bargello was built in 1255 as the first seat of Florence's government, and it once housed the law courts. In 1574 it passed to the police department and served as a prison until 1859. Renovated and restored, it opened as a museum in 1865. Today it houses Italy's finest collection of Renaissance sculpture. Airy rooms

It's good luck to drop a coin in the snout of Il Porcellino, the bronze boar in Mercato Nuovo

WALK: THE HEART OF FLORENCE

Refer to route marked on city map on page 89.

This walk (about 2 hours long) takes you through the heart of historic Florence and is useful for getting your bearings and choosing sights.

Start in the Piazza della Signoria.
This square is the historic center of Florentine power, as is evident from the looming Palazzo Vecchio, the elegant Logge dei Lanzi and the numerous sculptures.

Head toward the Arno river through the Piazzale degli Uffizi, with the Galleria degli Uffizi on your left. Turn right onto the Lungarno Archibusieri to the Ponte Vecchio, Florence's oldest bridge.
Cross the bridge and walk along the Via de' Guicciardini to the monumental Palazzo Pitti, which houses another of Florence's major art collections. Cross the Piazza dei Pitti to the Piazza San Felice, then cut right down the Via Mazzetta to Piazza Santo Spirito, with its lively atmosphere and great Brunelleschi church. Walk down Via del Presto di San Martino to the church's right, and across

Piazza Frescobaldi to re-cross the river on the beautiful Ponte Santa Trinita. Continue along Via de' Tornabuoni, where you'll find stores such as Versace and Gucci. Then take a right along Via Porta Rossa to the Mercato Nuovo, with its famous brass boar, the Porcellino. This is a great place for souvenir shopping.

A left turn here onto Via Calimala leads through the grandiose 19th-century Piazza della Repubblica, scattered with tempting pavement cafés, to Via Roma. This street opens up onto the Piazza San Giovanni, where you turn right to visit the religious heart of the city, the Piazza del Duomo, with the city's cathedral, Baptistery and campanile.

An option for hearty walkers is a detour north from the cathedral to San Lorenzo, the great Medici church, and up Via dell' Ariento to Florence's wonderful Mercato Centrale, the city's major produce market, housed in a superb 19th-century cast-iron structure. Return to the cathedral.
For a shorter route from the cathedral, turn left onto the Via dei Calzaiuoli. A few blocks down on the right is the church of Orsanmichele, Florence's medieval guild church, with its Renaissance sculptures and Bernardo Daddi fresco. Via dei Calzaiuoli leads back to the Piazza della Signoria.

surround a spacious courtyard and you'll find works by Michelangelo, Cellini and the flamboyant Giambologna. The vaulted first-floor hall contains the museum's masterpieces. Here are Donatello's jaunty bronze *David*, the first free-standing nude to be modeled since Roman times, his fine *St. George*, and the competition baptistery door reliefs by Ghiberti and Brunelleschi. Upstairs there are bright enameled terracottas by the della Robbia family.

✚ D2 ✉ Via del Proconsolo 4 ☎ 055 238 8606
🕐 Tue.–Sun. 8:15–1:50 🍴 Dino, see page 204
🚌 19 🎫 $$

PALAZZO MEDICI–RICCARDI

Many visitors bypass the Palazzo Medici, designed by Michelangelo in 1444. The solid exterior of heavy rusticated stonework is by the graceful courtyard, with its *sgrafitto* decoration. Many other Florentine palazzi, such as the Strozzi and Pitti, were influenced by this structure. The interior contains the *Cappella dei Magi*, a tiny chapel totally covered with charming frescoes. Executed by Benozzo Gozzoli from 1459 to 1463, they show the Magi, gorgeously dressed in contemporary high fashion, walking through an idealized Tuscan landscape rich with flowers and birds.

✚ C4 ✉ Via Cavour 3 ☎ 055 276 0340
🕐 Thu.–Tue. 9–7 🚌 1, 6, 7 🎫 $$

PALAZZO PITTI

Built for the Pittis, this opulent palace was the Medici residence from 1550 until their fall in 1743, when they bequeathed their collections to the city. It now houses five museums, the most important being the Galleria Palatina and the Museo degli Argenti. The former is primarily a painting gallery, where you'll find Raphael's sweet-featured *Madonna of the Chair*, a sexy Mary Magdalene by Titian and some fine portraits. The art objects in the Museo degli Argenti mostly represent a triumph of expensive bad taste, although the Roman glass and cameo collection are worth tracking down. The Pitti also houses the Appartamenti Monumentali (State Rooms), the Galleria del Costume (Costume Museum) and the Galleria d'Arte Moderna (Modern Art Gallery).

✚ B1 ✉ Piazza dei Pitti ☎ Galleria Palatina 055 238 8614; Museo degli Argenti 055 238 8709
🕐 Galleria Palatina: Tue.–Sun. 8–6:15. Museo degli Argenti: daily 8:15–1 hour before sunset (closed first and last Mon. of the month) 🚌 B, C, 11, 36, 37
🎫 Palatina $$$; Argenti $$

Jewelers' shops line the Ponte Vecchio, one of the world's most famous bridges

PIAZZA DELLA SIGNORIA

The logical place to begin or end your sightseeing, the Piazza della Signoria was the physical center of Medici and Florentine power. The council met in the Palazzo Vecchio, which overlooks the square where executions took place, riotous crowds assembled and religious fanatics preached. The square itself and the graceful Loggia dei Lanzi display an impressive range of sculptures. The mounted horseman, a statue by Giambologna dated 1595, is Duke Cosimo I, the Medici who brought all Tuscany under military rule. Don't miss Benvenuto Cellini's sinuous *Perseus*, who holds aloft Medusa's head.

✠ C2 ✉ Piazza della Signoria 🍴 Bars and restaurants nearby ♿ In pedestrian zone

PONTE VECCHIO

Not the most beautiful Florentine bridge, but certainly the most photographed, the Ponte Vecchio (Old Bridge) was built in 1345 to replace an earlier one. It is lined with shops, exclusively goldsmiths and jewelers since 1593. Above them runs a corridor used by the Medici to travel from the Pitti to the Uffizi. It was the only bridge not destroyed by the Germans in World War II, and it also survived the floods in 1966.

✠ C1 ✉ Ponte Vecchio ♿ In pedestrian zone

SANTA CROCE

This huge, plain Franciscan preaching church, damaged by the 1966 floods, was built in 1294 – although the colorful marble facade dates from 1863, funded by a Florence-loving Englishman, Sir Francis Sloane. The interior contains superb early Gaddi frescoes that tell the story of the Santa Croce (Holy Cross). Seek out the Bardi and Peruzzi chapels, which feature beautiful frescoes by Giotto. Michelangelo is buried here, as are Machiavelli, Galileo Galilei and the composer Antonio Rossini. In the serene cloisters stands the Cappella dei Pazzi (Pazzi Chapel), designed by Brunelleschi in the 1430s and among the most beautiful of Renaissance buildings.

✠ E1 ✉ Piazza Santa Croce ☎ 055 244 619 🕐 Mon.–Sat. 9:30–5:30, Sun. 1–5:30 🍴 Enoteca Pinchiorri, see page 204

🚌 23, 13, B 💰 $$

Tuscany, Umbria and the Marche

THE FLOOD OF 1966

As you walk the streets of Florence, keep an eye open above your head for the small stone plaques on many buildings; they mark the height to which the floodwaters of the Arno river rose on the night of November 4, 1966. It was an event that proved a catastrophe for the city and its art.

October 1966 was a very wet month throughout Italy, while the first two days of November saw 18 inches of rain fall in the Florence area. Water pressure rose dangerously in an upstream reservoir, and the authorities, fearing its dam might break, opened the sluices. They failed to warn anyone in the city of Florence; only the jewelers whose shops lined the Ponte Vecchio were alerted by their own night watchman who noticed that the bridge was shaking as the waters rose. As the traders cleared their stock, they asked watching police if the alarm had been officially raised, only to be told that no orders had been received. Shortly after, the banks of the Arno could no longer contain the unprecedented tons of water. They broke, releasing a flash flood of more than 500,000 tons of water and mud that poured with startling speed through the city.

Thirty-five Florentine citizens were drowned in the first onrush, many trapped in the underpass of Santa Maria Novella railroad station. The muddy floodwaters mixed with heating oil stored in cellars and basements, and it was this ghastly cocktail that did the damage.

Damage to homes, shops and businesses was huge, with many families losing all their possessions. The world's attention, though, was focused on the damage to works of art, particularly in the Santa Croce area, one of the lowest parts of Florence. More than 3,000 paintings were damaged, some irretrievably.

Antiquities were destroyed, and thousands of priceless books and manuscripts lost. Within days, voluntary workers, many of them art students, were arriving to begin the rescue operation.

Above: Cars re-emerging in the city center as water levels start to fall
Right: The devastated shops on the Ponte Vecchio

They worked nonstop in appalling conditions heaving artworks to safety and starting the drying-out process on books and manuscripts.

Money poured in from all over the world, and by the following summer Florence was itself again – at least superficially. Behind the scenes, however, the task of art restoration was immense, and more than 35 years later work still continues on paintings, sculpture, books and manuscripts.

One beneficial result of the disaster was the tremendous strides made in the development of restoration techniques to cope with the flood's effects. Frescoes had to be stabilized, oil paintings painstakingly reassembled from fragments, and priceless books dried and cleaned.

Later projects throughout Italy, such as the restoration of such major works as Michelangelo's frescoes in the Sistine Chapel in Rome and Piero della Francesca's frescoes in Arezzo, owe much to the efforts in Florence. International co-operation among restorers all over the world forged ahead, and galleries and museums worldwide have profited from the city's restoration challenges.

REGIONAL SIGHTS

Key to symbols

⊞ map coordinates refer to the region map on page 84; sights below are highlighted in yellow on the map
✉ address or location ☎ telephone number
⏰ opening times 🍴 restaurant on site or nearby
🚢 ferry 🖐 admission charge: $$$ more than €6, $$ €3 to €6, $ less than €3 ℹ information

AREZZO

Prosperous Arezzo, its modern wealth based on the fact that it is the world's largest gold manufacturing center, spreads down a hill above the Arno valley in eastern Tuscany. A major Etruscan city, it thrived under the Romans and was a prosperous medieval republic until 1384, when it was annexed by Florence. Today, Arezzo's chief glory is the superb fresco cycle, *The Legend of the True Cross*, by the enigmatic Renaissance artist Piero della Francesca, in the church of San Francesco. Newly emerged from a lengthy restoration, these luminous paintings, executed between 1452 and 1466, tell the story of the cross used to crucify Christ.

   Near San Francesco you'll find the Pieve di Santa Maria, an earlier Romanesque church with an exuberant facade and Pietro Lorenzetti's glowing high altar polyptych showing the *Madonna and Child with Saints*. The church is backed by the Piazza Grande, a sloping medieval square with a loggia on its north side. The piazza is the scene of Arezzo's major festival, the *Giostra del Saraceno*, a splendid jousting display preceded by costumed processions.

   The Duomo (Cathedral) stands at Arezzo's highest point; this harmonious building was constructed over more than four centuries, its facade finally finished in the 20th century. Inside there are glowing stained-glass windows; Guido Tarlati's lovely tomb, said to have been designed by Giotto; and the tiny fresco *Magdalene*, another work by Piero della Francesca.

   Elsewhere, Arezzo's shops offer plenty of temptations; the town is a noted antiques center, with many classy showrooms and a monthly antiques fair, the *Fiera Antiquaria*.

The distinctive medieval towers of San Gimignano

⊞ C3
Tourist information ✉ Piazza della Repubblica 28 ☎ 0575 377 678 ⏰ Mon.–Sat. 9–1 and 3–7, Sun. 9–1, Apr.–Sep.; Mon.–Sat. 9–1 and 3–6 (also first Sun. of month 9–1), rest of year
San Francesco ✉ Via Cavour ☎ 0575 352 727 ⏰ Mon.–Fri. 9–6, Sat. 9–5:30, Sun. 1–5:30; fresco cycle by guided tour only (sometimes in English, check for details). Tickets must be booked in advance by phone, online or from the office at San Francesco 🖐 $$
Pieve di Santa Maria ✉ Corso Italia ☎ 0575 22 629 ⏰ Daily 8–1 and 3–6:30 🖐 Free
Duomo ✉ Piazza del Duomo ☎ 0575 23 991 ⏰ Daily 7/8:30–12:30 and 3–6:30/7 🖐 Free
ℹ *Giostra del Saraceno* is held on the first Sun. in Sep. Smaller-scale versions are staged throughout the summer

ASCOLI PICENO

Ascoli Piceno stands in a steep hollow 25 kilometers (15 miles) from the Adriatic coast. Today's street plan still follows that of the Roman colony established here after the defeat of the Picini, an early tribe. The heart of the town is the lovely Piazza del Popolo, a serene ensemble of medieval and Renaissance buildings, all made of the travertine stone of which Ascoli is constructed. On the piazza's north side stands the lovely Gothic San Francesco church, with its graceful five-arched loggia and slender bell towers. Other delights include the Duomo (Cathedral), which contains an art gallery and an archeological museum; and the tangle of beguiling streets at the top of the Via del Trivio above the Tronto river.
⊞ E2
Tourist information ✉ Piazza del Popolo 1 ☎ 0736 253 045 ⏰ Mon.–Fri. 8:30–1 and 3–7, Sat. 9–1 and 3–7, Sun. 9–1
San Francesco ✉ Piazza del Popolo ☎ 0736 259 496 ⏰ Daily 8–12:30 and 3–7 🖐 Free
Duomo ✉ Piazza Arringo ⏰ Daily 8–12:30 and 4–8
Pinacoteca Civica ✉ Palazzo Arringo, Piazza Arringo 7 ☎ 0736 298 213 ⏰ Mon.–Fri. 9–1 and 3–7:30, Sat. 8–1, Sun. 3–7, Jun.–Sep.; Mon.–Sat. 9–1, Sun. 9–12:30, rest of year 🖐 $
Museo Archeologico ✉ Piazza Arringo 28 ☎ 0736 253 562 ⏰ Tue.–Sun. 8:30–7:30 (closed Sun. p.m.), Jun.–Sep.; mornings only, rest of year 🖐 $
ℹ *Quintana* is held on the first Sun. in Aug.

Medieval civil engineering at its best – the Basilica di San Francesco in Assisi

ASSISI

Assisi is inextricably linked with St. Francis (1182–1226), the founder of the Franciscan order. The town is visited by pilgrims from all over the world. In late 1997, Assisi was damaged by a series of earthquakes. The wonderful Basilica di San Francesco bore the brunt, with some of its lesser treasures lost forever. The lower church, built around 1228, and the upper church have reopened, and the 28 panels of Giotto's *Life of St. Francis* have been completely restored (with only the loss of 36 square feet). The most powerful of the lower church frescoes are Simone Martini's *Life of St. Martin* and Lorenzetti's heart-rending *Deposition* and *Crucifixion*, fitting companions to the tomb of St. Francis.

At the opposite end of town is Santa Chiara, the burial place of St. Clare, the companion of St. Francis and the founder of the Poor Clares, the Franciscan nuns. The square outside this pink-and-white striped Gothic building offers lovely views. Above the square stands the Duomo (Cathedral); built from 1140 to 1253, it has a beautiful Romanesque facade. Inside you can see the font used to baptize St. Francis and St. Clare.

Back toward the basilica is the Piazza del Comune, a lovely medieval square on the probable site of Assisi's Roman forum. The focal point is the superb first-century Tempio di Minerva, a perfectly preserved Roman temple facade with six Corinthian columns and a graceful pediment. The Pinacoteca Comunale (Art Gallery) occupies an old town house.

The evocative San Damiano is a country church and convent where St. Francis composed the *Canticle to the Sun*. Equally lovely is the Eremo delle Carceri, a monastery standing in oak woods and a place of retreat for St. Francis.

➕ D2

Tourist information ✉ Piazza del Comune 9 ☎ 075 812 450 or 075 812 534 🕐 Mon.–Fri. 8–2 and 3–6, Sat. 9–1 and 3–6, Sun. 9–1

Basilica di San Francesco ✉ Piazza Inferiore di San Francesco ☎ 075 819 001 🕐 Daily 6:30 a.m.–7 p.m. 🖐 Free

Basilica di Santa Chiara ✉ Piazza Santa Chiara 🕐 Daily 6:30–dusk or 7:30 🖐 Free

Duomo ✉ Piazza San Rufino 🕐 Daily 7–noon and 2–7 🖐 Free

Pinacoteca Comunale ✉ Via San Francesco 10 ☎ 075 812 273 🕐 Daily 10–1 and 2:30–7, Jul.–Aug.; 2:30–7, mid-Mar. to Jun. 30 and Sep. 1 to mid-Oct.; 10–1 and 2–5, rest of year 🖐 $$

San Damiano ☎ 075 812 033 🕐 Daily 10–noon and 2–6 (closes 4:30 in winter) 🖐 Free

Eremo delle Carceri ☎ 075 812 301 🕐 Daily dawn–dusk 🖐 Free

CHIANTI

Between Florence and Siena lies Chianti, an area of wooded hills and vineyards, dotted with intriguing villages and threaded by winding back roads. The most famous product is wine; trademark Gallo Nero (Black Cockerel) is known all over the world.

Chianti's good climate and fascinating surroundings have been attracting northern Europeans since the 1960s, and international visitors have bought and converted many of the lovely old houses, while once-unspoiled hill towns such as Radda in Chianti and neighboring Gaiole are now packed with visitors. The best way to enjoy this still-lovely region is to leave the main roads. Explore the woods and smaller villages and sample the wines at any of several hundred vineyards as you go. Wine lovers will enjoy Greve in Chianti; in September it's the scene of the area's biggest wine fair. Greve has a lively Saturday market in its main piazza, where you'll also find a statue of Giovanni da Verazzano, the discoverer of New York Harbor. He was born in the neighboring village of the same name.

Greve in Chianti 🛡 C3
Tourist information ✉ Via Verrazzano ☎ 055 854 6287 🕔 Mon.–Fri. 10:30–12:30 and 3–7, Sat. 10:30–12:30 🎏 Greve Wine Fair is held in Sep., further details available from the tourist office

GÚBBIO

Few tourists venture as far as Gúbbio, tucked beneath rolling mountains near Umbria's eastern border. But this charming town, once the most important *comune* between Rome and Ravenna, is rich in quaint streets, superb old palaces, churches and paintings. Start a tour at the bottom of the Old Town, where you'll find the church of San Francesco, with an engaging fresco (1410) by Ottaviano Nelli, and the 14th-century Loggia dei Tiratori, Italy's best-preserved example of a weaver's shed, where wool was spread to dry away from direct sunlight.

Up the hill stands the solid bulk of the 14th-century Palazzo dei Consoli, Gúbbio's civic masterpiece, fronted by the sweeping Piazza Grande. It now houses the town's museum and art gallery. Nearby stand the cathedral and the Palazzo Ducale, built by Federico da Montefeltro from neighboring Urbino (see page 115) in 1470. From here, you can climb Monte Ingino, which rises above the town, to visit the Basilica di Sant' Ubaldo, Gubbio's patron saint. The gigantic wooden *ceri* (candles), used in the *Corsa dei Ceri*, a famous and exuberant festival held May 15, are stored here.

🛡 D2
Tourist information ✉ Piazza Odersi 3–5 ☎ 075 922 0790 or 075 922 0693 🕔 Mon.–Fri. 8:30–1:45 and 3:30–6:30, Sat. 9–1 and 3–6, Sun. 9:30–12:30
Museo Civico ✉ Piazza Grande ☎ 075 927 4298 🕔 Daily 10–3 and 3–6, Apr.–Sep.; 10–1 and 2–5, rest of year 🎟 $$

LAGO TRASIMENO

Italy's fourth largest lake is a shallow expanse of warm water fringed with beaches and laid-back little towns. Lago Trasimeno (Lake Trasimeno) makes an excellent stopping point for a couple of days of relaxation. Castiglione del Lago, on the western shore, has a fine fortified 16th-century castle jutting into the lake and nice swimming beaches. Passignano, on the opposite shore, is a friendly town with a lakeside promenade and good bars and restaurants. In the hills behind Passignano you'll find Castel Rigone, a pretty village with fantastic views. Tuoro is another hill village above the lake; between here and Passignano is the site of Hannibal's great defeat of the Romans in 217 BC. Village names like Sanguineto (Place of Blood) and Ossaia (Place of Bones) are permanent reminders of the great Carthaginian general.

🛡 C2
Castiglione del Lago tourist information ✉ Piazza Mazzini ☎ 075 965 2484 🕔 Mon.–Fri. 8:30–1 and 3:30–7, Sat. 9–1 and 3:30–7, Sun. 9–1 and 4–7
Passignano tourist information ✉ Piazza Trento e Trieste 6 ☎ 075 827 635 🕔 Mon.–Sat. 10:30–12:30 and 4–7, Sun. 10:30–12:30, Jun.–Sep.; Fri.–Sat. 3–6:30, Sun. 10–12:30, rest of year 🚢 Boats run daily to Isola Maggiore, Trasimeno's largest island, from Passignano. Contact APM (☎ 075 827 157) for further information

Vines bearing Sagrantino grapes clothe the slopes below pretty Montefalco

DRIVE: EASTERN UMBRIA TO THE VALE OF SPOLETO

Duration: 3½ to 4 hours

This drive starts in remote Gúbbio (see page 101), a stone-built, fortress-like town in the hills of northeast Umbria.

> *From Gúbbio, take the SS298 heading southwest through the hills toward Perúgia.*

This scenic road takes you past tiny villages and farms to join the *superstrada* (highway) SS3bis in the upper valley of the Tiber river. The highway proceeds to Rome and the sea at Ostia.

> *Turn left onto the SS3bis and continue for 10 kilometers (6 miles) before joining the SS147 south (marked Assisi, Foligno and Spoleto). At the Assisi exit, follow the signs up the hill toward the town.*

The huge domed church in the lower modern part of Assisi is Santa Maria degli Angeli. It was begun in 1569, although the present building dates from 1832. The basilica is constructed around the *Porzuincola*, the tiny chapel where St. Francis lived in the earliest days of the Franciscan movement. In the garden outside you can see thornless rose bushes; according to legend they are the descendants of those into which the saint threw himself while grappling with temptation. As he fell they lost their spines, while their leaves became stained with drops of blood.

Tuscany, Umbria and the Marche

From Bevagna, continue 6.5 kilometers (about 5 miles) southeast to Montefalco. Montefalco is a superbly located town packed with artistic delights and noted for its fine wines. Made with the Sagrantino grape, found nowhere else in Europe, the pick of these full-flavored reds is perhaps Sagrantino Passito, a stunning sweet red dessert wine. Montefalco's chief attraction is the colorful and charming fresco cycle by Benozzo Gozzoli in the church of San Francesco, now a museum. Painted in 1452, the cycle depicts scenes from the life of St. Francis with charming detail. Other treasures include Perugino's 1503 *Nativity*, complete with a fine view of Lake Trasimeno (see page 101) in the background. The nearby church of Sant'Agostino contains mummies of local holy people, while the church of Santa Chiara contains the preserved body of St. Chiara of Montefalco.

From Montefalco, head east across the plain through San Luca to Trevi (see page 115). Pick up the SS3, which will take you south to Spoleto (see page 114).

Montefalco
San Francesco 🕐 Daily 10:30–1 and 3–7, Jun.–Jul.; 3–7:30, Aug.; 10:30–1 and 2–6, Mar.–May and Sep.–Oct. 🎫 $$

Do not drive into Assisi unless you have hotel reservations; the streets are narrow and steep, and there is no municipal parking. Leave your car in one of the pay parking lots outside town and walk (see page 100). From Assisi you can take the unclassified, part-dirt road over Monte Subásio to Spello (see page 111), and then join the SS75 to Foligno.
This beautiful route leads through upland meadows, carpeted in spring and early summer with spreads of wild narcissus, gentians, cistus and myriad orchids. From the road there are wide views over the plain. It's the perfect spot for a picnic. Above the treeline, you can see for miles and wander on the grassy slopes and along the little trails on the mountain's heights.

Alternately, head straight for Foligno on the SS75. Turn right at Foligno across the plain and continue for 7.5 kilometers (about 5 miles) to Bevagna.
The main square of this sleepy and undiscovered town contains two of Umbria's finest Romanesque churches, San Silvestro and San Michele. They were both built at the end of the 12th century. The facade of San Silvestro, now deconsecrated, was constructed using old fragments of Roman buildings; its shadowy interior has a marvelous sunken crypt. San Michele's facade was embellished with a rose window in the 18th century; look for the quirky gargoyles over the doorway.

An old Umbrian farmhouse amid vineyards

The riotously embellished facade of the church of San Michele in Foro, Lucca

LUCCA

Set in northern Tuscany at the foot of the Alpi Apuane, Lucca, with its tree-lined encircling walls, magnificent churches and solid provincial prosperity, is instantly appealing. There are three outstanding churches here, all built and decorated in the ornate 13th-century style known as Pisan Romanesque.

San Michele in Foro dominates the main piazza. Its exuberant facade is a riot of intricate columns, grotesques and carvings. Nearby, the Duomo (Cathedral) is fronted by a superb portal carved by Nicola Pisano. The interior houses the Tempietto, a shrine containing the venerated icon known as the Volto Santo (Holy Face), and the wondrous Renaissance tomb of Ilario del Carretto by Jacopo della Quercia. To the north is San Frediano; its facade glitters with 13th-century mosaics and its interior boasts a 12th-century font. Near here, just off Via Fillungo, Lucca's main shopping street, you'll find the Piazza Anfiteatro, a glorious oval built around the original Roman amphitheater. Lucca's best museum is the Museo Nazionale Guinigi, a wide-ranging collection of paintings, sculpture and furniture.

Be sure to leave time to walk the 16th-century walls and look for the Torre Guinigi, a 15th-century tower with a holm oak growing from the top.

Near Lucca is a group of elegant country villas, the summer homes of wealthy citizens of the 15th through 18th centuries. Many have superb gardens that are open to the public. Details about the gardens can be obtained from the Tourist Information office.

➕ B3

Tourist information 📧 Piazzale Verdi, Porta S Donato Vecchia ☎ 0583 583 150 🕐 Daily 9–7, Mar.–Oct.; 9:30–5:30, rest of year 🛈 An English-language audio guide to Lucca is available from the tourist office

San Michele in Foro 📧 Piazza San Michele 🕐 Daily 7:40–noon and 3–6 🎟 Free

Duomo di San Martino 📧 Piazza San Martino 🕐 Daily 7–7, Apr.–Sep.; 7–5, rest of year 🎟 Cathedral: free. Tomb of Ilaria Carretto $$

San Frediano 📧 Piazza San Frediano 🕐 Mon.–Sat. 8:30–noon and 3–7, Sun. 10:30–5 🎟 Free

Museo Nazionale Guinigi 📧 Via della Quarquonia ☎ 0583 496 033 🕐 Tue.–Sat. 8:30–7:30, Sun. 8:30–1:30 🎟 $$

Casa Natale di Puccini 📧 Corte San Lorenzo 9 ☎ 0583 584 028 🕐 Daily 10–6, Jun.–Sep.; 10–1 and 3–6, rest of year 🎟 $$

MONTALCINO

Hilltop Montalcino, encircled by walls and dominated by its *rocca* (fortress), was independent until 1260, when it became part of Siena. Montalcino heroically held out until 1555 as the last bastion of Sienese independence against the Florentines. This role is still commemorated during Siena's Palio (see page 117). Centuries of stagnation followed, until the 1960s saw the revival of its famous wine, Brunello di Montalcino, and the growth of tourism.

First explore the 14th-century fortress, and be sure to climb the walls for superb views over the idyllic southern Tuscan landscape. The fortress also contains the *enoteca*, a wine cellar where you can sample a range of superlative red wines. Montalcino's Museo Civico houses high-quality Sienese paintings and sculpture; among the finest is Sano di Pietro's *Madonna dell'Umiltà*, a rare portrayal of a kneeling Mary, the Blessed Mother.

For an architectural treat, take the road south to the Abbazia di Sant'Antimo, a 12th-century Benedictine abbey that stands alone amid olive trees and cypresses on the Francigena, one of Europe's ancient pilgrim routes. This glorious Romanesque building is noted for the carving on its pillars (don't miss Daniel in the lion's den) and its luminous interior. Much of the stone is alabaster, which helps suffuse the whole church with light.

✚ C2

Tourist information ✉ Costa del Municipio 8 ☎ 0577 849 331 🕓 Tue.–Sun. 10–1 and 2–4, May–Sep.; 10–1 and 3–5, rest of year ℹ *Torneo della Apertura della Caccia* (second Sun. in Aug.) and *Sagra del Tordo* (last Sun. in Oct.) feature costumed processions, archery tournaments and street banquets

Rocca ✉ Piazzale Fortezza 🕓 Tue.–Sun. 9–8, Apr.–Oct.; 9–6, rest of year 🎟 $

Museo Civico ✉ Via Ricasoli 31 ☎ 0577 846 014 🕓 Tue.–Sun. 10–1 and 2–5:50, Apr.–Oct.; 10–1 and 2–5:40, rest of year

Abbazia di Sant'Antimo ✉ Castelnuovo dell'Abate 🕓 Mon.–Sat. 10:30–12:30 and 3–6:30, Sun. 9 a.m.–10:30 a.m. and 3–6, Apr.–Sep.; Mon.–Sat. 11–12:30 and 3–5, Sun. 9 a.m.–10:30 a.m. and 3–6, rest of year 🎟 Free

MONTEPULCIANO

The highest of southern Tuscany's hilltop towns, Montepulciano sprawls down a narrow ridge, its picturesque side streets opening to gracious squares where you'll find a fascinating mixture of medieval, Renaissance and baroque architecture in churches and palaces. Following an alliance with Florence in 1511, money poured into the town, resulting in superb civic and private buildings designed by the architects Sangallo and Vignola. The focus is the Piazza Grande, where there are wonderful views from the Palazzo Comunale. The brick-faced cathedral has a serene Renaissance interior containing some great works of art, notably the glowing *Assumption* painted by Taddeo di Bartolo in 1401.

You can see more art displayed in the Museo Civico before heading outside of the walls to San Biagio (St. Blaise), a glowing, honey-colored pilgrimage church designed by Antonio da Sangallo in 1518. Leave time to taste the town's red wine, the Vino Nobile, which you'll find in wine shops all over town.

✚ C2

Tourist information ✉ Piazzale Don Minzoni 1 ☎ 0578 757 341 🕓 Daily 9–8, in Aug.; Mon.–Sat. 9–12:30 and 3–8, Sun. 9–12:30, May–Jul.; Mon.–Sat. 9–12:30 and 3–7, Sun. 9–12:30, rest of year ℹ *Cantiere Internazionale d'Arte*, a contemporary music festival, is held Jul.–Aug.; *Bravío delle Botti*, with elaborate costumed processions, a barrel race and street banquets, is held on the last Sun. in Aug.

Palazzo Comunale ✉ Piazza Grande ☎ 0578 712 243 🕓 Mon.–Sat. 10–noon and 4–6 🎟 Free

Museo Civico ✉ Palazzo Neri-Orselli, Via Ricci 10 ☎ 0578 717 300 🕓 Tue.–Sun. 10–1 and 3–6, Apr.–Oct.; Tue.–Sat. 11–12:30 and 3:30–4:30, Sun. 10–1 and 3–6, rest of year 🎟 $$

San Biagio ✉ Via di San Biagio 🕓 Daily 9–noon and 3–6 🎟 Free

NÓRCIA

For lovers of low-key, friendly towns, Nórcia should be high on the list. Tucked away in eastern Umbria at the foot of some of the region's most dramatic mountains, this solid little walled town is famed as the birthplace of St. Benedict, founder of the Benedictine order and patron saint of Europe.

The church of San Benedetto lies on Nórcia's harmonious main piazza; its lovely Gothic facade dates from 1389. Within the interior are the remains of a Roman building, reputedly the birthplace of the saint and his sister, St. Scholastica. Across the square looms the Castellina, a massive fortress designed by Giacomo da Vignola in 1563, which houses an intersting museum. Nórcia is famous for food – prosciutto, salami, sausages, pungent mountain cheeses and above all truffles, the black gold of Umbrian cuisine. You could fuel your appetite by hiking on the Piano Grande to the east; this unique upland plain, surrounded by grassy flower-covered mountains, is one of Umbria's least-known and most beautiful areas.

Tuscany, Umbria and the Marche

There are plenty of shopping temptations along Orvieto's quiet back streets

ORVIETO

A crag formed by an ancient volcano first attracted the Etruscans to the site of modern Orvieto, where they built a settlement, Volsinii. You can still view Etruscan tombs here, but most visitors are lured to Orvieto by what is arguably Italy's finest Gothic Duomo (Cathedral).

Construction started in the 13th century to celebrate the Miracle of Bolsena. During Mass, the communion host dripped blood on the altar cloth; this was the origin of the feast of the Body of Christ, which continued for centuries. The facade alone, glittering with mosaics and liberally endowed with sculpture, took more than 300 years to complete. The best-known interior work is Luca Signorelli's fresco *Last Judgment* (1504), a taut and technically stunning masterpiece that has been superbly restored.

Orvieto's other highlights include the Etruscan collection in the Museo Faina and the Pozzo di San Patrizio (St. Patrick's Well), an engineering tour de force with an impressive double ramp leading 62 feet into living rock. Orvieto is noted for its colorful *maiolica* pottery and other ceramics; you'll find a wealth of tempting stores in the streets around the Piazza del Duomo.

🚇 C1

Tourist information ✉ Piazza del Duomo 24 ☎ 0763 341 772 🕐 Mon.–Fri. 8:15–1:30 and 4–7, Sat. 10–1 and 3–6, Sun. 10–noon and 3–6

Duomo ✉ Piazza del Duomo 🕐 Daily 7:30–12:45 and 2:30–7:15, Apr.–Sep.; 7:30–12:45 and 2:30–6:15, Mar. and Oct.; 7:30–12:45 and 2:30–5:15, rest of year (Capella Nuova open as Duomo but opens at 10 a.m. and is closed Sun. a.m. year round) ♿ Cathedral free; Cappella Nuova (Signorelli's *Last Judgment*) $$

Museo Claudio Faina ✉ Piazza del Duomo ☎ 0763 341 511 🕐 Tue.–Sun. 9:30–6, Apr.–Sep.; 10–5, rest of year ♿ $$

Pozzo di San Patrizio ✉ Piazza Cahen ☎ 0763 343 768 🕐 Daily 10–7, Mar.–Sep.; 10–6, rest of year ♿ $$

PERÚGIA

Umbria's capital, Perúgia, is surrounded by ugly modern suburbs, but it's worth negotiating these to explore the unspoiled – and traffic-free – historic center. Parking is difficult, so leave the car in the lower town and use the escalators (*scala mobile*) to rise painlessly up to the hilltop core. Most of the main sights are on or near Corso Vannucci, a wide and gracious street running to Piazza IV Novembre, where you'll find the Duomo (Cathedral) and the exquisite 13th-century Fontana Maggiore. This two-basin fountain was sculpted by Nicola and Giovanni Pisano and is surrounded by statues and carvings; those showing the months of the year are particularly charming. The Palazzo dei Priori, the town hall, also houses the Galleria Nazionale dell'Umbria, one of central Italy's most important art collections, stunningly presented in light and airy galleries. Here you can trace the development of Umbrian painting, with some superb Sienese and Florentine works as an added bonus. Highlights include Duccio's lovely *Madonna and Child*, Fra' Angelico's heavenly blue triptych *Madonna with Angels and Saints*, and the radiant symmetry of Piero della Francesca's great polyptych *Madonna and Child with Saints* – note the use of perspective in the Annunciation panel.

Umbria's great duo, Perugino and Bernardino Pinturicchio, are represented by numerous paintings, suffused with light and color and perfectly encapsulating the distinct Umbrian style. Perugino also is the star of the Collegio del Cambio just down the street. He was commissioned in 1496 to decorate Perúgia's money changers' guild home, and he covered the walls and ceiling with figures, landscapes and decoration in a fusion of classical and Christian themes.

Close by, you can visit the Collegio della Mercanzia, the Merchants' Guild, to admire some superlative 15th-century wood paneling. Perúgia's other treasures include the graceful Renaissance Oratorio di San Bernardino, the grand and opulent church of San Pietro, and San Domenico, whose cloisters house the Galleria Nazionale Archeologico dell'Umbria. Perúgia has a wide choice of shops, bars and cafés along the Corso Vannucci, where you can buy locally made chocolates.

➕ D2

Tourist information ✉ Piazza IV Novembre 3 ☎ 075 572 3327 🕒 Mon.–Sat. 8:30–1:30 and 3:30–6:30, Sun. 9–1

Duomo ✉ Piazza IV Novembre 🕒 Daily 8–noon and 3:30–6 🎫 Free

Galleria Nazionale dell'Umbria ✉ Palazzo dei Priori, Corso Vannucci ☎ 075 574 1247 🕒 Daily 8:30–7:30; closed first Mon. of the month 🎫 $$$

Collegio del Cambio ✉ Corso Vanucci 25 ☎ 075 572 8599 🕒 Mon.–Sat. 9–12:30 and 2–5:30, Sun. 9–12:30 🎫 $$

Collegio della Mercanzia ✉ Corso Vanucci 15

☎ 075 573 0366 🕒 Mon.–Sat. 9–1 and 2:30–5:30, Sun. 9–1, Mar.–Oct.; Tue. and Thu.–Fri. 8–2, Wed. 9–1, rest of year 🎫 $$

Oratorio di San Bernardino ✉ Piazza San Francesco 🕒 Daily 8–noon and 3–6 🎫 Free

San Pietro ✉ Corso Cavour 🕒 Daily 8–noon and 3–6 but often closed, so check times 🎫 Free

San Domenico and Museo Archeologico Nazionale dell'Umbria ✉ Corso Cavour ☎ 075 572 7141 🕒 Mon. 2:30–7:30, Tue.–Sun. 8:30–7:30 🎫 $

PIENZA

The pocket-size Renaissance village of Pienza stands in the fertile rolling landscape of southern Tuscany, with the shapely peak of Monte Amiata to the south. Once known as Corsignano, it was the birthplace of the redoubtable Pope Pius II, Aeneas Sylvius Piccolomini, born in 1405. Elected to the papacy in 1458, Pius embarked on a scheme to transform his native village into an "ideal city." He commissioned the architect Bernardo Rossellino to design a cathedral, papal palace and town hall. This core of the existing town is harmoniously grouped around a charming square and named after the Pope. You can walk through the entire place in about 10 minutes, but Pienza merits more time than this. Start at the Duomo (Cathedral), with its lovely facade and interior inspired by the northern churches Pius had seen on his

Tuscany, Umbria and the Marche

Hilltop Perúgia is the gateway to Umbria's high mountain ranges

Tuscany, Umbria and the Marche

The unmistakeable silhouette of the Leaning Tower of Pisa

travels. The side chapels have some outstanding altarpieces by contemporary artists. Pius' residence, the Palazzo Piccolomini, stands next door; you can visit the papal apartments and admire the views from the triple-tiered loggia.

➕ C2

Duomo ✉ Piazza Pio II 🕐 Daily 8–1 and 3–7 (closed during services) 🎟 Free

Palazzo Piccolomini ✉ Piazza Pio II ☎ 0578 748 503 🕐 Tue.–Sat. 10–12:30 and 4–7, Apr.–Oct.; Tue.–Sat. 10–12:30 and 3–6, rest of year 🎟 $

PISA

Pisa's famous structure, the Leaning Tower, is just one of a quartet of beautiful buildings that make up the Campo dei Miracoli (Field of Miracles). The Duomo (Cathedral), Battistero (Baptistery), Campo Santo and the tower itself date from Pisa's Golden Age. In the 11th through 13th centuries, the city was still a port and one of the leading Mediterranean maritime powers.

Today Pisa is a busy industrial and university city, surprisingly unspoiled in many areas. The earliest building of the cathedral complex is the black-and-white striped cathedral itself, begun in 1064 in the unmistakable Pisan-Romanesque style.

The interior is mainly Renaissance, but the magnificent pulpit by Giovanni Pisano dates from 1302 and shows scenes from the life of Christ; look for the apse mosaic by Florentine Cimabue. Construction started on the Torre Pendente (Leaning Tower) in 1173; the spongy subsoil caused it to lean before it was half completed. By 1989 it was leaning more than 16 feet from upright and nearing its limits. The tower was stabilized in the 1990s and re-opened in December 2001.

The Baptistery, with its dome and Romanesque arcades, was built between the 12th and 13th centuries and is the largest in Italy. Along the north edge of the Campo dei Miracoli runs the perimeter wall of the cemetery, or Campo Santo, once lavishly decorated with frescoes but sadly destroyed during World War II.

It's worth venturing south from here toward the Arno river, where there are attractive streets and squares and a great daily food market. The riverbank is lined with fine palaces.

➕ A3

Tourist information ✉ Airport ☎ 050 503 700 🕐 Daily 10:30–4:30 and 6 p.m.–10 p.m. ✉ Piazza Stazione ☎ 050 42 291 🕐 Mon.–Fri. 9–7, Sat 9–1:30 ✉ Piazza del Duomo 1 ☎ 050 560 464 🕐 Daily 9:30–5:30

Pisa Duomo ✉ Piazza del Duomo 1 ☎ 050 560 547 🕐 Mon.–Sat. 8–7:30, Sun. 1–7:30, Apr.–Sep.; Mon.–Sat. 10:30–5:30, Sun. 1–5, Mar. and Oct.; Mon.–Sat. 10–12:45 and 3–4:30, Sun. 3–4:30, rest of year 🎟 $

Torre Pendente (Leaning Tower) ✉ Piazza del Duomo 17 ☎ Reservations: 050 560 547 🕐 Daily 8:30–8:30, Apr.–Sep. (also 8:30 p.m.–11 p.m., mid-Jun. to mid-Sep.); 8:30–7:30, Mar. and Oct.; 9:30–5, rest of year 🎟 $$$ ℹ 30-minute guided tours only

Battistero and Campo Santo ✉ Piazza del Duomo ☎ 050 560 547 🕐 Daily 8–7:30, Apr.–Sep.; 9–5:30, Mar. and Oct.; 9–4:30, rest of year 🎟 $$

PISTÓIA

Encircling walls enclose historic Pistóia, one of Tuscany's least-visited cities. The town displays a 12th-century zebra-striped Duomo (Cathedral), a Gothic baptistery and some impressive palaces. Inside the Pisan-Romanesque cathedral you'll find sculpture by masters such as

Colorful 16th-century reliefs by the della Robbia workshop over the door of the cathedral in Pistóia

Verrocchio and Rossellino, although the most astounding artwork is the Dossale di San Jacopo (St. James' Altarpiece). This solid silver altar weighs almost a ton and is covered with 628 sculpted figures; started in 1287, it took almost 200 years to complete. The Piazza del Duomo also contains a 14th-century baptistery and a much older belltower, once a Lombard watchtower. Other churches include San Giovanni Fuoricivitas, a wonderful green-and-white, 12th- to 14th-century structure, and Sant'Andrea, which contains a 1297 pulpit by Giovanni Pisano. July sees the town's famous *Giostro dell'Orso*, a medieval jousting tournament, preceded by spectacular processions.

➕ B3

Tourist information ✉ Piazza del Duomo 4 ☎ 0573 21 622 🕐 Mon.–Sat. 9–1 and 3–6 (also Sun. 9–1, Jul.–Aug.)

Duomo ✉ Piazza del Duomo 🕐 Daily 9–noon and 4–7. Cappella di San Jacopo: Mon.–Sat. 10–noon and 4–6, Sun. 11–noon and 4–6 🎫 $ Cappella di San Jacopo

SAN GIMIGNANO

Even without the famous towers, hilltop San Gimignano, known as "Medieval Manhattan," would be a town worth visiting. Crowded all year, your best

option may be to stay a day or two. Once the day-trippers have gone, the town takes on a completely different atmosphere.

San Gimignano once boasted 72 towers, built by rival nobles in the 12th and 13th centuries. Fifteen of them have survived. You can climb one of the towers, the Torre Grossa, for astounding views. San Gimignano's picturesque streets are full of tempting shops, cafés and picturesque houses and the town also is rich in art and history.

Sights cluster around the two main squares, the Piazza della Cisterna and the Piazza del Duomo. On the latter you'll find the 13th-century Collegiata, one of the most comprehensively frescoed churches in Tuscany, with scarcely an inch of wall left undecorated. Themes include the Creation and the Old and New Testaments, while the tiny Chapel of St. Fina depicts the life of San Gimignano's own saint. Other highlights include the Museo Civico, packed with lovely Gothic and Renaissance paintings, and the church of Sant'Agostino, on the northern end of town. It has luminous 15th-century Benozzo Gozzoli frescoes showing the life of St. Augustine, and the bonus of having few visitors.

➕ B3

Tourist information ✉ Piazza del Duomo 1

Tuscany, Umbria and the Marche

☎ 0577 940 008 ⏰ Daily 9–1 and 3–7, Mar.–Oct.; 9–1 and 2–6, rest of year

Torre Grossa and Museo Civico ✉ Piazza del Duomo ☎ 0577 940 008 ⏰ Daily 9:30–7:30, Mar.–Oct.; 10–5:30, rest of year 🖗 $$

Collegiata ✉ Piazza del Duomo ☎ 0577 942 226 ⏰ Mon.–Fri. 9:30–7:30, Sat. 9:30–5:30, Sun. 12:30–5:30, Apr.–Oct.; Mon.–Sat. 9:30–4:30, Sun., rest of year 🖗 $

Sant' Agostino ✉ Piazza Sant'Agostino ⏰ Daily 7:30–noon and 3–7, Apr.–Sep.; 7:30–noon and 3–6, rest of year 🖗 Free

SIENA

The warm colors of Siena's stones and brickwork and the exuberant black-and-white stripes of its Duomo (Cathedral) make it instantly more appealing to many visitors than its larger neighbor, Florence. Large and prosperous in the 13th and 14th centuries, the city's population was devastated by the 1348 Black Death; Siena never recovered, thereby leaving a legacy of one of Europe's most perfectly preserved cities.

The sloping square known as the Campo is the heart of Siena. Its south side is dominated by the magnificent 14th-century Palazzo Pubblico and the 320-foot belltower, the Torre del Mangia.

Once the seat of civic government and still the city's town hall, the palace also is home to the Museo Civico, which contains many frescoed rooms. The chief draws are Simone Martini's 1315 *Maestà*, the charming equestrian portrait of *Guidoriccio da Fogliano* and Ambrogio Lorenzetti's great 1338 frescoes *Allegories of Good and Bad Government*.

It's worth lingering in the Campo to enjoy an overpriced drink while you visualize Siena's ebullient medieval horse race, the Palio, which takes place in July and August. From here, head to the cathedral, a wonderful mix of Romanesque and Gothic, its splendid facade a riot of statuary. Inside you'll find masterpieces by Donatello, Pisano and the young Michelangelo. The cathedral's floor is entirely covered with a sumptuous marble pavement showing biblical and allegorical scenes. These were completed from 1349 to 1547 by just about every leading artist of the time. Don't miss the Libreria Piccolomini, built to house the books of Pope Pius II (Enea Silvio Piccolomini). The walls were painted by Bernardino Pinturicchio in 1502 with scenes of the life of Pope Pius II. Near the cathedral you'll find the baptistery and the Museo dell'Opera, which contains works

Siena's zebra-striped cathedral presides over a medieval huddle of rosy-red rooftops

from the cathedral, including Duccio di Buoninsegna's supreme *Maestà*. Opposite the cathedral stands Siena's medieval hospital, Santa Maria della Scala, which closed in the late 1990s. It's now a museum where you can admire lively frescoes showing everyday medieval hospital life. Nearby there are more paintings in the Pinacoteca Nazionale, with a collection that traces the whole development of Sienese painting.

➕ B2

Tourist information ✉ Piazza del Campo 56 ☎ 0577 280 551 🕐 Mon.–Sat. 8:30–7:30, Sun. 9–3, Apr.–Sep.; Mon.–Fri. 8:30–1 and 3:30–6:30, Sat. 8:30–1, rest of year

Duomo ✉ Piazza del Duomo 🕐 Mon.–Sat. 6:30–7:30, Sun. 2–7:30 (except during sevices) mid-Mar. to Oct. 31; Mon.–Sat. 7:30–1:30 and 2:30–5, Sun. 2–7:30 (except during sevices), rest of year. Libreria Piccolomini 🕐 Mon.–Sat. 10:30–7:30, Sun. 1:30–6:30, Mar.–Oct. (closes 1 hour earlier rest of year) 🎫 Cathedral: free. Libreria Piccolomini $$

Museo dell'Opera ✉ Piazza del Duomo 8 ☎ 0577 283 048 🕐 Daily 9–7:30, mid-Mar. to Sep. 30; 9–6, Oct.; 9–1:30, rest of year 🎫 $$$

Ospedale di Santa Maria della Scala ✉ Piazza del Duomo ☎ 0577 224 811 🕐 Daily 10:30–6:30, mid-Mar to Oct.; 10:30–4:30, rest of year 🎫 $$$

Museo Civico ✉ Piazza del Campo ☎ 0577 292 263 🕐 Daily 10–7:30, Jul.–Aug.; 10–7, mid-Mar. to Jun. 30 and in Sep.; 10–6:30, rest of year 🎫 $$$

Pinacoteca Nazionale ✉ Palazzo Buonsignori, Via San Pietro 29 ☎ 0577 281 161 🕐 Tue.–Sat. 8:15–7:15, Sun.–Mon. 8:30–1:30 🎫 $$

Torre del Mangia ✉ Piazza del Campo ☎ 0577 292 263 🕐 Daily 10–7, mid-Mar. to Oct.; 10–4, rest of year 🎫 $$$

SOVANA

Tiny Sovana rests in far southeast Tuscany, in the sparsely inhabited and undeveloped area called the Maremma. The area prospered in Etruscan, Roman and early medieval times, but its prosperity was later eroded by malaria. Don't miss Sovana, although neighboring Pitigliano, built on a spectacular rugged rock, also is worth a visit.

Less than 130 people live in Sovana; their houses line the broad brick expanse of the Via di Mezzo, which widens to form the tiny piazza. Here you'll find Santa Maria, a tranquil 13th-century church that houses a unique ninth-century pre-Romanesque stone canopy over the altar. Opposite the church is a small museum. A flower-edged lane leads to the huge Duomo (Cathedral), which was built from the eighth to 12th centuries. From here you can explore the labyrinth of sunken Etruscan roads carved out of the tufa, which lead to Etruscan tombs. These date from the seventh century BC and range from *colombari*, niches for funerary urns, to elaborately carved structures such as the famous Tomba Ildebranda.

➕ C1

Santa Maria ✉ Piazza del Pretorio ☎ 0564 614 074 🕐 Daily 9–1 and 3–6 🎫 Free

Museo del Palazzo Pretorio ✉ Piazza del Pretorio 🕐 Tue.–Sat. 10–12:30 and 3–6 🎫 $

Duomo 🕐 Daily 9–1 and 3–6 🎫 Free

Tomba Ildebranda 🕐 Tue.–Sat. 10–12:30 and 3–6 🎫 $

SPELLO

The enchanting medieval town of Spello rambles down the lower slopes of Monte Subasio in the Vale of Spoleto, the perfect place to catch a taste of unspoiled Umbria. Narrow streets lined with flower-hung houses, some classy food shops, and good bars and restaurants all combine to make the town a tempting stopping point.

Five Roman gates give access; head through Porta Consolare to Via Cavour, the main street, where you'll find the church of Santa Maria Maggiore. Inside, three walls of the Cappella Baglioni are decorated with Pinturicchio's glowing frescoes (1501) showing scenes of the life of Mary, the mother of Jesus. Next door is the Pinacoteca Civica, with more works of art; farther uphill, the church of Sant'Andrea has another Pinturicchio.

➕ D2

Tourist information ✉ Piazza Matteotti 3 ☎ 0742 301 009 🕐 Mon.–Sat. 9:30–12:30 and 3:30–6

Santa Maria Maggiore ✉ Via Cavour 🕐 Daily 7:30–12:30 and 2:30–6 🎫 Free

Pinacoteca Civica ✉ Piazza Matteotti 10 ☎ 0742 301 497 🕐 Closed for restoration 🎫 $$

Sant'Andrea ✉ Via Cavour 🕐 Daily 8–12:30 and 3–7 🎫 Free

The Benedictine abbey of Monte Oliveto Maggiore set amid cypresses, south of Siena

DRIVE: RENAISSANCE TUSCANY

Duration: 2½ to 3 hours

Start this drive in Monteriggioni, a walled town lying just off the Siena – Florence raccordo (link road).

You can walk from one end of Monteriggioni to the other in five minutes, as the town consists of little more than a spacious square with a tranquil old church, two dozen houses, two excellent restaurants and a hotel, all encircled by impressive walls punctuated by towers. Beneath the walls, vegetable gardens flourish and the tiny streets are decorated with flowers. Built by the Sienese in 1213 as a border outpost againt Florence, Monteriggioni was immortalized by Dante in *The Inferno*, where he refers to its towers as giants in an abyss; the verse is inscribed over the town's main gateway.

From Monteriggioni, take either the SS2 or the Siena to Florence raccordo (link road) to Siena (see page 110). If you are not visiting Siena, take the tangenziale (bypass) to bypass the city; watch for the exit back to the SS2, signposted Roma.

The SS2 follows the route of the Cassia, one of the great Roman consular roads that fanned out all over the Roman Empire; the road is still known by this name.

About 28 kilometers (17 miles) south, the Cassia skirts Buonconvento, well worth a stop.

Buonconvento was another of Siena's key outposts; today it's a bustling small town with some lovely old buildings and a tiny and exquisite museum displaying lovely Sienese paintings with grave-eyed Madonnas.

Turn left into the hills at Buonconvento, following the signs through woods and past cypresses to the Abbazia di Monte Oliveto Maggiore.

The great abbey of Monte Oliveto is set in the *crete*, the strange landscape of clay landslips and escarpments that characterizes this part of Tuscany. The abbey was founded in the early 1300s by a branch of the Benedictines and soon became one of Italy's most powerful religious foundations, falling from influence in the 19th century. Monks still live here, restoring books and producing wine and olive oil.

The main artistic attraction is the Chiostro Grande (Great Cloister), which has scenes of the life of St. Benedict. The frescoes were started by Luca Signorelli, who completed nine panels before handing the job over to Il Sodoma, who painted the other 27. These paintings are full of life – look for the birds and animals. The monastery also has a lofty church with some wonderful inlaid choir stalls and a fine Renaissance library.

Tuscany, Umbria and the Marche

Hot thermal springs feed the central pool at the tiny hamlet of Bagno Vignoni

Return to Buonconvento and head south to follow the SS2 for 2 kilometers (about a mile) before branching right to Montalcino (see page 104).
As this road climbs to approach the town, you'll pass wineries advertising the famous Brunello wine.

Leave Montalcino by the main road back to the SS2, a lovely stretch through vineyards, olive groves and wide views over southern Tuscany. Turn right on the S2 and continue for 6 kilometers (4 miles) before turning left at San Quírico d'Órcia onto the SS146 heading toward Pienza (see page 107) and Montepulciano (see page 105).
You could stay on the SS2 south for 5 kilometers (3 miles) before making a detour to Bagno Vignoni, one of Tuscany's most memorable hamlets. It's built around a hot spring, which was well known to the Romans and Renaissance popes and rulers. The central square is a huge Renaissance *piscina*, or bath, overlooked by a charming loggia. It's best seen in cool weather, when whisps of steam rise from the gently bubbling waters.

Buonconvento
Museo d'Arte Sacra ✉ Via Soccini 18 🕐 Tue.–Sun. 10–1 and 2:30–6, Apr.–Oct.; Sat.–Sun. only 10–1 and 3–5, rest of year 💶 $$ ℹ️ Opening times may change ☎ 0577 807 181
Abbazia di Monte Oliveto Maggiore ✉ Monte Oliveto Maggiore 🕐 Daily 9:15–noon and 3:30–6, Apr.–Sep.; 9:15–12:30 and 3:30–5, rest of year 💶 Free

Todi's winding streets tumble down the hillside high above the Tiber valley

SPOLETO

Spoleto's fine old town spreads down the hill from the hilltop Rocca (castle) to the charming Piazza del Mercato on the site of the Roman forum, with the still-intact Roman Arco di Druso nearby.

The 12th-century Duomo (Cathedral) is one of central Italy's loveliest; the entire apse features the blues and golds of Filippo Lippi's frescoes: Sant' Eufemia is a superb Romanesque building, while Sant'Ansano features sixth-century frescoes. You can walk outside town to San Pietro, with its Lombard-Romanesque carvings on the facade; your route will take you across a wooded gorge spanned by the magnificent 250-foot arches of the Ponte delle Torri, a monumental bridge and aqueduct rebuilt in the 14th century. June and July see the Festival of the Two Worlds, Italy's most prestigious international arts festival.
➕ D1

Tourist information ✉ Piazza della Libertà 7
☎ 0743 238 920 ⏱ Mon.–Fri. 9–1 and 4–7 (3:30–6:30, Nov. 1 to mid-Mar.), Sat.–Sun. 10–1 and 4–7
Rocca Albornozicina ✉ Piazza Campello 1 ☎ 0743 46 434 ⏱ Guided tours only: daily 10–8, mid-Jun. to mid-Sep.; Mon.–Fri. 10–1 and 3–7, Sat.–Sun. 10–7, Apr. to mid-Jun. and mid-Sep. to Nov.; Mon.–Fri. 2:30–5, Sat.–Sun. 10–5, Nov. to mid-Mar.; Mon.–Fri.

10–1 and 3–6, Sat.–Sun. 10–6, rest of year ✋ $$
Duomo ✉ Piazza del Duomo ☎ 0743 44 307
⏱ Daily 7:30–12:30 and 3–6 (3–5, Nov.–Feb.) ✋ Free
Sant' Eufemia ✉ Via Aurelio Saffi ☎ 0743 231 022
⏱ Daily 10–12:30 and 3:30–7, Apr.–Sep.; 10–12:30 and 2:30–6, rest of year ✋ $
Sant'Ansano ✉ Piazza Fontana ⏱ Daily 7:30–noon and 3–6:30, Apr.–Sep.; 7:30–noon and 3–5:30, rest of year ✋ Free
San Pietro ✉ On east side of N3 outside town
⏱ Daily 10–12:30 and 3:30–7, Apr.–Sep.; 10–12:30 and 2:30–6, rest of year. Times can change, so check with the tourist office ✋ Free

TODI

Once an important Etruscan outpost, ancient Todi is stunningly situated on a great bluff above the Tiber river, its mellow roofscape and towers inviting exploration. It reached its heyday in the 13th century, when the superb ensemble of buildings around the main square, the Piazza del Popolo, were constructed. Here you'll find the lovely Romanesque-Gothic Duomo (Cathedral). The interior has a lovely carved choir, but it's the pink facade and great rose window that draws the eye. The square has some fine medieval palaces, particularly the Palazzo dei Priori and the Palazzo del Capitano, which houses Todi's superb museum and art gallery.

San Fortunato, a huge 13th-century church, is nearby; from here you can walk through public gardens to reach Santa Maria della Consolazione, one of the best Renaissance churches in Italy.

🟦 D1

Tourist information ✉ Piazza Umberto I 6
☎ 075 894 5416 🕐 Daily 9:30–12:30 and 3–6
Duomo ✉ Piazza del Popolo ☎ 075 894 3041
🕐 Daily 2:30–6, Apr.–Sep.; 8:30–12:30 and 2–5:30, rest of year 🎟 Free
Museo Pinacoteca di Todi ✉ Palazzo del Capitano, Piazza del Popolo ☎ 075 894 4148 🕐 Tue.–Sun. 10:30–1 and 2:30–6:30, Apr.–Oct.; Tue.–Sun. 10:30–1 and 2–4:30, rest of year 🎟 $$
San Fortunato ✉ Piazza San Fortunato 🕐 Daily 9:30–12:30 and 3–6 🎟 Free
Santa Maria della Consolazione ✉ Viale della Consolazione 🕐 Daily 9–1 and 3–7 🎟 Free

TREVI

All travelers heading through the Vale of Spoleto notice Trevi, a perfect town perched on a cone-shaped hill. Wend your way up through the olive groves (which produce some of Umbria's best oil) and spend a couple of hours wandering around an unspoiled hill town. You'll find narrow streets, intricately paved with patterned cobblestones, and an unhurried small-town atmosphere. Like many Umbrian towns, there are some treasures, notably an art gallery, the Pinacoteca Comunale, and adjoining museum devoted to olives (Museo della Civltà).

🟦 D2

Tourist information ✉ Piazza Mazzini 6 ☎ 0742 781 250; www.protrevi.com 🕐 Daily 9–1 and 3–6 or 7
Pinacoteca Comunale ✉ Largo Don Bosco 14
☎ 0742 381 628 🕐 Daily 10:30–1 and 3:30–7, Aug.; Tue.–Sun. 10:30–1 and 3:30–7, Jun.–Jul.; Tue.–Sun. 10:30–1 and 2:30–6, Apr., May and Sep.; Fri.–Sun. 10:30–1 and 2:30–5, rest of year 🎟 $$ 🎫 Ticket includes admission to the Museo della Civltà (same opening hours as Pinacoteca Comunale).

URBINO

Nowhere outside Tuscany did the Renaissance flower as vividly as in beautiful Urbino, the Marche's most stately and distinguished small city. The birthplace of Raphael, Urbino flourished

The hill town of Trevi is distinguished by its honey-colored houses

in the 15th century under the rule of Duke Federico da Montefeltro to become one of Europe's most sophisticated and enlightened courts.

This university city is dominated by Duke Federico's 1465 Palazzo Ducale, still among central Italy's most sublime buildings. Federico hired some of the greatest Renaissance artists and architects to construct and decorate his palace. The Museo Nazionale delle Marche is housed in elegant rooms around the central courtyard. Its two outstanding treasures are Piero della Francesco's *Madonna di Senigallia* and his tiny *Flagellation*, both in Federico's private apartments, where you also can admire the stunning wood inlay in the study. His portrait hangs nearby (he was always painted in profile, having lost his right eye in battle), while Luciano Laurana's *View of an Ideal City* perfectly encapsulates the Renaissance ideal.

Other masterpieces include Titian's *Resurrection* and Raphael's *La Muta*. Away from the palazzo, Urbino has a large 18th-century Duomo (Cathedral), while Raphael devotees can visit the artist's birthplace. Climb to the Fortezza Albornoz gardens for views over the city, then pause for a drink in the Piazza della Repubblica.

✚ D3
Tourist information ✉ Piazza Rinascimento 1
☎ 0722 24 401 ⏱ Mon.–Sat. 9–1 and 3–6, Sun. 9–1,
May–Sep.; Mon.–Sat. 9–1, rest of year
Palazzo Ducale, Galleria Nazionale delle Marche
✉ Piazza Duca Federico ☎ 0722 22 760
⏱ Tue.–Sun. 8:30–7:15, Mon. 8:30–2 🎟 $$
Duomo ✉ Piazza Rinascimento ⏱ Daily 9–1 and 3–6
🎟 Free
Casa Natale di Raffaello ✉ Via Raffaello
☎ 0722 320 105 ⏱ Mon.–Sat. 9–1 and 3–7, Sun. 10–1,
Apr.–Oct.; daily 9–1, rest of year 🎟 $

THE VALNERINA

If you're looking for wild, mountainous
country, steep gorges and rushing rivers,
this is the place. The Valnerina has the
bonus of a handful of delectable villages
and imposing artistic sights thrown in.
Bustling Terni marks the start of the
Valnerina; from Terni the scenic SS209
follows the valley floor.

Your first stop should be the Cascate
delle Marmore, a 545-foot waterfall
created by the Romans in 271 BC. The
falls now feed a hydroelectric plant and
are sometimes diverted, but at full power

Roman remains are a vivid reminder of Volterra's
long history

are truly dramatic. Farther up the valley
stands the evocative abbey of San Pietro in
Valle. The hillside location is breathtaking,
and the abbey church contains some of
Umbria's most important 12th-century
frescoes. Pause at the medieval village of
Scheggino, with its trout-filled canals and
warren of alleyways. The hills on either
side become steeper and the valley narrows,
with tiny hamlets clinging to the slopes.
✚ D1

VOLTERRA

Imposing and isolated, Volterra stands on
a plateau surrounded by *balze* (cliffs),
which have steadily eroded over
thousands of years. This ancient
settlement has signs of Etruscan and
Roman occupation in the shape of walls,
gates and a theater. It also has one of the
most comprehensive Etruscan museums
in central Italy, the Museo Guarnacci.
The town's heart is Piazza dei Priori; on
this square stands the battlement town
hall, built in the first half of the 13th
century, and other impressive medieval
palaces. Behind the square is the black-
and-white striped 12th-century Duomo
(Cathedral), its dim interior lit through
alabaster windows.

The Pinacoteca Comunale has a
pleasing collection of Sienese and
Florentine paintings; Domenico
Ghirlandhaio's and Luca Signorelli's
serene Madonnas make a sublime contrast
to the angular forms and acidic colors of
Rosso Fiorentino's superlative *Deposition*.
This part of eastern Tuscany has always
been mining country, and you'll see
transluscent alabaster carvings for sale in
many of the local workshops.
✚ B2
Tourist information ✉ Piazza dei Priori 20 ☎ 0588
86 099 ⏱ Daily 9–1 and 2–7, Apr.–Oct.; 10–1 and 2–6,
rest of year
Museo Guarnacci ✉ Via Don Minzoni ☎ 0588 86 347
⏱ Daily 9–7, mid-Mar. to Oct. 31; 9–2, rest of year
🎟 $$$ (includes Pinacoteca and Museo d'Artesacra
Duomo ✉ Piazza San Giovanni ⏱ Daily 9–1 and 3–6
🎟 Free
Pinacoteca Comunale ✉ Via dei Sarti 1
☎ 0588 887 580 ⏱ Daily 9–7, mid-Mar. to Oct. 31;
8–1:45, rest of year 🎟 $$

SIENA'S PALIO

The Siena Palio is no mere tourist attraction; this spectacular bareback horse race, dating from medieval times, is a truly Sienese festival.

The Palio is named after the victory *pallium*, a banner embroidered with the image of the Blessed Virgin. The contest is between the city's wards, the *contrade*. The race runs on July 2 and August 16, each occasion preceded by weeks of preparation, bets and pageantry. The 17 wards each have their own church, museum and social center. Allegiance to your native *contrade* is absolute; children are baptized in the *contrade* fountain, and each neighborhood holds an annual parade. Ten neighborhoods take part in the Palio; they are chosen by lot, as are the horses. The jockeys are protected before the race for fear of bribes or worse. Each group has its traditional enemies and allies, and the pre-race weeks are filled with intrigue as alliances are forged and broken.

The days before the race are filled with processions and trial races. On race day the horses are blessed in the church. It's considered the best of luck if the horse defecates during the service. In the late afternoon a stunning procession, the *corteo storico*, takes place in the *campo* (town square), with drummers, flag-throwers and costumed captains and grooms. Huge bets are placed, and once the race starts anything goes. Ninety seconds of incredible excitement follow as the horses gallop three times around the square, which has a temporary surface of sand and mattresses to protect the most dangerous corners. The winning horse, with or without the jockey, is handed the Palio and mobbed by its jubilant supporters. Parties and parades go on all night and into the following weeks; the *contrade* hold street banquets as they relive every moment of the day.

You can watch the procession and race from the *campo*, which means standing for at least two hours prior to the race, and up to six hours if you want to be near the rails, with no exit once the barriers are closed. There are seats in the windows of the houses overlooking the *campo*; these are sold out for months before the race and should be booked a year ahead. (Contact Palio Viaggi at Gramsci 7 ☎ 0577 280 828.)

Tuscany, Umbria and the Marche

A historical procession heralds the start of the frenetic excitement of the Palio

CENTRAL ITALY

"LAZIO is a thriving area rich in history, while the neighboring regions of Abruzzo and Molise offer scenic beauty and undiscovered attractions."

The Emperor Constantine, under whose rule the Roman Empire adopted Christianity

Central Italy

CENTRAL ITALY

Three regions bridge the gap between northern and southern Italy – Lazio, the Abruzzo and Molise. Rome and its attractions tend to overshadow the rest of the Lazio region, with its gentle landscape and quiet towns. Across the Apennines lies the Abruzzo, one of the least known areas of Italy, a region of rugged mountainous scenery and villages where tourists are still a novelty. Abruzzo's smaller neighbor, Molise, offers more remote rolling hill country and economically has much more in common with southern than central Italy. All three of these regions have long coastlines, relatively undiscovered by international visitors.

Lazio

Until the 1860s, Lazio was part of the Papal States, the territory held by the Vatican. During the process of Italian unification, Rome – with its historical connotations of centralized power – became the symbol of the new united

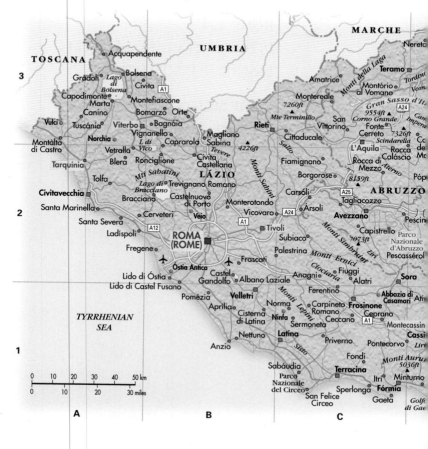

Italy and the obvious choice as the country's new capital. In fact, Rome had to wait until 1870 to join the united Italy, the last but symbolically most important part of the Italian peninsula to do so.

Like other areas that were once part of the Papal States, Lazio was traditionally poor and had little sense of identity and few historic towns, although its economy has made major strides in recent years.

The countryside varies from the gentle rolling hills of the north to steep mountains south and east of Rome. Lake Bolsena in the north attracts many visitors, as does Lazio's coastline, which is more attractive south of Rome.

A classically inspired summer house in the gardens of Rome's Villa Borghese

Abruzzo and Molise

Abruzzo and Molise were one region until 1963. Since then, the Abruzzo has forged ahead at the expense of Molise – the contrast between the two on every level is startling. They are both sparsely populated, mountainous areas prone to earthquakes, with a tradition of standing outside the mainstream of Italian affairs. Over the last 40 years, Abruzzo has emerged from poverty, developing the tourist potential of its national park's mountain wilderness and expanding a string of lucrative resorts along its sandy coastline.

Despite this, huge areas are still remote and unspoiled, and you'll find a true sense of pride and regional identity manifested in local festivals, crafts and costumes. The landscape, a wilderness of upland plains, remote valleys and high peaks, is superb.

Molise is poor, disorganized and undeveloped, and ranks fairly low on the tourist trail. More than 40 percent of the terrain is covered by mountains and industrial cities. If you're heading south to Apulia (Puglia), you'll pass through Térmoli, a small fishing port and attractive beach resort.

A Sense of the South

If you're traveling into central Italy from the north or from Rome itself, you'll at once sense an almost indefinable difference and grasp why this central area is viewed as "southern" by northern Italians. Towns are not as stylish or prosperous, villages are not so spic-and-span. There's more remote countryside and less cultivated land. The pace seems slower and the people more laid-back, noisy and ebullient. In some parts of the mountainous areas, the high-tech world seems to have barely impinged and foreigners still cause comment.

The tourist infrastructure is not as good as that, say, in Tuscany and Umbria, with fewer hotels of international standard. This area is well-served by *autostrade* (freeways); the A24/25, which cuts through the Apennines east of Rome to penetrate the Abruzzo, is one of Italy's finest and most scenic. Good roads run down both the west and east coasts, and the whole of Lazio is easy to explore. In Abruzzo and Molise, the roads in remoter areas are often steep, winding and narrow.

Highlights

Rome is going to be your number one stop in this part of Italy, and you should set aside four or five days to explore the city and what it has to offer. It makes sense to do most of your exploring into Lazio from a Roman base; Tivoli, the Castelli Romani, Óstia Antica and Tarquínia are all potential day trips from Rome via public transportation. If you're heading farther afield, a rental car may be better. Abruzzo National Park and the Gran Sasso are good choices. If you're looking for a few days of relaxation, there are charming, tranquil resorts south of Rome and all along the Abruzzo coast.

Capodimonte stands on the shore of Lake Bolsena in northern Lazio

When To Go

If you're planning to spend most of your time in Rome, there's much to be said for a winter trip, when the city is less crowded and the stifling heat won't be a problem. Late November and December can be wet, but January and February are generally crisp and dry, with surprisingly warm midday sun. Spring comes early to Rome, making

Central Italy

April and May lovely months to enjoy the city. Crowds and heat build in summer, which is the best time to visit the Abruzzo mountains if you're interested in fresh air and exercise. Avoid Rome in July and August, when the city is crammed with tourists but Romans themselves are on vacation, leaving many stores and restaurants closed. Fall, with its soft light and golden colors, can be a magical time to visit the region.

The People

The inhabitants of this central area are notably different from northerners. Romans have a reputation for surliness and impatience with visitors. It pays to go out of your way to charm by using a few key Italian phrases. If you're exploring remoter areas, few people speak English. This all adds to the delight, and there are few places in Italy where you'll get a better sense of traditional attitudes.

Central Italy

ROME

The capital of Italy provides magic and frustration in almost equal measure. Packed with art, steeped in history, humming with life, this most beautiful of cities will ensnare you with its charms, even if its traffic, noise and confusion sometimes make you wonder why you came. A heady mixture of classical, medieval, Renaissance and baroque sights fills the streets and squares. Golden light filters through pine trees to ancient stones; fountains splash quietly in sun-dappled piazzas. But traffic also roars up polluted streets, crowds push and shove, and heat levels

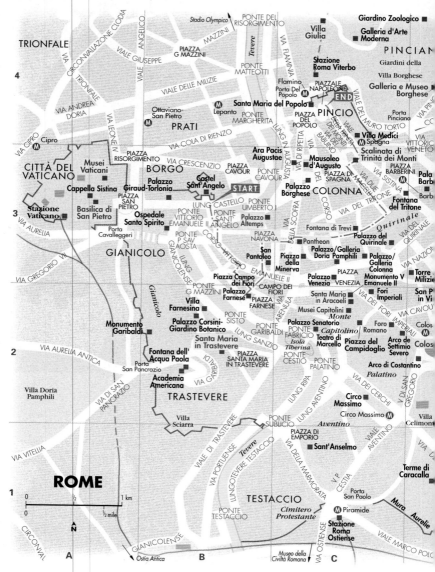

Central Italy

and noise can be intense. Accept this mixture and put aside your preconceptions. Rome (Roma) is a living city, not a museum, and therein lies its enchantment.

Getting Your Bearings

It shouldn't take you long to realize that Rome, laid out and built long before the automobile age, is not a huge city in terms of area. It lies on either side of the Tiber (Tevere) river and sprawls across seven hills. The Vatican, St. Peter's and the Trastevere quarter (with its excellent restaurants) lie on the west bank of the river; everything else you'll want to see is to the east.

This eastern part is roughly dissected by Via del Corso, which runs from Piazza del Popolo to Piazza Venezia and is dominated by the vast "wedding cake" of the Victor Emmanuel Monument. South of the monument are the Forum, the Colosseum and the heart of classical Rome. Between the Corso and the Tiber river lies the *centro storico* (historical center), a wonderful mix of medieval streets, Renaissance palaces and beguiling squares. East of the Corso there are more fine buildings and palaces, Rome's most elegant shopping streets, verdant parks, splendid viewpoints and the elegant Via Vittorio Veneto, home to the American Embassy and the smartest hotels.

Sightseeing

There are hotels scattered all over the city, but bear in mind that nowhere is going to be quiet. The *centro storico* is perhaps the best for its proximity to just about everything, and has a good selection of hotels. The only area to avoid is around the Stazione Termini train station.

To start your visit, spend a couple of hours on an organized tour. Several companies offer "get on and off" options, with tickets valid all day. Once oriented, it's important to prioritize. There's no way you're going to be able to see everything, so decide what's important to you and see it properly. Big sights such as the Vatican and the Forum are best tackled early in the day while you're fresh, and be sure to rest for a

The great dome of St. Peter's reflected at sunset in the Tiber river

couple of hours during the midday heat. Most people directly involved with tourism speak English and are generally helpful, although you may not get quite such an enthusiastic response from city dwellers going about their business.

You shouldn't miss St. Peter's Basilica, the Vatican museums or classical sights such as the Roman Forum and Colosseum. Add to these a couple of other major museums and churches and you'll be busy for at least three days. In addition, there's a wealth of delights ranging from ancient churches and idiosyncratic museums to lovely parks, elegant shops and jolly markets. Rome hosts splendid temporary exhibitions and shows; pick up a copy of the monthly *l'Evento* from a tourist office to find what's happening.

Culinary Pleasures

Like all Italians, Romans eat out regularly, so choose a restaurant patronized by locals to enjoy some specialties. There's an excellent choice in Trastevere and the old streets around Piazza Navona and the Pantheon, while more obviously upscale choices can be found nearer Via Vittorio Veneto. Roman cooking often features offal, tripe and brains, but there are other dishes, such as the delicious *saltimbocca alla Romana* – veal cooked with prosciutto and sage – that are more appetizing.

Do sample the mixed vegetable *antipasti,* often found in family-run restaurants, and pasta dishes such as spicy *rigatoni all'amatriciana,* or the delicious and familiar *spaghetti alla*

Mosaics

Rome's oldest churches are rich in mosaics. They serve as reminders of the early Christian church and the last days of the Roman Empire, when faith went hand in hand with Byzantine skill. Mosaics are composed of tiny pieces of polychrome stone, marble and gilding, shaped so that they will lock together on a vault or curved roof. They are built to create pictures and images of Christ and the saints and are usually set against a gold background and filled with charming details of plants, birds and animals. To see them at their best, visit the churches of Santa Prassede, Santa Costanza, San Clemente (see page 131), Santa Maria in Trastevere (see page 132) and Santa Pudenzia, where the mosaics were created between the fourth and ninth centuries.

carbonara with bacon and egg. Artichokes, often eaten deep-fried or raw, are a great Roman specialty. Food-to-go includes fabulous pizza by the slice, an ideal quick lunch. As everywhere in Italy, ice cream is wonderful, with a great range of flavors available. Local wines come from the Castelli Romani, the hills outside Rome, but you'll find wines and liqueurs from all over Italy, as well as international brands.

Retail Therapy

Shop till you drop in hedonistic Rome, where elegant women devote most of their lives to the art. The smartest stores cluster around Via Condotti and Via Frattina near Piazza di Spagna, where you'll find the top names in fashion, lingerie, leather and jewelry, as well as luxury housewares. Prices are lower, but quality and style are still good along Via del Corso and Via Nazionale. Department-store fans should try La Rinascente, Coin, Upim or Standa. Souvenir shops abound all over the city, although if you're looking for religious mementos, buy them in the shops in the vicinity of St. Peter's. Be sure to take in a food market; the daily one in the Campo dei Fiori is tops for color and atmosphere.

Peace and Quiet

Rome has its parks and gardens, and you'll occasionally stumble across a grassy square complete with benches to rest your weary feet. To escape the traffic's roar, head for the Villa Borghese (see page 130), the Botanical Gardens in Trastevere or the Colle

Oppio near the Colosseum. Best of all, take a picnic to the Forum, and eat it among the grassy ruins and wildflowers on Palatine Hill.

Entertainment

Dinner and a quiet stroll may be all you're after, but there's plenty of entertainment available – *l'Evento* will fill you in. Opera is a superb option in summer, when performances are held outdoors, and concerts and recitals take place all over the city. Several theaters show films in their original language, and there's also live rock and jazz and nightclubs for dancing.

Campo dei Fiori, Rome's most attractive market

ESSENTIAL INFORMATION

TOURIST INFORMATION
•Largo Goldoni ☎ 06 6813 6061
•Piazza Pia, Castel Sant' Angelo
☎ 06 6880 9707; www.romaturismo.it
•Via Parigi 5 ☎ 06 488 991
•Piazza Cinque Lune ☎ 06 6880 9240
•Piazza del Tempio della Pace ☎ 06 6992 4307
•Piazza S Giovanni in Laterano ☎ 06 7720 3535
•Piazza Sonnino (Trastevere) ☎ 06 5833 3457
•Stazione Termini, Galleria Gommata
☎ 06 4890 6300
•Via dell'Olmata, Santa Maria Maggiore
☎ 06 474 0955
•Via Nazionale ☎ 06 4782 4525
ATAC's 110 City Tour ☎ 06 4695 2256

URBAN TRANSPORTATION
Public transportation – orange buses and trams and a two-line subway system – can be slow. Bus tickets must be purchased before boarding; you'll find them at automatic machines or shops and newsstands displaying an ATAC sticker. They are valid for any number of bus journeys plus one subway journey within a 75-minute period and must be validated on boarding at the rear of the vehicle. The *biglietto integrato* is valid for a day's unlimited travel on buses, trams, the subway and suburban rail service. A weekly

pass, the *carta integrata settimanale*, is valid for buses and the subway only. Taxis are yellow or white and can be picked up from one of the stands indicated by a blue-and-white sign; they do not stop on the street. You can call a taxi from Radio Taxis (☎ 06 3570, 06 4994, 06 88 177, 06 5551 or 06 8822). The meter will start running immediately after your call. Do not trust anyone offering a private taxi service and be sure the meter is at zero if you pick up a taxi at a stand.

AIRPORT INFORMATION
Rome has two airports, Leonardo da Vinci (☎ 06 6595 4455), at Fiumicino to the west of the city, and Ciampino (☎ 06 794 941), south of Rome. You are most likely to arrive at Leonardo da Vinci. The easiest way to get to and from Leonardo da Vinci is by train from Stazione Termini; there are daily departures every 30 to 60 minutes between 6:51 a.m. and 10:37 p.m. Trains also run from the airport to Fara Sabina and Tiburtina suburban railroad stations; if you use these you will have to get a connection. There is a nightly bus service between the airport and Stazione Termini. To reach Rome from Ciampino, take subway line A to Anagnina and connect with the COTRAL bus service, which runs daily from about 6:50 a.m.–11:40 p.m.

CLIMATE – Average highs and lows

JAN.	FEB.	MAR.	APR.	MAY	JUN.	JUL.	AUG.	SEP.	OCT.	NOV.	DEC.
13°C	13°C	15°C	17°C	21°C	25°C	28°C	28°C	26°C	21°C	17°C	14°C
55°F	55°F	59°C	63°F	70°F	77°F	82°F	82°F	79°F	70°F	63°F	57°F
4°C	4°C	5°C	8°C	12°C	16°C	19°C	19°C	17°C	13°C	8°C	5°C
39°F	39°F	41°F	46°F	54°F	61°F	66°F	66°F	63°F	55°F	46°F	41°F

ROME SIGHTS

Key to symbols

⊞ map coordinates refer to the Rome map on page 124; sights below are highlighted in yellow on the map

✉ address or location ☎ telephone number

◉ opening times 🍴 restaurant on site or nearby

Ⓜ nearest subway station

🚌 nearest bus or tram route

💰 admission charge: $$$ more than €6, $$ €3 to €6, $ less than €3 ℹ information

BASILICA DI SAN PIETRO

The present Basilica di San Pietro (St. Peter's Basilica), the heart of the Catholic church worldwide, stands on the site of the saint's burial place. It was built between 1506 and 1626. The principal architects were Donato Bramante and Giovanni Bernini, working to Michelangelo's concepts; the soaring dome is his creation. The sweeping colonnades, fountains and triumphant facade are a fitting prelude to the vast and opulent interior, dominated by Bernini's great high altar *baldicchino* and its spiraling columns. Don't miss Michelangelo's sublime *Pietà*, the bronze statue of St. Peter with his right foot worn away by caresses, and the crypt where numerous popes are buried around the tomb of St. Peter.

⊞ A3 ✉ Piazza San Pietro, Città di Vaticano ☎ 06 6988 4466 ◉ Basilica: daily 7–7, Apr.–Sep.; 7–6, rest of year. Closed during religious services Ⓜ Ottaviano 🚌 23, 64, 81, 492 💰 Basilica: free; dome: $$ ℹ Dress code: no shorts, short skirts or bare shoulders

COLOSSEO

Every modern public stadium's design ultimately copies that of the Colosseo (Colosseum), a massive structure dating from AD 72. Its tiers of seats held 55,000 people, while the sophisticated "backstage" facilities allowed the arena to be flooded. Shows here featured gladiators, slaves and animals often fighting to the death; few Christians were martyred here. The Colosseum served as a source of building material during the Middle Ages, hence the missing sections.

It's traditional to throw a coin into the Fontana di Trevi before you leave Rome to ensure your return

⊞ D2 ✉ Piazza del Colosseo ☎ 06 3996 7700 ◉ Daily 9 to 1 hour before sunset Ⓜ Colosseo 🚌 1, 13, 15, 27, 30, 81, 85, 110, 118, 186, 673 💰 $$$ (ticket also valid for Palatino); ground floor free

FONTANA DI TREVI

You'll hear the Fontana di Trevi (Trevi Fountain) before you see it. Tucked into a tiny piazza amid a warren of narrow streets, it's a wonderful array of figures, tritons and horses set against an architectural backdrop. The latest in a series of fountains here since Roman times, Trevi dates from 1732 and gets its name from the three streets – *tre vie* – that converge here.

⊞ C3 ✉ Piazza Fontana di Trevi 🍴 Al Moro, see page 207 Ⓜ Spagna or Barbarini 🚌 52, 53, 71, 95

FORO ROMANO

The Foro Romano (Roman Forum), today a romantic jumble of fallen columns and tumbling walls, was the heart of the Roman Empire and contained all the most important political, religious and municipal buildings. Time and imagination are needed to puzzle it out, but be sure to track down the House of the Vestal Virgins, home to the guardians of the sacred flame, and the second-century

Temple of Antoninus and Faustinus (AD 141). Other highlights include the fine Arch of Septimius Severus, and all of The Palatine Hill. Once covered with palaces, today the ruins of the Palatine lie among oleanders and cypresses, an evocative reminder of the transience of glory.

➕ C2 ✉ Largo Romolo e Remo 1 ☎ 06 699 0110 🕐 Mon.–Sat. 9–6, Sun. 9–1, Apr.–Sep.; Mon.–Sat. 9–sunset, Sun. 9–1, rest of year 🚇 Colosseo 🚌 75, 81, 85, 87, 117 🎟 Palatine $$$ (ticket also valid for the Colosseum); Forum free ℹ English audio guide

GALLERIA E MUSEO BORGHESE

Built in 1613 by Cardinal Scipione Borghese as a summer retreat, the Villa Borghese is now a museum housing the cardinal's superb art collections. The cardinal's favorite sculptor was Giovanni Bernini, whose works dominate; the *David* is said to be a self-portrait, and there's an *Apollo and Daphne*, full of flight and panic. Don't miss Antonio Canova's *Pauline Borghese*, a likeness of Napoleon's sister; the statue perfectly captures her seductive looks. The paintings also are spectacular, with treasures by Raphael, Titian's sensuous *Sacred and Profane Love* and Caravaggio's famous *Boy with a Fruit Basket*.

➕ D4 ✉ Villa Borghese, Piazzale Scipione Borghese 5 ☎ 06 841 7645 🕐 Tue.–Sun. 9–7 🍴 Restaurant in museum 🚇 Spagna 🚌 3, 52, 53, 56, 57, 116, 319, 490, 495 🎟 $$$ (booking fee) ℹ Advance booking necessary

MUSEI CAPITOLINI

Occupying two palaces on opposite sides of Piazza del Campidoglio, the Capitoline Museums boast outstanding Greek and Roman sculptures. The Palazzo Nuovo contains most of the finest pieces, none greater than the second-century bronze equestrian statue of Marcus Aurelius. A tunnel links this museum to the Palazzo dei Conservatori, the former seat of Rome's medieval magistrates, which has an art gallery and more classical sculpture.

➕ C2 ✉ Piazza del Campidoglio 1 ☎ 06 6710 2475 🕐 Tue.–Sun. 9–8 🚇 Colosseo 🚌 44, 46, 62, 80, 160 🎟 $$$

MUSEI VATICANI

Allow plenty of time to enjoy the 1,400 rooms that make up the Musei Vaticani (Vatican Museums). You can follow one of the color-coded routes to the museum's highlights, the Cappella Sistina (Sistine Chapel) and the Stanze di Raffaello (Raphael Rooms). The walls and ceiling of the lofty Sistine Chapel are entirely frescoed, most notably by Michelangelo. His extraordinary creation scenes from the Old Testament cover the rear wall of the chapel and were painted from 1508 to 1512; they show more than 300 figures and include his extraordinarily powerful *Last Judgment*. Raphael's Rooms, all symmetry and harmony, provide a balance to the huge energy of the Sistine. Elsewhere you'll find classical sculpture, paintings and much more (there's even a piece of moon rock presented by the U.S. government), while the richness of the building itself is an added bonus.

➕ A3 ✉ Viale Vaticano, Città del Vaticano ☎ 06 6988 3332 🕐 Mon.–Sat. and last Sun. of the month 8:45–4:45, Apr.–Oct.; 8:45–1:45, rest of year 🚌 23, 49, 64, 81, 492 🎟 $$$; free last Sun. of month ℹ English audio guide available

PALAZZO ALTEMPS

A beautifully restored 15th- through 16th-century palazzo houses Cardinal Ludovisi's classical sculpture collection, augmented by those of other private collectors. The building is a joy in itself; charming rooms with vaulted ceilings surround a frescoed loggia above an inner courtyard. Don't miss the famous sculpture *Dying Gaul* and the tender Greek *Aphrodite Rising from the Waves*, dating from the fifth century BC. The museum is best visited as darkness falls, when the statues are lit by spotlights.

➕ B3 ✉ Piazza Sant'Apollinare 44 ☎ 06 3996 7700 🕐 Tue.–Sun. 9–7:45 🚌 70, 81, 116, 186 🎟 $$ ℹ English audio guide available

PALAZZO MASSIMO

The Museo Nazionale Romano (National Roman Museum), housed in the 19th-century Palazzo Massimo, is the showcase

Central Italy

for a breathtaking collection of sculptures, bronzes, mosaics and frescoes dating from Roman times. Beautifully displayed with excellent information in English, the artifacts are displayed so as to trace different themes running through Roman history from the Republican era up to the fifth century. Here you'll find superlative busts and bronze figures alongside fine Roman copies of the best of ancient Greek sculpture. Highlights include the *Discus Thrower*, a sensuous *Sleeping Hermaphrodite* and a wonderfully languid *Apollo*. The third floor is devoted to frescoes and mosaics; the beautiful first-century BC garden paintings from the dining room of Livia's villa could grace any modern house.

🛐 D3 ✉ Piazza dei Cinquecento 67, Largo di Villa Peretti ☎ 06 4890 3500 🕐 Tue.–Sun. 9–7:45 🍴 Café 🚇 Termini, Repubblica 🚌 16, 38, 90, 92, 105 👑 $$$ ℹ English audio guide available

PANTHEON

The greatest surviving complete Roman building, the Pantheon was erected from AD 119 to 128. This superbly engineered building gives a vivid impression of the grandeur of ancient Rome. Built as a temple, it survived the fall of Rome due to its early conversion in AD 609 to a Christian church. The stately portico leads to a huge dome; here you'll find the tombs of Raphael and two Italian kings.

🛐 C3 ✉ Piazza della Rotunda ☎ 06 6830 0230

🕐 Mon.–Sat. 8:30–7:30, Sun. 9–6, holidays 9–1 🚇 Spagna 🚌 64, 70, 81, 86, 87, 90, 119, 170 👑 Free

PIAZZA NAVONA

The elongated shape of the Piazza Navona follows the lines of the Roman racetrack that once occupied this site. Today's piazza was rebuilt in 1644 by Pope Innocent X, who commissioned its lovely fountains from Bernini in 1651. The central one, known as the Fountain of the Four Rivers, shows the Nile, Ganges, Danube and the Plate. The Nile's head is veiled, as the source had yet to be discovered. Francesco Borromini's baroque church of Sant'Agnese stands on the west side.

🛐 B3 ✉ Piazza Navona 🚌 70, 81, 87, 116, 186

SAN CLEMENTE

No other church gives a better sense of Rome's layers of history than the ancient church of San Clemente. This shadowy 12th-century basilica has columns, a marble choir and fine pulpit, with Byzantine mosaics in the apse above. Beneath San Clemente you'll find a fourth-century church with eighth-century frescoes, while lower still are the remains of Roman streets and a Mithraic temple have been excavated.

🛐 D2 ✉ Via di San Giovanni in Laterano ☎ 06 7045 1018 🕐 Mon.–Sat. 9–12:30 and 3–6, Sun. 10–12:30 and 3–6 🚇 Colosseo 🚌 85, 117, 186 👑 Church free. Excavations $

Surrounded by splendor in the Piazza Navona, these elderly Romans enjoy a chat

SANTA MARIA IN ARACOELI

The 124 steep steps leading up to the church of Santa Maria in Aracoeli (Our Lady of the Altar of Heaven) were built in 1348 as a thanksgiving at the end of a plague. Medieval pilgrims climbed them on their knees to the church, which was built in 1260 and whose plain facade hides a sumptuous interior. The huge columns in the nave were taken from Roman buildings; against their solidity, the gilded 16th-century ceiling provides a contrasting note of grandeur.

➕ C2 ✉ Piazza d'Aracoeli ☎ 06 679 8155
🕐 Daily 7–noon and 4–6 (or dusk) 🚌 44, 62, 80

SANTA MARIA MAGGIORE

Santa Maria Maggiore (St. Mary Major) was first built in the fifth century on a site miraculously marked by a summer snow. Much has been added over the years, but it still retains the fifth-century mosaics in the nave, while those in the apse represent the best of 13th-century mosaic art. The ceiling is said to be gilded with the first gold to arrive from the New World as a gift from Spain. Pause to reflect that this is Rome's only church where Mass has been celebrated every day since the fifth century.

➕ D3 ✉ Piazza di Santa Maria Maggiore 42
☎ 06 446 5836 or 06 481 4287 🕐 Daily 7–7 or 8 p.m., Apr.–Sep.; 7–6:30 or 7, rest of year 🍴 Agata e Romeo, see page 207 🚇 Termini, Cavour 🚌 16, 70, 71, 75, 105

SANTA MARIA IN TRASTEVERE

If you're exploring the neighborhood of Trastevere, make a point of visiting the church of Santa Maria in Trastevere. A pleasing 18th-century portico fronts the mosaic facade of this ancient church; the nave columns, like so many in old Roman churches, once supported classical buildings. The Byzantine-style 12th-century mosaics in the apse show the glorification of the Virgin Mary.

➕ B2 ✉ Piazza Santa Maria in Trastevere
☎ 06 581 4802 🕐 Daily 7:45–8 or 9 p.m. (may close 12:30–3:30 in winter) 🚌 44, 75, 170, 280, 780

SCALINATA DI TRINITÀ DEI MONTI

The elegant Scalinata di Trinità dei Monti (Spanish Steps) curve gracefully up from the Piazza di Spagna to the church of Trinità dei Monti, a focal point for Rome's smartest shopping area. Built in 1723, the steps got their name from the piazza, which once housed the Spanish embassy. The poet Keats died in lodgings overlooking the steps in 1821; the building now houses a small museum devoted to Keats and Shelley. The piazza's fountain, built in 1627, resembles a sunken boat.

➕ C3 ✉ Piazza di Spagna 26 ☎ 06 678 4235
🕐 Museo Keats–Shelley: Mon.–Fri. 9–1 and 3–6, Sat. 11–2 and 3–6 💵 $$ 🚇 Spagna 🚌 116, 117, 119

VIA APPIA ANTICA

A section of the Via Appia Antica (Old Appian Way) still survives just outside the city. It's one of the many roads that fanned out to all corners of the Roman Empire. Built in the fourth century BC to link Rome and Brindisi, today it's a picturesque cobbled way, shaded by pines and lined with tombs and monuments. It was here that St. Paul marched on his way to prison, and Spartacus and his slaves were executed in 71 BC. Nearby you can visit two sets of catacombs.

➕ D1 ✉ Via Appia Antica 136 ☎ 06 5130 1580
🕐 Catacombs: San Sebastiano (Mon.–Sat.) and San Callisto (Thu.–Tue.) 8:30–noon and 2:30–5 (5:30 in summer) 💵 Catacombs: $$ 🚌 118

VILLA GIULIA

The beautiful Villa Giulia, set in peaceful gardens, houses one of Italy's great museums devoted to the enigmatic Etruscans. The collection includes the Castellani exhibits, with striking Minoan jewelry, fine Greek vases and the seventh-century BC gold and silver from the Barbarini tombs. Most touching of all is the Sarcofago degli Sposi, a sixth-century BC sarcophagus featuring a married couple reclining on a banqueting couch.

➕ C4 ✉ Piazzale di Villa Giulia 9 ☎ 06 322 6571
🕐 Tue.–Sat. 8:30–7:30 🚇 Flaminio 🚌 19, 30, 52, 926
💵 $$ ℹ English audio guide available

The Vatican

Until Italian unification, the papacy held territory, known as the Papal States, throughout central Italy. In 1870 these lands became part of the new united Italy, and Pope Pius IX retreated to the Vatican as a virtual prisoner. As supreme head of Catholics worldwide, the pontiff clearly needed his own independent sovereign territory to retain his spiritual authority, and in 1929 the Treaty of the Lateran was signed with Mussolini. This established the Vatican State (Città del Vaticano), an area covering 110 acres around the Basilica of St. Peter and the Vatican Palace, today the world's smallest state.

Opulent gilded plasterwork decorates the ceiling of the Galleria delle Carte in the Vatican Museums

The Vatican Today

The pope is Europe's sole remaining absolute monarch, with complete power over this tiny state.

In April 2005, 78 year old Cardinal Joseph Ratzinger of Germany was elected Pope following the death earlier in the month of Pope John Paul II who had reigned for 26 years. The new Pope, who has taken the name Pope Benedict XVI, is well known for his conservative views and dislike of liberal reform. Even so, he is a popular choice among the faithful and was greeted by the cheers of tens of thousands of followers when he stepped onto the balcony of St. Peter's Basilica to give his first blessing, proclaiming that he was but "a simple, humble worker."

Latin is still the official language in the Vatican, which has all the appertenances of an independent state including a daily news-paper and a broadcasting service.

The Pope's Army

The pope and the Vatican itself are defended by the Swiss Guard, a 90-strong brigade drawn from Switzerland's four Catholic cantons since 1506. Young men aged 19 to 25 sign up for a term of two to 20 years; their duties are largely ceremonial, but they are highly trained for all contingencies. They normally wear a picturesque navy-blue uniform. Their instantly recognizable red-, yellow- and blue-striped dress uniform, said to have been designed by Michelangelo, is reserved for state occasions.

The Agenti di Vigilanza, formed in 1816, augment the Swiss Guard.

Seeing the Pope

When he is in Rome, the Pope traditionally gives a midday Sunday blessing from the window of his rooms overlooking the piazza. Since the 1970s, weekly audiences have been held in the vast Aula Paolo VI (Paul VI Hall). Up to 7,000 people attend these moving occasions; tickets are free and obtainable from the Prefetura della Casa Pontifica, in the right-hand colonnade of the Piazza San Pietro.

Colorful Swiss Guards are responsible for the pope's safety

Central Italy

WALK: THE BEST OF ROME

Refer to route marked on city map on page 124.

This walk takes you from Papal Rome through medieval Rome to some of the city's Renaissance splendors. You could spend a whole day walking the route, stopping for museum visits en route and lunching at one of the cozy neighborhood restaurants near the Pantheon. Or you could just tackle part of it, picking up bus 119 or 116 (a minibus that trundles through the narrow streets of the historic center) at the Pantheon or in Piazza di Spagna.

Start at the Castel Sant'Angelo.
The Castel Sant'Angelo was built by the Emperor Hadrian in AD 130 as a mausoleum; it got its present name when Pope Gregory the Great had a vision of an angel on its summit in AD 590. Beginning in the ninth century, it was a papal fortress; it was linked in 1277 to the Vatican by a passage. After

The gateway of the Palazzo del Quirinale is the setting for pomp and pageantry

spells as a prison and barracks it became a museum in 1933.

> *Cross the Ponte Sant'Angelo and walk straight across the Piazza Ponte Sant'Angelo into Via Banco Santo Spirito. Continue left to Largo Tassoni, then turn left onto the busy Corso Vittorio Emanuele II. Continue for five blocks, then cross the corso and turn right down Via Sora, then left onto Via del Pellegrino. This will bring you to the Campo dei Fiori.*

One of the city's most alluring squares, the Campo dei Fiori stood at the heart of medieval Rome, surrounded by private palaces, inns and brothels. The statue in the center is the philosopher Giordano Bruno, who was burned here for heresy in the 17th century. The square has a daily fruit, vegetable and fish market. Neighborhood stores abound in the surrounding streets, and it's the perfect place to experience local life and have a *cappuccino*.

> *Turn right down Via Farnesi Gallo to Piazza Farnese, one block south.*

Piazza Farnese is dominated by the Palazzo Farnese, a Renaissance architectural masterpiece partly designed by Michelangelo and begun in 1516. It's now the French Embassy. The beautiful baths forming the fountains are Roman and came from the ruins of the Baths of Caracalla.

> *Retrace your steps to the Campo dei Fiori, cross the square and head down Via dei Baullari back to Corso Vittorio Emanuele. Cross the corso and walk past the church of San Pantaleo and down Via Cuccagna into Piazza Navona (see page 131). After visiting the piazza, go back to where you entered it, face the square and turn right to reach Corso del Rinascimento. Cross the road and head up Via Sediari. Turn left at the end onto Via della Scrofa, then take the second road on the right to reach the Piazza della Rotonda and the Pantheon (see page 131). With your back to the Pantheon, turn right and walk along Via dei Pastini and Via di Pietro to Via del Corso; this section is marked with brown pedestrian signs to the Fontana di Trevi (see page 129).*

Via del Corso runs from the Piazza del Popolo to the Piazza Venezia, bisecting the northern half of the city. Partially pedestrian-only, it's a

The Spanish Steps are always thronged with visitors

favorite shopping street with a good variety of clothes, shoes and accessories.

> *Cross Via del Corso and follow Via della Muratte (and the brown signs) to the Fontana di Trevi. Keep the fountain on your left and head up Via Lavatore and Via delle Scuderie, with the bulk of the Palazzo del Quirinale on your right, then branch left to Via del Tritone with the Quirinale behind you.*

The Palazzo del Quirinale is home to the president of Italy; it was built in the 16th and 17th centuries as the papal residence. Opposite the palace are the 18th-century Scuderie (Papal Stables), restored and converted in 2000 to an exhibition hall.

> *Cross Via del Tritone and head straight down Via Due Macelli to the Piazza di Spagna. Climb the Spanish Steps (see page 132) on your right and turn left at the top of the steps. Follow Viale della Trinità dei Monti all the way along, keeping the Giardini della Villa Borghese on your right, until you reach Piazzale Napoleone.*

En route, you'll pass the Villa Medici on your right, a gracious 16th-century villa that houses the French Academy. From the Piazzale Napoleone you could visit the Museo Etrusco at the Villa Giulia (see page 132), the Galleria Borghese (see page 130) or simply enjoy the tranquility of the park.

Central Italy

REGIONAL SIGHTS

Key to symbols

🞢 map coordinates refer to the region map on page 120; sights below are highlighted in yellow on the map

✉ address or location ☎ telephone number

🕐 opening times 🍴 restaurant on site or nearby

🎟 admission charge: $$$ more than €3, $$ €3 to €6, $ less than €3 ℹ️ information

GRAN SASSO D'ITALIA

The highest peak on the Italian peninsula is the 9,554-foot Gran Sasso d'Italia (Etna on Sicily and many Alpine summits are higher). It rises above the Campo Imperatore, a huge upland plain. This is snowcapped mountain scenery at its best, and the area attracts thousands of hikers and climbers, although motorists also can enjoy some inspiring vistas.

The best access point is the tiny settlement of Fonte Cerreto, where a cable car runs up to the Albergo-Rifugio Campo Imperatore. It was here that Mussolini was imprisoned after the Italian surrender in 1943, only to be lifted out in a daring aerial raid by an ace German pilot dispatched by Hitler.

From the Rifugio, trails lead higher into the massif. Take number 10 to Monte della Scindarella (7,326 feet) for a taste of the area – it's a two-hour hike. You could drive farther across the rock-strewn landscape of the Campo Imperatore to explore some of the crumbling and semi-deserted villages that fringe it; Castel del Monte, crowned with a ruined castle and church, and the abandoned settlement of Rocca Caláscio, with its crumbling castle, make interesting stops.

🞢 C3

Tourist information ✉ Piazza Santa Maria Paganica 5, L'Aquila ☎ 0862 410 808 🕐 Mon.–Fri. 8–2 and 4–6, Sat. 8–2 ℹ️ For information on hiking in the Gran Sasso massif contact the Italian Alpine Club ✉ Via Sasso 34, L'Aquila ☎ 0862 24 342

L'AQUILA

L'Aquila is the capital of the Abruzzo and a relatively undeveloped and unexplored region on central Italy's east coast. It lies in the shadow of the Gran Sasso mountain, a dour stone-built city that proves more attractive on closer inspection, with good shops, a wonderful market and the thriving atmosphere a university brings.

Founded in 1242 by German Emperor Frederick II, L'Aquila is said to have been created by amalgamating 99 villages; the number remains significant today. The town hall clock chimes 99 times nightly, and the Fontana delle 99 Cannelle (Fountain of the 99 Spouts) is still a major attraction. You'll also want to visit the Museo Nazionale d'Abruzzo (Abruzzo National Museum), housed in the 16th-century castle. The museum is a splendid hodgepodge of exhibits; the main draw is the skeleton of a mammoth discovered nearby in the 1950s. Other sights include the lovely rose-and-white marble church of Santa Maria di Collemaggio and the sumptuous San Bernardino, burial place of St. Bernardino of Siena. The Sienese still come here on the saint's feast, bearing gifts of Tuscan olive oil. Leave time in L'Aquila to visit the daily market, held in the central Piazza del Duomo.

🞢 C3

Tourist information ✉ Piazza Santa Maria Paganica 5 ☎ 0862 410 808 🕐 Daily 8–1 and 3–6, Apr.–Sep.; closed Sun. afternoon, Oct.–Mar.

Museo Nazionale d'Abruzzo ✉ Viale B Croce ☎ 0862 6331 🕐 Tue.–Sun. 9–7 🎟 $$

Santa Maria di Collemaggio ✉ Piazza di Collemaggio ☎ 0349 732 5007 🕐 Daily 8:30–1 and 3–8

San Bernardino ✉ Piazza del Teatro ☎ 0862 222 255 🕐 Daily 6:30–11:45 and 3:30–7:30

Cattle are released in the early days of spring in the mountains around the Gran Sasso

Left: Preparing for the market in the Piazza del Duomo, the focal point of L'Aquila

The impressive bulk of the Abbey of Montecassino, scene of bitter fighting in World War II

MOLISE

Part of the Abruzzo until 1963, Molise is Italy's newest region, an undeveloped area that has more in common with its neighbors to the south than those to the north. Forty percent of Molise is mountainous; these mountains offer great hiking possibilities, particularly around the lakes, woods and high plains of the Matese chain. From the town of Boiano you can hike up Monte Gallinola, a two-hour climb that culminates in a coast-to-coast view across the whole Italian peninsula.

Molise's main centers are Isernia and Campobasso, sprawling modern cities surrounded by factories built with northern money. To taste the best of the region, head for the rolling countryside or the coastal resort of Térmoli, with its long sandy beach and medieval heart. Other attractions in Molise include Saepínum, Italy's best-preserved example of a Roman provincial town.

✚ D1–E1

Campobasso tourist information ✉ Piazza della Vittoria 14 ☎ 0874 415 662 🕐 Mon.–Sat. 8–2
Isernia tourist information ✉ Palazzo della Regione (6th floor), Via Farinacci 9 ☎ 0865 3992 🕐 Mon.–Sat. 8–2
Saepinum ✉ Altilla, 3 kilometers (2 miles) from Sepino 🕐 Site always open

MONTECASSINO

Scene of one of World War II's most bitterly fought battles, the Benedictine Abbey of Montecassino was founded in AD 529 by St. Benedict; legend maintains he was led to this impregnable spot by three ravens. It quickly became one of the most important monasteries in Europe, sending monks far and wide to disseminate Benedictine ideals. Its strategic mountaintop position between Rome and Naples made it a target over the centuries for repeated attacks, and the abbey has been rebuilt many times.

During World War II the abbey became the German regional headquarters and was besieged by the Allies for more than six months. It was completely destroyed by Allied bombs in May 1944. Its destruction, although vital to the Allies' cause, has caused controversy ever since. The old monastery complex has been faithfully rebuilt and still looms impressively over the valley. The views from the central cloister are as exceptional as ever. The area around and to the south of Montecassino is scattered with much-visited war cemeteries.

✚ D1

Abbazia di Montecassino
✉ Via Montecassino ☎ 0776 311 529 🕐 Daily

8:30–12:30 and 3:30–6 (to 5 p.m. Nov.–Mar.). Closed during services 🚷 $

PARCO NAZIONALE D'ABRUZZO

The 99,000 acres of the Parco Nazionale d'Abruzzo (Abruzzo National Park) make up one of Europe's great wilderness areas. If you love the great outdoors, this is a must-see. Once a royal hunting reserve, the park was established in 1917 and comprises a jumble of Apennine mountain massifs, with the Sangro Valley cutting through its heart.

Here lie the villages of Pescassèroli, Opi and others, where you can pick up information on hiking and viewing wildlife; there are more than 150 well-marked trails of different standards. You'll likely see a subspecies of chamois (a type of antelope) native to the Abruzzo. Wolves are harder to spot, though some are kept in reserves near Pescassèroli. Rarest of all is the Apennine brown bear; there are 100 in the park and numbers are increasing. Spring and fall are probably the best times to explore. The spring flowers are stunningly beautiful, while fall sees mountain slopes glowing with colors.
🚩 D2

Information office ✉ Via Consultore, Pescassèroli ☎ 0863 91 955 🕐 Daily 9–noon and 3–7 ℹ There are smaller summer-only offices at Opi, Barrea and Civitella Alfedena

TARQUÍNIA

It's hard to imagine that 5,000 years ago unassuming Tarquínia boasted a population of more than 100,000 and was the most important of the 12 Etruscan cities. Today's town retains its medieval walls and the 12th-century Romanesque church of Santa Maria di Castello, but most visitors are drawn here by the Etruscan tombs and the superlative Museo Nazionale Tarquiniense (National Tarquinian Museum), which is housed in the 15th-century Palazzo Vitelleschi. This museum has a significant collection of treasures discovered in the Etruscan necropolis to the east of town. There are sarcophagi, ceramics and delicate gold

Wall paintings in 5,000-year-old tombs at Tarquínia show the firm Etruscan belief in an afterlife

jewelry, although pride of place must be given to the beautiful pair of winged terracotta horses, a breathtakingly sophisticated piece of sculpture.

The necropolis itself, just outside town, is an underground honeycomb of tomb chambers, many of which have been opened so you can admire the colorful wall paintings that adorn them. Steps lead down into the earth to allow you to see these lively 5,000-year-old paintings. Excavation of the tombs continues today.
🚩 A2

Tourist information ✉ Piazza Cavour 1 ☎ 0766 850 080 🕐 Mon.–Sat. 8:30–2
Santa Maria di Castello ✉ Piazza Santa Maria di Castello ☎ Obtain key from guardian in house next to church
Museo Nazionale Tarquiniense ✉ Palazzo Vitelleschi, Piazza Cavour 1 ☎ 0766 856 036 🕐 Tue.–Sun. 8:30–7:30; closed Jan. 1, May 1 and Dec. 25 🚷 $$$ ℹ Ticket also is valid for the necropoli in the Zona Archeologica
Zona Archeologica ✉ Via Ripagretta ☎ 0766 840 000 🕐 Tue.–Sun. 8:30–1 hour before dusk 🚷 $$ or $$$ with combined ticket with museum ℹ The tombs are opened in rotation to help conserve the paintings, and there is no way of knowing in advance which will be open on any particular day

Sunlight sparkling on water dazzles the eye in the gardens of the Villa d'Este at Tivoli

TIVOLI

The main attractions of Tivoli, a small town in a lovely wooded location some 30 kilometers (18 miles) from Rome, are the Villa d'Este and the vast classical site of the Villa Adriana (Hadrian's Villa). Both are usually crowded with day-trippers from Rome, so come early to appreciate them at their best. The Villa d'Este, built in 1550 and now rather shabby, has superb gardens with terraces, cascades and fountains; wherever you are in its shady green coolness, you'll hear the refreshing splash of falling water. The two Bernini fountains, the elegant Fontana di Biccierone and the Fontana dei Draghi, are the most splendid, but make sure you don't miss the breathtaking Viale delle Cento Fontane (Avenue of a Hundred Fountains).

Just outside town are the vast and rambling ruins of the Villa Adriana (Hadrian's Villa), built by the emperor in AD 125 as a retirement home. During his imperial travels he had been impressed with buildings all over the known world, and the villa was designed to incorporate copies of many of these. It eventually covered as much ground as imperial Rome itself. This fascinating place is vast, rambling, green and romantic, and you'll need a map to make sense of it all.

✚ B2

Tourist information ✉ Largo Garibaldi ☎ 0774 311 249 🕓 Tue.–Sat. 8:30–2:30 (also 3–6 Tue. and Thu.)
Villa d'Este ✉ Piazza Trento ☎ 0774 312 070 🕓 Tue.–Sun. 8:30 or 9–6:45, Apr.–Sep.; 8:30 or 9–4, rest of year 🍴 Refreshments available in gardens ✋ $$$
Villa Adriana ✉ Via di Villa Andriana 204 ☎ 0774 530 203 🕓 Daily 9 a.m.–90 minutes before dusk 🍴 Refreshments available at villa site ✋ $$$

VITERBO

Capital of northern Lazio, Viterbo's heyday was in medieval times, when it was a favored place for different popes to escape troubles in Rome. Their legacy is a collection of grand palaces and fine churches still enclosed by intact city walls. The entire city has an intensely medieval atmosphere, which you'll best appreciate by exploring the San Pellegrino neighborhood, a tight mass of hilly streets dotted with towers and elevated medieval walkways. At the heart of the city, Piazza del Plebiscito is a fine square surrounded by 15th- and 16th-century buildings. The decorative lions, which you'll see all over the city, are Viterbo's symbol.

From here, head to Piazza San Lorenzo to see the 13th-century Palazzo dei Papi (Papal Palace); its Gothic loggia overlooks the green gorge cutting into the city's center. The Duomo (Cathedral) stands opposite the palace, an austere and serene Romanesque church of great beauty. The city's Museo Civico is mainly devoted to exhibits from the surrounding area, including Etruscan artifacts.

✚ A3

Tourist information ✉ Piazza San Carluccio ☎ 0761 304 795 🕓 Mon.–Sat. 9–1
Duomo ✉ Piazza San Lorenzo ☎ 0761 325 462 🕓 Daily 9–12:30 and 3:30–6 ✋ $$
Museo Civico ✉ Piazza Crispi ☎ 0761 348 275 🕓 Tue.–Sun. 9–7 ✋ $$

THE ETRUSCANS

While traveling in Lazio and other parts of central Italy, you'll come across frequent signs of the Etruscans in the shape of monuments, tombs and museums. Who were these enigmatic and mysterious people?

History

The Etruscans stepped into history's limelight around the fifth century BC. They were a people probably made up of indigenous tribes and seafarers from Asia Minor. Inhabiting an area of central Italy called Etruria and stretching from modern Tuscany down to Rome, they formed a confederacy of 12 cities, building towns, passing laws and trading overseas. They were a lively and imaginative people with sophisticated cultural, political and social systems. That much is clear, but little else of their everyday life is known. This is explained by two factors. First, the Romans so admired them that they absorbed much of Etruscan culture as they rose to power. By the third century BC, the Romans had virtually assimilated all of Etruria, together with much of its language, customs and religious beliefs. Secondly, the Etruscans built their cities of wood, not stone, and nothing remains.

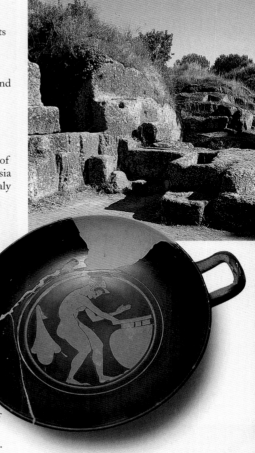

Top: Tombs laid out to form a city for the dead
Inset: Sophisticated Etruscan ceramics

Monuments

We also know that the Etruscans were deeply religious, firmly believing in an afterlife and burying their dead, as did the Egyptians, with all they would need for the future. Their tombs (necropoli), unlike their wooden cities, were permanent, made either of stone or carved out of the soft tufa rock found all over ancient Etruria. Wonderful finds have been made in these tombs – jewelry, vases, sculpture and wall paintings. From these, historians have learned much about the Etruscan way of life. The artifacts from the tombs are preserved in on-site museums, although the finest have gone to the Vatican Museums (see page 130) and the Villa Giulia (see page 132) in Rome.

Wonderful Sites

You can explore Etruscan sites all over central Italy, but the most interesting are found in Lazio. Tarquínia (see page 139) has wonderful painted tombs. Orvieto, in Umbria (see page 106), has streets carved from tufa, while in Sutri a 6,000-seat amphitheater is carved from the living rock. Cerveteri, north of Rome, is literally a "city of the dead," complete with streets, houses and piazzas. There are more than 5,000 tombs here, although only around 50 have been systematically excavated.

DRIVE: THE COAST TO THE ALBAN HILLS

Duration: 4½ to 5 hours

Start this drive in San Felice Circeo, a honey-colored coastal village with a good beach, an hour's drive south from Rome.

From San Felice, you have access to the Parco Nazionale del Circeo (Monte Circeo National Park), named after the limestone headland of Monte Circeo, which looms above the town. Monte Circeo was reputedly the home of the sorceress Circe, who lured Ulysses with her guiles and siren song. You can drive to the summit for wonderful views up and down the coast. The park, the smallest of Italy's national parks, was established in 1934 to preserve some of the natural beauty of the neighboring marsh and wetland area, as well as to preserve the woodlands and wonderful flora of Monte Circeo itself. It's of special interest to bird enthusiasts, as the lakes and lagoons provide marvelous habitats for many varieties of waterfowl. With luck you'll spot herons, storks and fish hawks.

Continue north along the coast to Anzio (signposted Sabáudia).

North of Monte Circeo, the road hugs the coast for more than 32 kilometers (20 miles),

then makes a brief detour inland before hitting the sea again at Nettuno. There's a big, peaceful and beautifully tended World War II cemetery at Nettuno where nearly 8,000 American GI's are buried, killed at the Anzio landings in 1944.

At Anzio, take the SS207 (signposted Aprília) and continue for 33 kilometers (20 miles) to Aprília and then Pavona. Turn right and follow signs to Castel Gandolfo.

Castel Gandolfo, set high above Lago Albano (Lake Albano) in the Alban Hills, is best

The pope's summer palace overlooks Castél Gandolfo's pretty piazza

Impressive Roman mosaics are one of Óstia Antica's attractions

known as the pope's summer retreat. Several pontiffs have come here to escape the broiling heat of the Roman summer. It's a pleasant little town, dominated by the Papal Palace, in whose courtyard the pope traditionally gives a Sunday blessing when he's in residence. Below the town, the picturesque lake is tempting, where you can have a swim or eat at one of the many lakeside restaurants.

Follow signs to Frattócchie, then branch right on an unnamed road across country to the junction with the SS215 and follow the signs to Frascati.

Frascati is another of the Alban hill towns; it's the nearest to Rome, and therefore often packed with day-trippers and Romans who flock there to eat Sunday lunch. It's attractive and picturesque, dominated by the bulk of the majestic Villa Aldobrandi, built in 1598. The villa's gardens today are romantically overgrown. The spectacular fountains are often switched off, but if the gardens are open it's worth going in for the sweeping views from the terrace in front of the house.

White wine has been made in Frascàti since Roman times, and is well known outside Italy. There are plenty of places where you can sample this light and clean-tasting wine; some growers offer tours.

Rejoin the SS215, this time following signs to the Grande Raccordo Annullare

(GRA), Rome's ring road, and turn left. Continue on the GRA for 18 kilometers (11 miles), then exit on the SS8 to Lido di Óstia, Óstia Antica and the coastline.

In Roman time the coastline lay farther inland than it does today, at the site of the Óstia Antica, the port of ancient Rome. You'll learn far more here, in perhaps far greater peace, than moving with the crowds in the Forum in Rome itself. The site is huge, evocative and dotted with grass-covered mounds and spreading umbrella pines. You could wander for hours (perhaps bringing a picnic with you), but if time is short, head for the Piazzale di Corporazione, the ancient city's commercial center. Ruined shops and offices still line it, and the mosaics in front indicate each building's purpose – ropemakers, grain merchants and chandlers. You can explore private houses (the Casa di Diana with its central courtyard is among the best), walk the streets and visit the Thermopolium, an ancient café.

Parco Nazionale del Circeo information office
✉ Via Carlo Alberti 107, Sabáudia ☎ 0773 511 386; www.parks.it 🕓 Mon.–Sat. 9–1 (also 4–7, Apr.–Oct.)

Frascati tourist information ✉ Piazza Marconi 1 ☎ 06 942 0331 🕓 Mon.–Sat. 8–2 (also Tue.–Fri. 3:30–6:30)

Óstia Antica ☎ 06 5635 8099 🕓 Tue.–Sun. 9–6, Apr.–Oct.; 9–4, rest of year 👋 $$

THE SOUTH

*"**I**N the deep south, climate, landscape, economy and way of life combine to form a startling contrast to the north. "*

The South

Clear blue seas surround the famous Faraglioni rocks off the coast of the island of Capri

THE SOUTH

The South

Southern Italy – the Mezzogiorno – starts south of Rome and includes four very diverse regions: Campania, with its breathtakingly beautiful coastline; the mountainous inland areas of Calabria and Basilicata; the empty flatlands along the Ionian coast; and the rolling Apulian (Puglian) seaboard. Its chief city is Naples, one of the most vibrant, frustrating but ultimately bewitching cities in Italy. Spiritually a million miles from the dynamic north, Italy's south, remote and little explored, provides a balance to the northern regions and the Renaissance perfection of the central areas.

Echoes of the Past

Invaders have poured into the south for more than 2,500 years. Greek, Arab, Norman, German and Spanish each systematically bled the region. However, these successive waves of invasion left behind a superb artistic legacy of temples, churches and palaces. They established a genetic mark on the population and incorporated the rhythms of their own speech in local dialects, and brought echoes of their tastes to the intense flavors of southern cuisine. Their absolutist regimes also bequeathed the very elements that kept the south one of the most economically depressed areas of Europe.

Today

Southern Italy is still poor. This is partly the result of centuries of foreign neglect, but it's also due to a policy of industrializing the north, while using the south as a convenient labor pool to fuel this industry. After World War II, millions of southerners emigrated north to find work, leaving the south increasingly depopulated, its industry and infrastructure undeveloped. The north-south divide is very real and will be only too apparent if you've already explored northern and central Italy.

Despite massive central government and European Union investment in recent years, the southern standard of living still lags far behind the rest of Italy. Organized crime and corruption still exist, although things are improving and the average visitor certainly won't be affected. You will notice the dilapidation and grime of many southern towns, while away from the tourist areas you'll have to bear in mind that you're traveling in the poorer

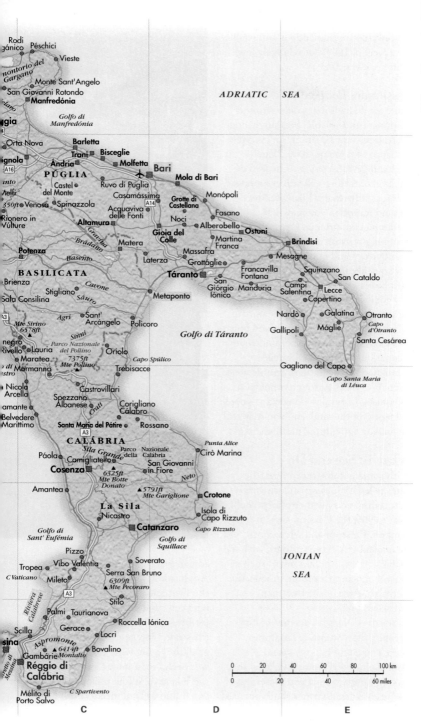

Rodi
gánico Péschici
Vieste
nontorio del
Gargano
Monte Sant'Angelo
San Giovanni Rotondo
Manfredónia
gia
Golfo di
Manfredónia
Orta Nova
Barletta
Trani **Bisceglie**
ignola
Molfetta
Andria **Bari**
A16
PÚGLIA **Mola di Bari**
into Castel
Aelfi del Monte Ruvo di Puglia Monópoli
350ft Venosa Spinazzola Casamássima **Grotte di** Fasano
Rionero in Acquaviva **Castellana**
Vúlture delle Fonti Noci Alberobello **Ostuni**
Altamura **Gioia del** Martina **Brindisi**
Matera **Colle** Franca
Potenza Massafra Mesagne
Laterza Grottáglie Francavilla Squinzano
BASILICATA **Táranto** Fontana Campi San Cataldo
Brienza San Manduria Salentina **Lecce**
Stigliano Metaponto Giórgio Copertino
Sala Consilina Iónico Nardò Galatina Otranto
Mte Sirino Sant' Policoro Gallipoli Máglie Capo
6578ft Arcángelo d'Otranto
negro Sinni Golfo di Táranto Santa Cesárea
Rivello Lauria Parco Nazionale Oriolo
Maratea del Pollino
7375ft Trebisacce Gagliano del Capo
di Mormanno Mte Pollino Capo Spúlico
astro Capo Santa Maria
Nicola di Léuca
Arcella Castrovillari
amante Spezzano
Albanese Corigliano
Belvedere Cálabro
Maríttimo Santa Maria del Pátire Rossano
CALÁBRIA Punta Alice
Sila Grande Parco Nazionale Cirò Marina
Páola della Calábria
Camigliatello San Giovanni
Cosenza 6325ft in Fiore
Mte Botte Neto
Amantea Donato 5791ft **Crotone**
Mte Gariglione
La Sila Isola di
Nicastro Capo Rizzuto
Catanzaro Capo Rizzuto
Golfo di
Sant' Eufémia Golfo di
Pizzo Squillace
Tropea Soverato **IONIAN**
Vibo Valéntia
C Vaticano Serra San Bruno **SEA**
Mileto 6309ft
Mte Pecoraro
A3
Palmi Stilo
Riviera Tauranova
Calábrese Roccella Iónica
Scilla Gerace
sina Aspromonte Locri
Gambárie Bovalino
6411ft Montalto
Réggio di
Calábria
Mélito di C Spartivento
Porto Salvo

ADRIATIC SEA

Gráuna
Brádano

Basento
Cavone
Agri Sáuro
Sinni

A3

Crati

Sila

0   20   40   60   80   100 km
0   20   40   60 miles

C   D   E

The South

half of the "two Italys." Persevere; the rewards are tremendous and you'll see a facet of Italy that relatively few visitors experience.

Passionate People

Southern Italians may come across as passionate and volatile. Seemingly huge altercations may be simply an everyday exchange of news or views. Watch the hand gestures to get some idea of the level of feeling – ill will evaporates as fast as it flares up. Likewise, the offhand reception you may first encounter can turn quickly to over-whelming warmth and friendliness. Spontaneous and open, southerners react quickly, their hearts often ruling their heads.

People tend to be smaller and darker complected than in the north, although red and blonde hair and blue eyes are the genetic legacy of northern occupation. Society is still male-dominated, particularly in remote areas where it's rare even to see women on the streets. In rural regions many people still work on the land, and you may still see archaic agricultural methods in use.

What To See and Do

With some notable exceptions, the south is less rich in artistic treasures than central and northern Italy. You'll want to visit the classical sites of Pompeii, Paestum and Metaponto, and the ancient city center of Bari, with its Arabic echoes. Apulian towns such as Alberobello and Lecce are unique, but it's the southern coast that many visitors will remember.

South of Naples stretches one of Europe's most stunning coastlines, where you could happily spend a week exploring the pretty villages and soaking up the sun. If you prefer less-chic resorts, head farther south and east to the homely little resorts along the

Ionian Sea coast and within Calabria. Apulia's long beaches and the cliffs of the Gargano strike a happy balance between rural charm and good facilities. Wilderness lovers will find the south's interior everything they could hope for, with great hiking in wonderful mountain scenery. Explore the Sila and Pollino inland areas, where you'll find upland meadows and forests reminiscent of northern landscapes.

Conical-shaped roofs of *trulli* – an architectural oddity found only in Puglia

When To Go

As in the rest of Italy, the best time to visit the south is in spring, early summer or fall. Spring reveals the country at its greenest and most beautiful; by May and June it's already warm enough to enjoy the beaches. September and October can be idyllic, with velvet-warm seas and balmy nights. July and August are months to be avoided; the south has a true Mediterranean climate, and temperatures can climb well into the 90s. These also are the Italian holiday months when coastal resorts are at their most crowded, and cities empty of their residents. Many hotels outside the main centers are closed during winter, when daylight hours are short and it can be wet and windy.

The South

NAPLES

Vibrant Naples (Nápoli), the capital of southern Italy and one of Europe's most beautiful cities, is light years removed from the dynamic, work-driven north. Ramshackle and confusing, in places, Naples can feel alien and intimidating, but most visitors are quickly won over by its exuberance, way of life and people.

Come to Naples with an open mind, remembering you'll find a big, sprawling city that suffered huge damage in World War II. Indiscriminate construction has wrecked some of the loveliest outlying areas, while 19th-century slum clearances by no means solved the problems of overpopulation and social deprivation. Concentrate instead on the superb monuments, churches, museums, galleries and the welcoming charm of the people. In no other major Italian city will you find such friendliness.

Getting Around

The horrific traffic makes all transportation excruciatingly slow, so it's best to tackle central Naples on foot. Sites are grouped together in different areas, so take a bus or cable car to reach them and then walk. Wandering around is an essential part

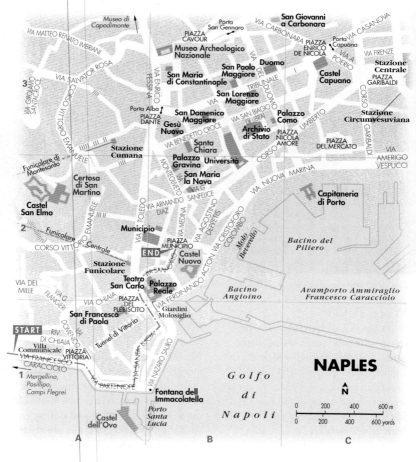

NAPLES

of the Naples experience, but stick to well-frequented areas. It is wise to avoid the labyrinthine back streets, the docks and the railroad station. Take great care crossing streets; Neapolitan drivers ignore pedestrian crossings, and scooter users appear to come out of nowhere and frequently use the pavement. The best way to appreciate the beauty of Naples' superb setting on the bay is from the sea; you could combine this with a boat trip to Sorrento (see page 165) or the ravishing islands of Capri (see page 157) and Ischia.

Mediterranean Flavors
Neapolitan cooking ranks among Italy's best, with intense flavors and a strong emphasis on the freshest fish and seafood, as well as local fruits and vegetables. It is home to thin, crisp pizza, baked in wood-fired ovens. Cakes and pastries, stuffed with *crema* and dripping with liqueurs, come from

a *pasticceria*, where you'll often find ice cream – best in summer when it's made with seasonal fruit. Local wines to try are *Lacryma Christi* (Christ's Tears) and *Greco di Tufo*. Be sure to sample *Limoncello*, a lemon-flavored liqueur.

Shopping and Entertainment
Head for the Via Toledo and the Via Chiaia for designer outlets, leather goods, knitwear and accessories; this area also is home to department stores such as la Rinascente and Coin, while the Vomero district has shopping centers at Galleria Vanvitelli and Galleria Scartelli. The San Biagio neighborhood is the place to hunt for coral jewelry and cameo brooches, as well as beautiful traditional nativity figures.

If you like opera and classical music, try to fit in a performance at the San Carlo opera house. Traditional music is easy to find, and many restaurants feature evening serenades.

ESSENTIAL INFORMATION

TOURIST INFORMATION
•Piazza dei Martiri ☎ 081 410 7211; www.inaples.it
•Stazione Centrale ☎ 081 268 779
•Stazione Mergellina ☎ 081 761 2102

URBAN TRANSPORTATION
It's best to walk in traffic-clogged Naples. Longer distances can be covered by subway, bus and cable car, all of which are slow. There are two types of *Giranapoli* tickets, valid for either 90 minutes or all day; they are interchangeable between the systems and are available from tobacconists or newsstands. Tickets must be validated at each system in the special machines used for this purpose. The Circumvesuviana railway runs every half-hour from Corso Garibaldi to Sorrento, an hour's

journey. You also can travel to Sorrento by ferry or hydrofoil from either Mergellina or the Molo Beverello docks. The same companies also serve Capri, Ischia and the other islands. There are taxi stands throughout the city, or you can phone Taxi Napoli (☎ 081 556 4444) or Taxi Free (☎ 081 551 5151). Taxis also will take you sightseeing outside Naples for fixed rates.

AIRPORT INFORMATION
Naples Capodichino Airport (☎ 081 789 6259), with internal and European flights, is northwest of the city center. Airport 'Alibus' shuttle buses leave every 30 minutes (6 a.m.–11:30 p.m.) and take 20 minutes to get to Piazza Garibaldi, depending on traffic or take a local ANM city bus number 35, which leaves every 15 minutes and takes between 30 and 45 minutes.

CLIMATE – Average highs and lows

JAN.	FEB.	MAR.	APR.	MAY	JUN.	JUL.	AUG.	SEP.	OCT.	NOV.	DEC.
12°C	13°C	15°C	18°C	22°C	26°C	29°C	29°C	26°C	22°C	17°C	13°C
54°F	55°F	59°F	64°F	72°F	79°F	84°F	84°F	79°F	72°F	63°F	55°F
4°C	5°C	7°C	9°C	13°C	17°C	19°C	19°C	17°C	13°C	8°C	5°C
39°F	41°F	45°F	48°F	55°F	63°F	66°F	66°F	63°F	55°F	46°F	41°F

NAPLES SIGHTS

Key to symbols

✚ map coordinates refer to the Naples map on page 150; sights below are highlighted in yellow on the map

✉ address or location ☎ telephone number

🕐 opening times 🍴 restaurant on site or nearby

Ⓜ nearest subway station

🚌 nearest bus or tram route

💵 admission charge: $$$ more than €6, $$ €3 to €6, $ less than €3 ℹ️ information

CASTEL DELL'OVO

Encircled by the sea, Castel dell'Ovo (Egg Castle) is on an island joined to the mainland by a causeway. It is Naples' oldest castle, built between the ninth and 16th centuries. The name is derived from the story that it was built on top of an egg placed here in Roman times; if the egg broke, Naples would fall. Run-down and dilapidated by the 1970s, it has now been extensively restored and is used for cultural events.

✚ A1 ✉ Borgo Marinaro 🍴 La Cantinella, see page 209 🚌 R3; tram 1 💵 Free

CASTEL NUOVO

The Castel Nuovo (New Castle), with its five massive chess-piece towers, dominates the Naples waterfront. First built in 1282, it was enlarged in the 15th century and was later the residence of the Aragonese monarchs. Today it's the home of the Naples city council. A magnificent Renaissance gateway opens onto the central courtyard, which is surrounded by buildings housing the Museo Civico (Civic Museum), the splendid Gothic Sala dei Baroni (Baron's Hall) and the Cappella Palatina (Palatine Chapel), the only surviving part of an earlier 13th-century building.

Nearby is the huge and imposing Palazzo Reale, a grandiose structure built in 1602 with a flamboyant but strangely dull interior. The famous San Carlo, Italy's largest opera house, is east of the castle.

✚ B2 ✉ Piazza Municipio ☎ 081 795 5877 🕐 Mon.–Sat. 9–7 🚌 R2, R3 💵 $$

CERTOSA DI SAN MARTINO

Visible from all over Naples, the hilltop complex of the Certosa di San Martino (St. Martin's Charterhouse) was mainly constructed between the 16th and 18th centuries. You can explore the Chiostro Grande (Main Cloister), the sumptuous baroque church and the lavishly decorated Quarto del Priore (Prior's Quarters). Don't miss the exhibition of *presepi* (Nativity figures), a charming collection of figures, animals and everyday objects fashioned for 19th-century Christmas nativity scenes, the highlight of a visit to the Certosa. Walk through the monastery to the terrace at the back; planted with shrubs and trees, it commands a sweeping view of the city and Bay of Naples.

✚ A2 ✉ Largo San Martino 5 ☎ 081 578 1769 🕐 Certosa: Tue.–Sat. 9–2, Sun. 9–1; Museum: Tue.–Sat. 8:30–7:30, Sun. 9–7:30 Ⓜ Montesanto 🚌 V1 💵 $$$

MERGELLINA

This waterfront area west of the city is a popular place to eat. The harbor is the focal point of the traditional fishermen's quarter, and it's a delightful place to stroll. Fishing boats and island ferries still leave from the harbor.

✚ A1 ✉ Via Mergellina 🍴 Don Salvatore, see page 209 Ⓜ Mergellina 🚌 R3, C21

MUSEO ARCHEOLOGICO NAZIONALE

The Museo Archeologico (Archeological Museum) houses one of the world's most important collections of classical sculpture, mosaics, gems, glass and silver. Buy an English-language guide before you start. The first floor is devoted mainly to sculpture, much from the 17th-century Farnese collections that were largely discovered in Rome. The stars are the muscular *Farnese Hercules* and the *Farnese Bull*. Dating from 200 BC, this is the world's largest classical sculptural group to have survived. Many rooms are filled with finds from Pompei and Herculaneum, including frescoes and mosaics; don't miss the graceful fresco of Flora scattering

Santa Chiara, one of the best-known churches in the city, stands at the center of historic Naples

spring flowers, and a mosaic of a fierce but friendly dog from a Pompeian front door.
✚ B3 ✉ Piazza Museo 19 ☎ 081 544 1494 or 081 440 166 🕐 Mon. and Wed.–Sat. 9–7, Sun. 9–8 🚌 1, 24, 42 💵 $$$ 🛈 English-language guidebooks are available at the museum shop

MUSEO DI CAPODIMONTE

Built in 1738 as the Bourbon King Charles III's palace and surrounded by a wooded park, Capodimonte has been restored and rearranged. You can wander freely through the opulent royal apartments on your way to the majolica and porcelain collection, much of it made by the Capodimonte factory and painted with local scenes. Upstairs is a collection of paintings spanning the 15th to 17th centuries, with an emphasis on Renaissance works. Some rooms are often closed, but with luck you'll get to see Botticelli's *Madonna*, Umbrian paintings by Perugino and Pinturicchio, and some sensitive portraits of Pope Paul III by Titian. There's a Raphael portrait of Pope Leo X, contrasting with Sebastiano del Piombo's worldly interpretation of Pope Clement VII.
✚ A3 ✉ Parco di Capodimonte, Via Miano 1 ☎ 081 749 9111 🕐 Museum: Tue.–Sun. 8:30–7:30. Park: daily 8 to 1 hour before sunset 🚌 R4, 24, 110, 161 💵 $$$. Park: free

POSILLIPO AND THE CAMPI FLEGREI

Posillipo and the Campi Flegrei (literally "Burning Fields," named because of the area's volcanic activity) are west of Naples on what is still a lovely stretch of coast. Dotted with classical ruins, fishing villages, beaches, inlets and grottos, this is an area well worth exploring.
✚ Off the map ✉ Posillipo 🚇 Mergellina, Campi Flegrei

SANTA CHIARA

The Franciscan church of Santa Chiara is a good starting point for exploring Spaccanapoli, the ebullient heart of historic Naples. Packed with squares and historic buildings, this entire area teems with life, noise and confusion. By contrast, the church is simple and austere. Rebuilt after a fire in 1943, it contains tombs and offers access to the 14th-century cloister, with its garden and 17th-century columns and seats. There also is a museum and a nativity scene.
✚ B3 ✉ Via Benedetto Croce 49 ☎ 081 797 1256 🕐 Church: daily 7–12:30 and 4–7. Cloister: Mon.–Sat. 8:30–12:30 and 3:30–6:30, Sun. 9:30–1. Museum: Mon.–Tue. and Thu.–Sat. 9:30–1 and 2:30–5:30, Sun. 9:30–1 🚌 R1, R4, 110 💵 Museum: $$; church and cloister: free

The Palazzo Reale, the former Royal Palace

WALK: WATERFRONT NAPLES

Refer to route marked on city map on page 150.

This walk beside the sea will take about an hour. Starting from the Villa Communale, it goes through the elegant neighborhood of Chiaia to Santa Lucia and on to Piazza Municipio.

Start on Via Francesco Caracciolo, a waterfront, pedestrian-only street west of the Castel dell'Ovo.

Via Francesco Caracciolo was constructed in the late 19th century; its broad elegance will help you to appreciate Naples' glorious location. Views stretch around the bay from the north headland to Vesuvius in the south.

From Piazza della Repubblica continue along Via Caracciolo's walkway. To your left you'll see the green oasis of the Villa Communicale, Naples' central park.

The gardens, with steps down to the sea, were laid out in 1778 with parallel walks, trees, shrubs and statues; they were enlarged in the 19th century when the promenade was built. The gardens are always crowded on summer evenings and on the third weekend of every month, when an antiques market takes place in the villa. In the middle of the park stands the 19th-century building housing the Aquarium, a rather dreary collection of fish and marine life.

Walk along farther to Piazza Vittoria and continue beside the sea along Via Partenope, a smart street lined with luxury hotels. To your right looms the Castel dell'Ovo (see page 152), which you'll pass on the right as the road swings around to reach the harbor of Santa Lucia.

There's a splendid fish market here in the mornings, while later in the day you can eat a delicious seafood lunch or dinner in one of the restaurants clustered along the waterfront. Every Neapolitan song you've heard seems to feature this area, including the best-known of all, *O Sole Mio*. Ahead of you stands the flamboyant fountain known as the Immacolatella.

Cross Via Partenope and turn left up Via Santa Lucia.

This area contains some of Naples' most elegant shops, where you'll find outlets for Italian and international designer names. Local stores specialize in more traditional Neapolitan products, such as coral necklaces, bracelets and earrings, and delicate cameo brooches.

Via Santa Lucia opens on Via Cesario Console, where you turn left to head up to sweeping Piazza del Plebiscito, with the Palazzo Reale to your right. Turn right onto Via San Carlo, which leads past San Carlo opera house and the Castel Nuovo (see page 152) to busy Piazza Municipio, with the grandiose city hall at the top of the square.

There's no best time to visit Naples, although spring and fall are ideal for those who don't enjoy extremes. July and August can be hot, with temperatures well over 95 degrees Fahrenheit (35 degrees Celsius), while winter can be cold and wet. But whenever you visit, you'll find the calendar punctuated by a series of feasts and festivals.

Dressed for the Easter Parade

SEASON BY SEASON

Spring and Summer

Carnival generally falls in February. March 19, the feast of San Giuseppe, is the traditional date for changing to spring clothes, and Good Friday sees religious processions through the streets of many city neighborhoods. This time of grief is followed by the joyous celebrations of Easter Sunday and Monday, affectionately known as *Pasquetta*, when families head to the country for huge feasts.

The first Sunday in May is the first of two annual celebrations of San Gennaro, the patron saint of Naples, when his statue is carried through the streets from the cathedral. Many buildings and churches are opened in May, an inspired idea to encourage locals and visitors to rediscover historic Naples. The *Estate a*

Napoli (Summer in Naples) festival, a series of arts events in and around the city, runs from July to September. July 16 is the feast of Madonna del Carmine; a fireworks display commemorates the saving of the church's belltower from fire by the Blessed Virgin Mary. August, the traditional vacation month throughout Italy, is Naples' quietest month, and many restaurants close.

Autumn and Winter

Autumn's biggest feast is on September 19, the feast of the miracle of the blood of San Gennaro. In front of huge crowds in the cathedral, accompanied by cheering and emotional scenes, a vial of the saint's normally solid blood liquidizes. December 8, the feast of the Immaculate Conception, is the start of the Christmas season, when the first of the *presepi* (Nativity figures) are made. Christmas itself sees more feasting, while the days before January 1 are marked by fireworks and bagpipers. Children get presents on January 6, the Epiphany, when Befana, a benevolent witch, brings gifts to good kids and "coal" (lumps of black candy) to bad kids.

Costumed processions parade through the streets on Good Friday

Alberobello's beguiling *trulli* are still homes for many local people

REGIONAL SIGHTS

Key to symbols

⊞ map coordinates refer to the region map on page 146; sights below are highlighted in yellow on the map
✉ address or location ☎ telephone number
🕐 opening times 🍴 restaurant on site or nearby
🚢 ferry 💲 admission charge: $$$ more than €6, $$ €3 to €6, $ less than €3 ℹ information

ALBEROBELLO

Driving inland south from Bari, you'll start to notice round, stone buildings with conical roofs topped with a stone symbol; these structures are *trulli*, found nowhere else in Europe except in this area of Apulia. Scattered across the landscape, there are more and more to be seen as you approach Alberobello. This little town, a UNESCO World Heritage Site, has more than 1,400 *trulli* in two different areas, the Rione Monti and the Aia Piccola.

The Rione Monti, a series of *trulli*-lined streets running down the hillside, is tourist heaven. Most of the *trulli* have been turned into craft shops, enabling you to wander through the interiors and even climb on their roofs, where you'll find perfect photo opportunities featuring a forest of these charming structures.

Aia Piccola is much more authentic; here, the *trulli* are still people's homes. Nobody really knows the origin of this architectural form, once thought to have been a form of tax evasion on permanent dwellings. The latest theories link them with ancient Greece or even Syria – Apulia was once part of Magna Graecia – or they may have been introduced by eastern monks or returning Crusaders.

⊞ D5

Tourist information ✉ Casa d'Amore, Piazza del Popoto ☎ 080 432 5171 🕐 Mon.–Fri. 9:30–1 and 3:30–5:30, Sat. 9:30–1

BARI

Ancient Bari falls into two sections: the grid-plan 19th-century town, with its straight avenues and seafront promenade; and the old city, one of southern Italy's most vibrant warrens. Explore the jumble of narrow streets, where life

Vacation villas overlook the colorful waterfront of Marina Grande's harbor on Capri

surges around you: flapping washing, crowded one-room apartments open to the street, women screeching from balconies and roaring scooters.

Here you'll find the great Basilica di San Nicola (St. Nicholas), built between 1087 and 1180 and the stunning prototype for many of Apulia's Romanesque churches. Behind the balanced facade lies a lofty, dim interior whose treasures include a 12th-century *ciborio* (altar canopy) and a superb episcopal throne. St. Nicholas is buried in the crypt. Each December the basilica is the focal point for the exuberant processions and festivities that celebrate the saint's feast. Nearby stands the more austere Cattedrale di San Sabino (St. Sabine's Cathedral), with a simple interior containing an eighth-century icon of the Virgin Mary, said to be a true likeness. Close by you'll find the huge 13th-century bulk of the

Castello (Castle), built by Frederick II, which stands on the site of a Roman fort. A word of caution: pay attention to what's going on around you and make sure your valuables are out of sight.

➕ C5

Tourist information ✉ Piazza Aldo Moro 33/A ☎ 080 524 2361 🕐 Mon.–Fri. 8–2 (also 3–6 Tue. and Thu.)

Basilica di San Nicola ✉ Piazza San Nicola ☎ 080 573 7111 🕐 Daily 9–1 and 5–7 💷 Free
ℹ Festivities with processions, concerts and fireworks are held during the week of Dec. 6

Cattedrale di San Sabino ✉ Piazza Odegitria 🕐 Daily 8:30–1 and 5–7 💷 Free

Castello ✉ Piazza Federico II di Svevio 2 ☎ 080 528 6111 🕐 Tue.–Sun. 8:30–7:30 💷 $$

CAPRI

A favorite of Roman emperors, the tiny island of Capri has spectacular scenery and is surrounded by crystal waters,

The South

easily reached as a day trip from Naples. The two main settlements are Anacapri and Capri; their whitewashed houses and narrow, winding streets are packed with tempting boutiques, cafés and restaurants. Many visitors take a boat trip to the Grotta Azzurra (Blue Grotto), a spectacular sea cave filled with refracted turquoise light.

Another highlight is the beautiful Villa San Michele, in Anacapri. Built in the late 19th century by Swedish physician Axel Munthe, this dream-like villa with its peaceful green garden is filled with classical statues. You can enjoy some of the island's loveliest views from its shady pergola.

Classical enthusiasts can walk to the ruins of Villa Jovis, emperor Tiberius' clifftop villa, from where he allegedly threw victims into the sea. Another stroll leads to a lookout above the Faraglioni, a cluster of offshore rocks jutting more than 360 feet out of the sea.

➕ A4

Tourist information ✉ Piazza Umberto 1 ☎ 081 837 0686 🕐 Daily 8:30–8:30, Jun.–Sep.; Mon.–Sat. 9–1 and 3:30–6:30, rest of year 🚢 Ferry operator: Caremar, from Molo Beverello, Naples (☎ 081 551 5384). Hydrofoil operators: Caremar, from Molo Beverello, Naples (☎ 081 551 3882); NLG, from Molo Beverello, Naples (☎ 081 552 7209); SNAV, from Mergellina, Naples (☎ 081 761 2348)

Blue Grotto ☎ 081 837 0634 🕐 Daily (weather permitting) 9 a.m.–1 hour before dusk 🚢 From Marina Grande 🎧 $$$

Villa San Michele ✉ Viale Axe Munthe 3, Anacapri ☎ 081 837 1401 🕐 Daily 9–6, May–Sep.; 9:30–5, Apr. and Oct.; 9:30–4:30, in Mar.; 10:30–3:30, rest of year 🎧 $$$

Villa Jovis ✉ Via Tiberio ☎ 081 837 0634 🕐 Daily 9 a.m.–1 hour before dusk 🎧 $

CASTEL DEL MONTE

The gentle, rolling landscape behind the coast near Bari is dominated by the huge bulk of Castel del Monte. Built of luminous ashlar stone by the Sicily-based German emperor Frederick II in 1240, this mighty building soars up against the blue sky on a windswept, lonely hill. The octagonal castle is built around an octagonal courtyard and is flanked by eight towers, which also are octagonal.

This mathematical precision is a mystery, as is the lack of defensive features normally associated with a medieval castle. Some scholars claim its proportions relate to the movement of the stars. Others think Frederick may have built it as a pilgrim hostel or to imitate a Jerusalem mosque. You can wander around the high, bare, interlinked rooms and look down to the courtyard through the windows and French doors on the upstairs floor. Windows also pierce the outer walls, giving panoramic views of the surroundings.

➕ C5

✉ Andria 🕐 Daily 10–7:30, Mar.–Sep.; 9–6:30, rest of year 🍴 Bar and restaurant outside gates 🎧 $$

LECCE

Elegant Lecce is packed with exuberant baroque architecture, the product of 17th-century mercantile money and the zeal of religious orders. Known as Leccese Baroque, the style is opulent and extravagant yet airy, with churches, palaces and houses all a riot of gamboling *putti*, windswept saints and angels, curlicues, garlands and wreaths. It's a joy to wander, but start with the Basilica di Santa Croce, the apotheosis of the style. It stands next to the wonderful Palazzo dei Celestini, which has a restrained courtyard that contrasts with its intricate facade. Both were designed by Giuseppe Zimbalo, who was responsible for many of Lecce's most successful buildings. From here, cross Piazza Oronzo, with its Roman amphitheater still used for concerts, and head up Corso Vittorio Emanuele II to Piazza del Duomo, a spacious and elegant square. Here the city's Duomo (Cathedral) is flanked by the lovely Seminario (Seminary) and Palazzo Vescovile (Bishop's Palace).

Lecce's other treasures include more fine churches such as Santa Chiara, the Rosario, the Gesù and the Carmine, Charles V's vast 16th-century castle and the interesting Museo Provinciale.

➕ E4

Tourist information ✉ Corso Vittorio Emanuele II 24 ☎ 0832 248 092 🕐 Mon.–Fri. 10:30–1 (also 5–7:30 Wed. and Fri.)

Basilica di Santa Croce ✉ Via Umberto I 🕐 Daily

A window of Lecce's Basilica di Santa Croce provides a perfect example of the city's flamboyant Baroque architecture

8–1 and 5–7 👋 Free
Duomo ✉ Piazza del Duomo 🕐 Daily 7–7 👋 Free
Museo Provinciale ✉ Viale Gallipoli 🕐 Mon.–Sat. 9–7:30, Sun. 9–1 👋 $$

MARATEA

Pretty Maratea is located on the Tyrrhenian Sea coast, where majestic mountains drop to the water – and lovely coves and beaches provide a sharp contrast to the flat lands along the Ionian Sea to the east. With its good hotels and restaurants, Maratea makes an ideal stopping point for a few nights if you're traveling south. The old village has a tangle of narrow streets, squares and stairways, with some fine old houses and churches. Below lies the port, along with attractive houses, shops and restaurants. Fine hotels and villas are tucked among the pine trees on either side of the port.

A winding coastal road connects everything and gives access to secluded bays and beaches. High above on Monte San Biagio stands a huge statue of Christ the Redeemer, which was erected in 1965. You can drive up the mountain to visit the Santuario di San Biagio, built on the site of a pagan temple, and take in the superb views up and down the coast. The nearby coastal village of Fiumicello is very pretty and full of activity in summer.

➕ B4
Tourist information ✉ Piazza del Gesù 40, Fiumicello ☎ 0973 876 908 🕐 Daily 9–1 and 3–8, Apr. 1 to mid-Sep.; 9–12:30 and 4–7, rest of year

The little coastal town of Maratea

DRIVE: THE UNDISCOVERED GARGANO PENINSULA

Duration: 7 to 9 hours

This drive will give you a chance to explore the incredible natural beauty of the Gargano peninsula, as well as take in a couple of its inland and coastal towns. All the roads are steep, twisting and occasionally vertiginous, so don't attempt the trip if you suffer from travel sickness. It would be a long drive to tackle in a day; both Vieste and Pèschici are good places to spend the night, with excellent swimming and seafood as enticements.

The Gargano is the "spur" on the boot of Italy. It's a limestone plateau bordered on the north by beaches and lagoons and on the south by steep pine-clad cliffs and rocky coves. The interior is mountainous, with high grassy meadows, intricate agricultural terraces cultivating almonds, olives and grapevines, and upland forests of oak and beech trees. The indigenous flora and fauna are outstanding, and there are plans to turn the whole area into a national park, a move that would help protect the environment from increasing development as more and more

Pilgrims have been visiting Monte Sant'Angelo since the fifth century

summer visitors come to enjoy the lovely coast and clear seas.

Start your drive at Monte Sant'Angelo, reached via the SS89 from Manfredónia on the coast.

Monte Sant'Angelo, one of the oldest Christian shrines in Europe, is dedicated to the Archangel Michael. Hordes of devout pilgrims have been journeying here since at least the fifth century to pray at the spot where Michael is said to have appeared. His sanctuary stands on the grotto where he was sighted; you approach through superb 11th-century bronze doors made in Constantinople. The town has some interesting streets of terraced medieval houses and a fine Norman castle.

Take the SS272 north of town into the valley. At the junction, branch right onto the SS528. Follow this until you reach the Foresta Umbra visitor center.

This is an exceptionally varied and lovely stretch

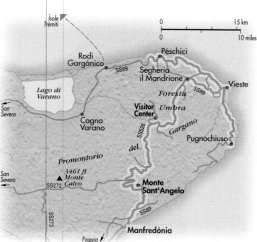

Péschici, just one of the many picturesque seaside towns along the rocky coastline of the Gargano Peninsula

through woods and meadowland and past ancient terraces. The Foresta Umbra (Forest of Shadows) stretches right across the upland heart of the Gargano. Stands of forest like this, mainly beech and oak, once covered much of Apulia. It's a wonderful wildlife habitat, home to a wide variety of animals and birds. The woods are rich in wildflowers; spring crocus gives way to numerous different orchids, and in autumn the woodland floor is carpeted with drifts of cyclamen. Foxes, wolves, deer and wild boar inhabit the deep forest, and you could easily spot woodpeckers, hawks and hoopoes. You can learn more at the visitor center. From here, easy hikes lead into the woods past a little lake and picnic tables.

Turn right onto an unclassified road running northeast and signposted "Segheria il Mandrione and Vieste." After 24 kilometers (15 miles), turn right onto the SS89 to Vieste.

Still a small fishing port, Vieste is a jolly and relaxed town with superb beaches and a range of hotels and restaurants. It's not yet swamped by international tourism, and the old center, which has narrow cobbled streets, a castle and an 11th-century cathedral, is well worth a stop. The coastline to the south is stunningly beautiful, with hidden beaches beneath high limestone cliffs and a series of watery caves and grottoes around the Testa del Gargano headland. You can take a boat trip to view them or venture farther offshore to the beautiful Trémiti Islands. Watch for the *trabuco* on Vieste's headland. This huge wooden structure, entwined with ropes and winches, is used for catching mullet; the design is said to date from Phoenician times.

Explore the road south of Vieste along the coast before retracing your route and heading north on the SS89 to Péschici.

The winding road follows more lovely coast and sandy beaches before you reach Péschici, a picturesque town tumbling down a headland to a sandy beach. It dates from the 10th century, when it was built as a defense against Saracen raids, and the claustrophobic labyrinth of alleys has a distinctly Arabian feel. Boats also run from Rodi Gargánico, farther along the coast, to the Trémiti Islands.

Vieste tourist information ✉ Piazza Kennedy ☎ 0884 708 806 🕐 Mon.–Sat. 8:30–1 and 3:30–8, Sun. 8:30–1, Jun.–Sep.
Trémiti Islands Ferries ✉ Tickets from Agenzia Sol, Via Trepiccionis, Vieste ☎ 0884 701 558 🚢 Daily departures from May to Sep.

Atmospheric lighting enhances the fascination of Matera's unique cave houses

MATERA

Matera, a UNESCO World Heritage Site, has been continuously inhabited since Paleolithic times, making it one of the world's oldest settlements. It's a provincial capital with an admirable dose of civic pride, and its *sassi* provide one of Europe's most bizarre urban features. *Sassi* are cave dwellings dug out of the sides of a ravine over the centuries. Many were inhabited until the 1960s, when the area was cleared and the people rehoused. Today, some *sassi* have been restored and people have moved back, living in very different conditions from some 40 years ago, when malaria, trachoma and dysentry were common. A road (Strada Panoramica dei Sassi) has been built through the *sassi* district, but to explore it thoroughly, you'll need to penetrate the maze of tiny streets. Be sure to see the *chiese rupestri* (rock-hewn churches), carved by monks from the eighth to the 13th centuries.

Leave time for the rest of the town, which centers around Piazza Vittorio Veneto, a lovely square. From here you can access both the *sassi* and the medieval *civita* area, whose winding streets lead to the 13th-century cathedral. Matera also boasts a superb archeological museum,

housed in the old convent of Santa Chiara. Recently restored, the collection covers local finds from the Paleolithic age to the full flowering of Greek civilization in Magna Graecia.

✚ C4

Tourist information ✉ Via de Viti de Marco 9 ☎ 0835 331 983 🕐 Mon.–Thu. 9–1 and 4–6:30, Fri.–Sat. 9–1 🚹 Guides hold keys to the churches in the *sassi;* apply at the tourist office. If approached, make sure it is an official guide wearing a badge

Museo Nazionale Domenico Ridola ✉ Via Ridola 24 ☎ 0835 310 058 🕐 Tue.–Sun. 9–7, Mon. 2–7 💲 $$$

METAPONTO

Ancient Metapontum (Metaponto) was one of the greatest of the sixth-century BC Greek cities of Magna Graecia. It was a thriving metropolis packed with temples, theaters and public buildings. Today Metaponto is a huge and confusing archeological site where you'll need a lot of imagination to visualize its heyday. Most evocative is the Tavole Paladine, a fifth-century BC temple that is dedicated to Hera and stands alone among flowery grass and oleanders. Metaponto's chief draw is the superb Museo Archeologico (Archeological Museum), which traces the history of Metapontum from its native pre-Greek civilization to its decline after Romanization. The jewelry is lovely – look for the charming headdress of gilded leaves decorated with berries and crickets (third century BC), as well as the gold bracelets and earrings. The red-and-black figured vases are very fine, and careful study of their decoration will tell you much about everyday Greek life.

➕ C4

Museo Archeologico Nazionale ✉ Via Aristea 21 ☎ 0835 745 327 🕐 Tue.–Sun. 9–7, Mon. 9–2 🎫 $$

PARCO NAZIONALE DEL POLLINO

The Parco Nazionale del Pollino (Pollino National Park), a 494,000-acre area of wild and unspoiled mountainous countryside in the southern Apennines, lies in both Basilicata and Calabria. Its highest point is Monte Pollino at 7,400 feet. The terrain varies from high mountain country through stony steppe and rich forests to gorges, river valleys, water meadows and dry river beds. The park's symbol is the Bosnian pine, a tree with scaled bark that grows on difficult terrain up to 6,000 feet; few exist elsewhere in Europe. Fascinating wildlife includes wolves, wild boar and otter; eagles, vultures and other raptors amy also occasionally be seen.

Twisting mountain roads link the scattered villages within the park, many of which are becoming popular as bases for hiking and climbing. The main villages are Terranova di Pollino, San Severino Lucano, Carbone, Latronico and Castelluccio. Even if you don't have time to explore this wonderful area, you can get a taste of its scenic grandeur from the A3 *autostrada*; a spectacular section of this freeway skirts the park's eastern edge.

➕ C4

RÉGGIO DI CALÁBRIA

Calábria's capital, an ancient Greek foundation, faces Sicily across the Straits of Messina. It's the only city of any size this far south, with a vibrancy that belies its grim reputation. Repeatedly devastated by earthquakes over the centuries, dogged by high unemployment and suffering

The head of a life-size, fifth-century BC bronze sculpture, one of the Réggio's treasures

from the octopus-like embrace of the Calabrian Mafia, physically it's a ramshackle and grubby city with a few redeeming features. But take time to stroll the superb seafront, with its Roman remains and tree-shaded garden, before heading down the main street, Corso Garibaldi, to Réggio's chief attraction, the Museo Nazionale. This wonderful collection includes material from all over Calábria and is well-presented, with plenty of English-language information. The highlights are the two antique male bronzes known as the Bronzi di Riace. These fifth-century BC sculptures were discovered underwater off the Ionian coast near Riace in 1972; after a lengthy restoration they were returned to Calábria in 1981. Naked, bearded and tautly muscled, these superb works are attributed to Phidias, the greatest sculptor of antiquity. On the top floor are canvases, primarily by southern Italian artists.

Réggio also has more shops and better bars than anywhere else in this region.

➕ C1

Tourist information ✉ Corso Garibaldi 329 ☎ 0965 892 012 🕐 Mon.–Sat. 8–1:30 and 2–8 **Museo Nazionale della Magna Graecia** ✉ Piazza de Nava ☎ 0965 812 255 🕐 Daily 9–7 (closed first and third Mon. of each month) 🎫 $$

The South

RIVIERA CALABRESE

The stretch of coast north from Réggio di Calábria is known as the Riviera Calabrese (Calabrian Riviera). It's a string of small resorts and coastal villages popular with Italian vacationers. Tropea to the north is the prettiest; this lively town is perched above golden beaches. On a clear day there are superb views of the Aeolian Islands and the cone of Stròmboli.

Don't miss the lovely church of Santa Maria dell'Isola, perched on a rocky massif near the sea, or the Norman cathedral, where you can see two unexploded American bombs dating from World War II within the walls. Farther south the coastline is more dramatic, with towering cliffs and views of Sicily. Tucked down at the shoreline lies Scilla, a picturesque village set around a castle, with a sandy beach that doubles as a fishing port at its foot. The northern end is dominated by a rock associated with the ancient Scylla of Homer's *Odyssey*, the lair of one of a pair of sea monsters. Charybdis, the other monster, in legend dwells across the Straits of Messina on Sicily.

🔰 C1

Tropea tourist information ✉ Piazza Ercole ☎ 0963 61 475 🕓 Daily 9:30–12:30 and 5–8; closed Sun. afternoon

ROSSANO

Modern Rossano is located on Calábria's east coast. It's a relaxed seaside resort with sandy beaches. Up a twisty road is old Rossano, a shabby and charming hillside town with elegant, if crumbling, 16th-century palaces and a spacious central square. From the eighth to 11th centuries Rossano was a great Byzantine center of scholarship and piety, and its greatest treasures date from this time. In the cathedral you can see a ninth-century Byzantine fresco of the Blessed Virgin Mary, while the tiny museum tucked behind contains the famous *Codex Purpureus Rossanensis* (Purple Codex). This is a sixth-century Greek manuscript written on reddish-purple parchment, from which it gets its name. The manuscript is illustrated with scenes from the gospels, and you can see how the *Last Supper* was originally depicted. From the museum, walk to ancient San Marco, a 10th-century Byzantine church, its triple-nave interior topped by five small cupolas. Few other buildings in southern Italy are so evocative.

🔰 C3

Museo Diocesano ✉ Piazza del Duomo ☎ 0983 525 263 🕓 Tue.–Sat. 9:30–12:30 and 4–6 or 7, Sun. 10–noon 🎫 $$

A cathedral dominates the old center of Tropea, a popular vacation town on the Riviera Calabrese

SORRENTO PENINSULA AND THE AMALFI COAST

One of Europe's most beautiful coastal roads runs around the Sorrento peninsula south of Naples. Every twist and turn opens up another spectaular vista of sea and cliffs, while the string of villages it links are among the most attractive and popular on all of Italy's coastline.

Castellammare di Stàbia, nearest to Naples, is an ancient spa town; its springs still draw people to the therapeutic waters. Sorrento, a good jumping-off point for Capri (see page 158), is the first of the truly charming towns along the coast. Its pretty streets, beaches, bars and restaurants have been drawing visitors for the past 200 years.

From here the main road cuts inland and south to emerge on the Amalfi side of the peninsula. Positano, the first town of any size, is a pyramid of colorful houses tumbling down the cliffs to a beach where sun worshippers share space with fishing boats. Tempting shops sell the town's famous brightly colored textiles. Bars and restaurants beckon, and boats sail to otherwise inaccessible swimming coves. To the east lies Praiano, where the cliff approaches are dotted with opulent private villas. Between here and Amalfi, you can visit the Grotta dello Smeraldo (Emerald Cave), a vividly green sea cave complete with stalagmites and stalactites. Amalfi, tucked between the mountains and the sea, is a cheerful small town whose only clue to its great past as a powerful maritime republic is the wonderful Duomo (Cathedral). Approached up a wide flight of steps, the cathedral was built in the 11th century, its bronze doors cast in Constantinople in 1066. Don't miss the 13th-century cloister known as the Chiostro del Paradiso (Cloister of Paradise), a peaceful enclave with whitewashed interlaced arches.

High above the coast east of Amalfi stands Ravello, offering perhaps the finest views of the coast. The 13th-century cathedral has a splendid pulpit donated by the Rufolo family, who also built the Villa Rufolo, where the courtyard and gardens inspired Richard Wagner's *Parsifal*. There

Amalfi cathedral's distinctive and colorful bell tower

are more gardens at the Villa Cimbrone, as well as incomparable views.

Castellammare di Stàbia ✚ A4
Tourist information ✉ Piazza Matteoti ☎ 081 871 1334 ⊙ Mon.–Sat. 9–1:30 and 4:30–7:30
Sorrento ✚ A4
Tourist information ✉ Via Luigi de Maio 35 ☎ 089 807 4033 ⊙ Mon.–Sat. 8:30–7
Positano ✚ A4
Tourist information ✉ Via Saraceno 4 ☎ 089 875 067 ⊙ Mon.–Sat. 8–2 and 3:30–8, Jul.–Aug.; 8–2, rest of year
Amalfi ✚ A4
Tourist information ✉ Corso Repubbliche Marinare 19/21 ☎ 089 871 107 ⊙ Mon.–Fri. 8:30–1:30 and 3–5:15, Sat. 8:30–12:30
Duomo di Sant'Andrea
✉ Piazza del Duomo ⊙ Daily 9:30–7, Jun.–Oct.; 9:30–5:15, rest of year. Chiostro del Paradiso: daily 9–8 ✋ $
Grotta di Smeraldo
✉ SS 163, 4 kilometers (2.5 miles) from Amalfi ⊙ Daily 9–4 ✋ $$$
Ravello ✚ A4
Tourist information ✉ Piazza Duomo 10 ☎ 089 857 977 ⊙ Mon.–Sat. 8–8
Duomo ✉ Off Piazza del Duomo ⊙ Daily 8:30–1 and 3–6:30 ✋ Free
Villa Rufolo ✉ Piazza del Duomo ☎ 089 857 096 ⊙ Daily 9–sunset ✋ $$
Villa Cimbrone ✉ Via Santa Chiara 26 ☎ 089 857 138 ⊙ Daily 9–sunset, May–Sep.; 9–6, rest of year ✋ $$

A forbidding glimpse of the crater on Vesuvius, where the ground is warm even in midwinter

VESUVIUS AND POMPEI

One of the world's best-known volcanoes, Vesuvius rises smoothly to 4,200 feet above the Bay of Naples. It has erupted more than 100 times since the Roman era, the last in 1944. You get a good view of the volcano from the Circumvesuviana railroad. Buses run up to within a half-hour's walk, which is worth it for the spectacular views and odd wisps of steam that come from the deep jumble of reddish rocks that form the crater.

Vesuvius is infamous for its devastating eruption in AD 79, when it engulfed the prosperous Roman city of Pompei (Pompeii) and neighboring Herculaneum, burying them under a thick layer of pumice and volcanic ash. Pompeii remained buried for more than 1,700 years, perfectly preserved beneath a hard layer of volcanic debris. Excavations started about 1750 and the city gradually emerged. Worth tracking down as you explore the town are the forum, theaters, covered market, bakery, laundry and numerous taverns advertising bargain prices on the walls outside.

The most interesting buildings are the houses; some are wonderfully preserved

and still decorated with wall-paintings in vivid reds and ochres. The House of the Vetii, with its lovely garden and frescoed dining room, is a highlight. Also notable is the House of the Tragic Poet, whose owners had a portrait mosaic of their dog by the front door with *cave canem* (beware of the dog) carefully inscribed.

Other houses worth seeing are the spacious House of the Faun; the House of Menander, with its elegant bath; and the Villa of the Mysteries. The villa lies outside Pompei's walls at the end of the tomb-lined Via dei Sepolcri; its rich frescoes are connected with the Dionysian cult. Magnificent statues and artifacts were found at Pompei, as were the bodies of those asphyxiated by the fumes; plaster casts of these are scattered throughout the city. Most of Pompei's artistic treasures have been relocated; you can see many at the Museo Nazionale Archeologico (see page 152) in Naples.

Vesuvius ✚ A5 🚃 Circumvesuviana railway to Ercolano; then a bus stops close to the summit
Pompei ✚ A5 ☎ 081 857 5347 🕐 Daily 8:30–7:30, Apr.–Oct.; 8:30–3:30, rest of year (last admission 90 minutes before closing) 🍴 Self-service restaurant and bar outside the forum 🚃 Circumvesuviana or FS train to Pompei Scavi Station 🎫 $$$

The Acropolis looms above the Greek city of Selinunte, Sicily

MAGNA GRAECIA

Throughout southern Italy and Sicily, you'll see ruins of great Greek temples and cities and a spectacular array of Greek artistic treasures in archeological museums. Why are they here? Where did they come from?

Greek Arrivals

Greece is mountainous country with little arable land. As the city-states grew in size and influence, they started to trade with parts of Italy and quickly realized that colonization was feasible in this flat and fertile land. Greeks moved into the modern regions of Campania, Basilicata, Calabria and Sicily in the eighth century BC, establishing a network of settlements. They absorbed the cultures and populations of the indigenous tribes and quickly established an efficient and high-yielding agricultural system. Grapes and olives were introduced, the colonies became successful, and cities such as Siracusa, Sybaris, Metapontum and Tarentum were soon richer and more sophisticated than those in Greece. The area was in every way Magna Graecia – "Greater Greece."

Decline

Like the city-states of mainland Greece, these colonies were split by internal rivalries and internecine war, uniting only when faced with the threat of outside invasion, sometimes from Greece itself. In 415 BC Siracusa and its allies trounced Athens in a great sea battle. The North African power of Carthage, founded by the Phoenicians, posed a continuous threat, often playing one of the Magna Graecia cities against the others. The colonies finally allied in the third century BC against the growing might of Rome. In 400 BC the Romans razed Sybaris, and in 211 BC the sack of Siracusa marked the effective demise of Magna Graecia.

The Legacy

You can see archeological and historical traces of these city-states all over southern Italy and Sicily. On the mainland, head for the great temples of Paestum, south of Salerno; Metapontum, with its fabulous archeological museum; or the scattered and sparse ruins of once-voluptuous Sybaris. Sicily is richest of all, with theaters at Taormina and Siracusa and wonderful temples at Segesta, Selinunte and Agrigento. Smaller sites are everywhere, and even obscure museums have superb collections of stunning Greek vases and sculpture.

SICILY AND SARDINIA

> *"I TALY'S two main islands contribute mountainous interior and beautiful coastline to enhance the rich cultural heritage of the people. "*

Snowcapped and smoking, Mount Etna's summit is a fitting backdrop for beautiful Taormina

SICILY AND SARDINIA

Sicily (Sicilia), one of the Mediterranean's largest islands, is also one of its most beautiful, with rugged mountain scenery, woodlands, a diverse coastline, and rich agricultural land producing wheat, olives, vines and citrus fruits. The eastern half is dominated by the graceful cone of Mount Etna, Europe's largest volcano, while the interior pushes north to the coast in the shape of the Monti Madonie. Good beaches are found all around the island, with some internationally renowned resorts on the east and north coasts, while the outlying islands are washed by some of the clearest waters in the Mediterranean. Sardinia (Sardegna) is only a little farther from the African coast of Tunisia than it is from the Italian mainland, making a trip here feasible only if you have plenty of time.

Sicily's Past

A succession of foreign invaders ruled this island from the fifth century BC until the process of Italian unification began in Sicily in 1860. The ancient Greeks, Carthaginians, Romans, Arabs, Normans and the Spanish all left their marks. These conquerors drained Sicily economically dry, while their rule left a legacy of resentment, oppression and insularity – an ideal breeding ground for the corruption of organized crime. Marginalized for centuries from mainstream Italy, Sicilians still see themselves as a people apart. Since World War II aid has poured in from the Italian government and the European Union, but poverty is still widespread.

Sicilians

Sicilians first and Italians second, the island's population is exuberant and outgoing. Tourism is important, and you'll find the people welcoming and friendly, although levels of accommodations and service may not be what you're used to. English is spoken in the main tourist centers and

good hotels, but otherwise very few people speak English. In remoter areas it's rare to see women on the streets or working; society is still male-dominated, with wives and daughters kept at home. Some young men consider foreign girls fair game, a point for women traveling alone to bear in mind.

When To Visit Sicily

The best time to visit Sicily is the spring, when the island is carpeted in wildflowers and the temperature ideal. Spring arrives in late February. July and August can be unbearably hot, with sirocco winds blowing in from Africa and little air-conditioning. Winters are mild on the coast, although there's snow in the interior and it can be wet

Sicily and Sardinia

A glimpse of Sardinia's Costa Smeralda, where traditional buildings mingle happily with glitzy resorts

and windy. Few tourists are around from November through February. Many coastal hotels are closed and daylight hours are short in winter.

What To See

You'll want to explore Sicily's diverse terrain, so renting a car is a good idea. Roads are generally uncrowded away from the towns, although the mountain roads can be very twisty. Sightseeing is a major attraction; Sicily has a wealth of ancient monuments, including some of the world's finest Greek archeological sites, and the museums are excellent. Later architecture is a major draw; this includes Roman mosaics, Norman churches and elegant baroque towns. Many tourists simply enjoy a beach holiday, with delicious food, hot sun and a relaxed pace of life.

Visiting Sardinia

Sardinia's main attraction is its beautiful coastline and well-organized resorts, which attract the rich and famous from all over Europe. But there's more than that to Sardinia, including archeological traces of its first endemic civilization, fine Romanesque churches built during the Pisan occupancy, a string of fortresses erected by the Genoans, and towns that are more Spanish than Italian. The island is increasingly geared to international visitors, and standards of accommodation and service are improving all the time. Spring, early summer and autumn are the best times to visit. If you want a beach vacation, summer is best for diving, sailing and windsurfing. Be sure to reserve well in advance, as Sardinia is a popular choice with mainland Italians.

Spring carpets inland Sicily with wildflowers

PALERMO

Redolent with history and filled with artistic treasures, vibrant Palermo is like no other European city. Unemployment and crime levels are high, and visitors are frequently shocked by the noise, grime and decay. But despite the dirt and chaos, Palermo is full of wonderful things to see. Few other cities have so many rich churches, dating from 12th-century Norman to 17th-century baroque. There are good museums and galleries, a lively arts scene and excellent restaurants.

Discovering Palermo

Pick up a copy of the free monthly tourist information magazine *Palermo* from the tourist office. Printed in English, it's packed with useful tips to help make Palermo more accessible, as well as arts, sports and entertainment listings. After dark, avoid the back streets and the dock and market areas, and use taxis to travel around the city. Driving in Palermo is not

recommended; traffic is chaotic, drivers are aggressive and parking spots are almost impossible to find.

The historic core of Palermo can easily be explored on foot. Indeed, to investigate the tangled lanes, walking is the only option, as the streets are too narrow for buses. Taxis are cheap and horse-drawn carriages, *carrozze*, ply the main historic center; agree on a price before your journey starts.

Shopping

Palermo has a good range of shops, including branches of nationwide department stores such as la Rinascente and Coin, and outlets for the big Italian designer names. Many stores cluster around Via Roma, Via Cavour and Viale della Libertà. Most tourists enjoy browsing in the Mercato delle Pulci (Flea Market), and take time to visit one of Palermo's food markets. Local crafts include ceramics, basketware and wrought iron, still made in the Via Cala and Via Calderai. Sculpted almond paste confectionery, called *frutta di Martorana*, is a real specialty.

Sicily and Sardinia

Entertainment and Excursions

Palermo's city streets empty early and can feel threatening late at night, although things are livelier in the newer areas. There's an excellent year-round choice of music, opera, theater, dance and open-air movies. The top venue is the Teatro Massimo, beautifully restored and reopened in 1997 after being closed for 23 years. The other main theaters are the Politeama and the Golden; both stage classical concerts. Contact tourist information offices for full details.

The quintessential Palermo entertainment is the puppet theater; you can see a performance at the Puppet Museum (see page 177) or search out the real thing at Opera dei Pupi. If time is short, take a city tour to see Palermo's high points.

Mondello

If the noise and dirt of Palermo starts to get you down, head for Mondello, a charming resort that's virtually a city suburb. Located west of Palermo beneath the bulk of Monte Pellegrino, Mondello has sandy beaches, pleasant walkways, a tiny harbor, a huge range of souvenir and food stalls, and wonderful *gelaterie* (ice-cream shops). Restaurants line the waterfront, where you can eat the freshest fish and seafood before heading to the beach for a swim. Mondello buzzes at night, with cruising cars, an animated *passeggiata* (parade) and outdoor discos.

ESSENTIAL INFORMATION

TOURIST INFORMATION
•Piazza Castelnuovo 34 ☎ 091 583 848 or 091 605 8111; fax 091 586 338
•Aeroporto Falcone Borsellino ☎ 091 591 698
•Stazione Centrale, Piazza Giulio Cesare ☎ 091 616 5914
www.regione.sicilia.it
•City tours: AMAT ☎ 091 350 415; CST ☎ 091 743 9611

URBAN TRANSPORTATION
You'll need to use buses to reach sights in the outlying areas; they are run by AMAT (☎ 091 729 1111) and cover every corner of the city. You can buy a single ticket or one valid all day; remember to validate it in the machine at the back of the bus each time you buy a new ticket. Tickets are available at AMAT sales booths at the Stazione Centrale and Piazza Verdi, where you'll see the sign "Véndita Biglietti AMAT," as well as at tobacconists and newsstands. The circular

routes served by minibuses, Linea Rossa (Red Line) and Linea Gialla (Yellow Line), cover the main tourist destinations and are useful. Taxis are inexpensive and can be hailed at stands all over the city, or you can call Autoradio Taxi (☎ 091 512 727, 513 311, 513 198, 513 374) or Radio Taxi Trinacria (☎ 091 225 460 or 091 682 5441).

AIRPORT INFORMATION
Palermo Falcone Borsellino Airport (☎ info line 091 702 0127), with national and international flights, is 19 miles west of the city center at Punta Raisa. There are no direct flights to and from the United States from Palermo or any other Sicilian airport. Buses (☎ 091 580 457) run into Palermo every 30 minutes daily from 5 a.m. until after the arrival of the last scheduled flight, a journey of 40 minutes. Buses also run twice daily to Agrigento. Taxis are available outside the airport.

CLIMATE – Average highs and lows

JAN.	FEB.	MAR.	APR.	MAY	JUN.	JUL.	AUG.	SEP.	OCT.	NOV.	DEC.
15°C	15°C	16°C	18°C	21°C	25°C	28°C	29°C	27°C	24°C	19°C	16°C
59°F	59°F	61°C	64°F	70°F	77°F	82°F	84°F	81°F	75°F	66°F	61°F
9°C	9°C	11°C	13°C	16°C	20°C	24°C	25°C	22°C	19°C	14°C	12°C
51°F	51°F	52°F	55°F	61°F	68°F	75°F	77°F	72°F	66°F	57°F	54°F

PALERMO SIGHTS

Key to symbols

➕ map coordinates refer to the Palermo map on page 174; sights below are highlighted in yellow on the map

✉ address or location ☎ telephone number

🕐 opening times 🍴 restaurant on site or nearby

Ⓜ nearest subway station 🚌 nearest bus or tram route ⛴ ferry 💵 admission charge: $$$ more than €6, $$ €3 to €6, $ less than €3 ℹ information

CAPPELLA PALATINA

The huge Palazzo dei Normanni (Norman Palace), a ninth-century Arab structure enlarged in the 12th century by the Normans, houses Sicily's regional parliament. On the first floor you'll find Palermo's most beautiful artistic gem, the tiny jewel-like Cappella Palatina, built as a private chapel for the Norman ruler Roger II in the 1130s. The apses, nave and cupola are entirely covered with iridiscent mosaics, glistening under the lights. The work of both Byzantine and local craftsmen, the mosaics show scenes from the Old and New Testaments. The chapel is dominated by a majestic Christ Pantocrator. The intricate marble floor dates from the same era, while the elaborate wooden ceiling is Arabic.

➕ A1 ✉ Piazza Indipendenza ☎ 091 705 4317 🕐 Mon.–Fri. 9–11:45 and 3–4:45, Sat. 9–11:45, Sun. 9–9:45 and noon–12:45 🚌 103, 105 💵 Free

CATTEDRALE

Palermo's Cattedrale (Cathedral) was founded in 1185 by English archbishop Roger of the Mill as a private power base. It wasn't finished for centuries, having been eclipsed by William II's magnificent cathedral at Monreale (see page 183). The lovely triple-apsed eastern end and matching towers are pure Norman, as are numerous exterior carvings and details. The dome was added in the 18th century when the interior was given a neoclassic facelift. Be sure to see the huge sarcophagi in the chapels to the left of the entrance. Here lie Sicily's great Norman rulers – Frederick II, Henry VI and Roger II.

➕ A1 ✉ Corso Vittorio Emanuele II ☎ 091 334 376 🕐 Mon.–Sat. 7–7, Sun. 8–1:30 and 4–7 🍴 'A Cuccagna, see page 211 Ⓜ Linea Rossa 💵 Free

CONVENTO DEI CAPPUCCINI

For hundreds of years, the Capuchin monks of the Convento dei Cappuccini (Capuchin Convent), on the western outskirts of Palermo, retained the right to place their dead – and many lay people as well – in the corridors beneath the church. But the bodies weren't buried in coffins; they were embalmed, dressed in clothes such as crumbling silks and dusty top hats that were provided before death, installed in niches and placed in glass cases. It's a bizarre and grotesque collection, some contorted figures fixing you with a basilisk stare, others grinning, while the various states of decomposition can be extremely unnerving.

➕ A1 ✉ Piazza Cappuccini 1 ☎ 091 212 117 🕐 Daily 9–noon and 3–5 (also 5–5:30 in summer) 🚌 327 💵 Free

GALLERIA REGIONALE DELLA SICILIA

Deep in the Kalsa district stands the imposing 15th-century Palazzo Abatellis, built from 1490 to 1495, which houses the Galleria Regionale Siciliana (Sicilian Regional Gallery). This is a lovely collection ranging from sculpture and woodcarvings to frescoes, mosaics and paintings. Look for Francesco Laurana's serene, white marble bust of Eleanor of Aragon; a clutch of paintings by Sicily's homegrown 15th-century master, Antonello da Messina; and some early 13th-century Madonnas. With their wide, dark eyes and long-fingered hands, these portraits clearly show the influence of Byzantine art.

➕ C2 ✉ Palazzo Abatellis, Via Alloro 4 ☎ 091 623 0011 🕐 Daily 9–1:30 (also Tue.–Thu. 3–7:30) Ⓜ Linea Gialla 💵 $$$

LA MARTORANA

The Norman church of La Martorana was built by ruler Roger II's admiral; its name comes from the Spanish convent that later owned it. It's easy to ignore the baroque encrustrations of the 16th-century remodeling inside and concentrate on the superb 12th-century Greek mosaics rioting over the dome and surrounding columns. The figure of Christ is surrounded by angels with splendid wings, their golds and greens highlighted by the sunlight streaming in, while the Virgin Mary and Apostles occupy the side spaces.

✚ B1 ✉ Piazza Bellini 3 ☎ 091 616 1692 ⏱ Daily 8–1 and 3:30–5, Sun. 8:30–1 🍴 'A Cuccagna, see page 211 🚊 Linea Gialla, Linea Rossa 💷 Free

MUSEO ARCHEOLOGICO

A converted church and its cloisters house Palermo's Museo Archeologico Regionale (Regional Archeological Museum). This small but excellent collection is essential viewing if you're planning on visiting Sicily's classical sites. Here are preserved wondrous fifth-century BC lion's-head waterspouts, *metopes* (stone carvings) and friezes from Selinunte temples, as well as artifacts from major Neolithic, Carthaginian, Greek and Roman Sicilian sites. A fierce bronze ram, a technical tour-de-force, comes from Siracusa; nearby you'll see Hercules grappling with a stag. Don't miss the fine Roman mosaic pavements, excavated from the center of Palermo itself.

✚ B2 ✉ Via Bara all'Olivella 24 ☎ 091 616 805 ⏱ Tue.–Sun. 8:30–1:45 (also Tue.–Fri. 3–6:45) 🚊 101, 102 💷 $$

MUSEO DELLE MARIONETTE

Puppet shows are a traditional Sicilian entertainment, usually centering on the exploits of the hero Orlando (Roland) and his struggles against the Saracens. The Museo delle Marionette (Puppet Museum) has Palermo's biggest collection of puppets, costumes and scenery. It also stages summer shows that are a great antidote to too much culture, even though it's unlikely you'll understand the rich dialect of the performers.

✚ C2 ✉ Piazzetta Niscemi 5 ☎ 091 329 060 ⏱ Mon.–Fri. 9–1 and 4–7, Sat. 9–1 🚊 103, 105 💷 $$

SAN CATALDO

The ancient church of San Cataldo, with its red domes, squats amid palm trees in the heart of the city. Built in the 12th century, it was never decorated, and its peaceful, plain interior and marble mosaic floor exude a sense of spirituality often lacking in some of Palermo's ornate baroque churches.

✚ B1 ✉ Piazza Bellini 3 ⏱ Mon.–Fri. 9–3:30, Sat. 9–12:30 🚊 Linea Gialla, Linea Rossa 💷 Free

SAN GIOVANNI DEGLI EREMITI

To appreciate the weight of Palermo's Arab-Norman legacy, visit the deconsecrated church of San Giovanni degli Eremiti (St. John of the Hermits), founded by Roger II and built in 1132. There are distinct Arab overtones in the church's five domes; it was built around an earlier mosque, part of which is still visible. It's an evocative place set amid lemon trees, with a delightful 13th-century cloister; twin columns and pointed arches echo both Arab and Norman architectural styles.

✚ A1 ✉ Via dei Benedettini ☎ 091 651 5019 ⏱ Daily 9–6:30 🚊 103, 105 💷 $

Spooky, fully clothed mummies inhabit the catacombs beneath the Convento dei Cappuccini

Sicily and Sardinia

Palermo's food markets are among the most exciting in the Mediterranean

WALK: FROM THE NORMANS TO A VIBRANT CENTER

Refer to route marked on city map on page 174.

This walk takes about 2 hours and offers you the chance to see some artistic treasures combined with a taste of Palermo's vibrant street life.

Start at the Porta Nuova (New Gate) at the west end of Corso Vittorio Emanuele II.
The New Gate was built in 1535 to commemorate Spanish ruler Charles V's Tunisian campaign; he stopped in Palermo on his way back to Spain, the only Spanish monarch to visit during the 400-year viceregal period.

Visit the Palazzo dei Normanni and the Cappella Palatina (see page 176), then continue east down Via Vittorio Emanuele II to the left of the cathedral (see page 176). Continue until you come to the Quattro Canti crossroads (see page 177). Turn right onto Via Maqueda.
The Via Maqueda was constructed in the 16th century to run straight through the old quarters of the Albergheria and the Capo. This area has changed little over the past several hundred years. Behind Via Maqueda there's a warren of narrow streets, crumbling buildings and tiny squares. You'll see evidence of World War II bomb damage, as well as houses that seem ready for

demolition. Try to ignore them and concentrate instead on the vibrant street life, surging crowds and intense atmosphere. Fifty yards along Via Maqueda on the left you'll see the Piazza Pretoria, recently cleaned and restored. The large building is the Municipio (City Hall), and the huge 16th-century church is Santa Caterina. The square's central fountain was designed in the 1500s.

Adjacent to Piazza Pretoria and also on Via Maqueda, cross Piazza Bellini to visit the churches of La Martorana (see page 176) and San Cataldo (see page 177). Cross the road and turn right a little farther down Via Ponticello, a grubby and run-down street, to reach the glorious church of Il Gesù.
Built in 1564, this church is a Sicilian baroque extravaganza of marble, relief work and wood inlay, topped by a magnificent green-and-white dome.

Continue down Via Ponticello to lively Piazza Ballarò.
Piazza Ballarò, nearby Piazza del Carmine and the surrounding streets are home to a daily food market, something you shouldn't miss. Palermo markets are among the most raucous in the Mediterranean. The stalls are piled high with a bewildering variety of meat, fish, fruit and vegetables of excellent quality and freshness. You'll find a huge choice of ready-to-go food and tiny eating places where you can lunch on local specialties such as *arancini* (see opposite), raw sea urchins, or rolls filled with spleen and liver.

Sicily and Sardinia

CUISINES OF PALERMO

Meals in Palermo and Sicily will be a highlight; possibly no other region of Italy has been so influenced by the civilizations that have lived here. Each has left ingredients, flavors and cooking methods that together make up one of the most inventive cuisines in the Mediterranean.

Main Meals

Meals follow the standard Italian pattern of *antipasto*, *primo*, *secondo* and *dolce*, and portions are large. The emphasis is on fish, although inland you'll find flavorful meat and game dishes. Pasta dishes include *spaghetti alle vongole* with tiny clams and a hint of spicy *peperoncino* (chili); *pasta con le sarde*, with a piquant sardine sauce; and *spaghetti con le seppie*, with an unctuous blackness that derives from the ink sac of the cuttlefish. *Pasta alla Norma* with eggplant, tomatoes and melted cheese is a real Palermo specialty. The main course *(secondo)* is often plain grilled fish, so a squeeze of lemon is all it needs, or a delicate *fritto misto*, deep-fried prawns and calamari. Swordfish and tuna are particularly good. Vegetable dishes are superb; be sure to sample *caponata*, a traditional vegetable stew featuring eggplant, celery, olives and capers; *zucchine in agro-dolce*, an Arab-influenced sweet-sour dish; or anything that includes huge, tender lime-green cauliflowers, a winter treat.

Snacks and Desserts

Pizza in Palermo makes an excellent snack – paper-thin, crisp and blackened at the edges from a wood-fired oven. It's a revelation to those used to the Americanized version. *Arancini*, another Sicilian specialty, are rice balls stuffed with meat sauce and peas, coated with egg and breadcrumbs, then deep-fried. *Focaccia*, a bread snack with various toppings, also makes a quick lunch. Sicilian desserts show the Arab legacy; heavy use is made of almonds and sugar, and you'll find trays of mouthwatering varieties in every *pasticceria*. *Cannoli* and *cassata Siciliana* both use ricotta cheese, heavily sweetened and studded with candied fruits and chocolate, while Sicilian *gelato* (ice cream) is some of the world's best.

Local Drinks

Wines are straightforward and often served by the carafe. If you want something special, look for the red Corvo; Etna, made from grapes grown on volcanic soil; or Donnafugata, from outside Palermo. Settle your dinner with a glass of Sicilian *amaro* (bitters). Averna, found throughout Italy, is made in Sicily, as is Limoncello, a lemon-based liqueur from the east coast.

A typical selection of fish found in Palermo restaurants

The Tempio della Concordia at Agrigento is a reminder of Sicily's fifth-century BC golden age

SICILY SIGHTS

Key to symbols

✚ map coordinates refer to the region map on page 170; sights below are highlighted in yellow on the map

✉ address or location ☎ telephone number

🕐 opening times 🍴 restaurant on site or nearby

🚌 nearest bus or tram route ⛴ ferry

💶 admission charge: $$$ more than €6, $$ €3 to €6, $ less than €3 ℹ information

AGRIGENTO

Agrigento's Greek temples and ruins once formed the Hellenistic city of Akragas, founded in the sixth century BC. The ancient city was spread along two ridges above the sea. Modern Agrigento stands on the higher ridge, with the temples known as the Valle dei Templi (Valley of the Temples) strung along the lower ridge a couple of miles down the hill. The site falls into two zones; head first for the eastern zone. Make your way along the path past the Tempio di Ercole (Temple of Hercules) to the superb Tempio della Concordia (Temple of Concord), built around 430 BC and converted to a Christian church in the sixth century, which explains why it is in such an excellent state of preservation.

Beyond the Temple of Concord stands the half-ruined Tempio di Giunone (Temple of Juno), its masonry still marked by the fire set by the Carthaginians in 406 BC. Down the hill you can explore the jumble of ruins that comprise the western zone. Here are the Tempio dei Dioscuri (the so-called Temple of Castor and Pollux) and the massive remains of the Tempio di Giove (Temple of Jupiter), the largest Doric temple ever. It was supported by huge male figures – one still lies abandoned amid the ruins.

From the temples, return back up the hill to visit the Hellenistic-Roman quarter, an excavated section of the original city, and the Museo Archeologico Regionale (Regional Archeological Museum), which has an excellent and varied collection. On the grounds you'll find the third-century BC, semicircular odeon and the lovely Norman San Nicola, a serene and solid church with a peaceful cloister.

Modern Agrigento is a mix of the medieval and baroque. Via Atanea runs through the heart of town, and off it old narrow alleys and steep stairs follow the Arabic layout past crumbling palaces to the vast cathedral, which stands at the town's highest point.

✚ C2
Tourist information ✉ Via Cesare Battisti 15
☎ 0922 204 541; www.agrigentosicilia.it
🕐 Mon.–Sat. 9–1:45 and 5–7
Valle dei Templi ✉ Via dei Templi 🕐 Daily
8:30–dusk 🍴 Bar at parking lot (summer only)
💲 $$$ (combined ticket with Museo Archeologico)
Hellenistic-Roman Quarter ✉ Via dei Templi
🕐 Daily 9–1 hour before dusk 💲 $
Museo Archeologico Regionale ✉ San Nicola,
Via dei Templi ☎ 0922 401 565 🕐 Tue.–Sat. 9–1 and
2–7:30, Sun. 9–1 💲 $$$ (combined ticket with
Valle dei Templi) 🛈 There is no English information
on any of the exhibits

CATÁNIA

Catánia, Sicily's second-largest city, is
an ancient settlement crouching in the
shadow of Mount Etna on the east coast.
Catánia makes a good base for visiting
Etna, and has some good-value hotels and
wholesome food choices. Etna's eruptions
and the 1693 earthquake have taken their
toll, leaving a largely 18th-century city
center with some fine baroque churches
and monuments. The top sites include the
Duomo (Cathedral), fronted by an
elegant piazza; the 18th-century church
of San Nicolò, Sicily's largest church; and
the Museo Civico, housed in the Castello
Ursino. Take care in this area, as the
castle is in a grim neighborhood. On a
lighter note, Catánia also has one of
Sicily's biggest and most ebullient food
markets.

✚ E2
Tourist information ✉ Via D Cimarosa 10
☎ 095 730 6211; www.turismo.catania.it
🕐 Mon.–Sat. 9–7, Sun. 10–6
Duomo ✉ Piazza del Duomo ☎ 095 320 044
🕐 Daily 8–noon and 5–7 💲 Free
San Nicolò ✉ Piazza Dante 🕐 Daily 8–noon
💲 Free 🛈 Restoration is ongoing (opening times
may vary)
Museo Civico ✉ Castello Ursino, Piazza Federico di
Svevia ☎ 095 345 830 🕐 Closed for renovation
💲 Free

CEFALÙ

Cefalù, on the northern coast, is an
ancient port with a strong sense of
identity. Its tangle of medieval streets
were built in the shadow of a huge crag,
and it offers good beaches, a lovely
coastline and better-than-average shops
and restaurants. Spend time exploring the
narrow alleys that lead down to the old
port before wandering up Corso Ruggero
to the palm-fringed Piazza del Duomo,
dominated by the magnificent Duomo
(Cathedral). Built by Norman ruler Roger
II in 1131, this beautiful building is a
fusion of Arab, Norman and Byzantine
styles, the different architectural elements
heavily influenced by the craftsmen who
built it. As much fortress as cathedral, its
twin towers and honey-colored facade
soar above the historic town. The
shadowy interior has surging columns and
glittering gold mosaics, dominated by the
huge image of Christ Pantocrator, his
right hand raised in blessing.

For more artistic treasures, head for
the Museo Mandralisca; its chief treasure
is the fine *Portrait of an Unknown Man*,
painted by Sicilian-born Antonello da
Messina in 1465. Energetic visitors can
climb the brooding outcrop above the
town to enjoy fine views and the ruins of
the fifth-century BC Temple of Diana.

You also could use Cefalù as a suitable
base for exploring the Madonie
Mountains, a magnificent upland area
with picturesque villages, high peaks and
excellent hiking.

✚ C3
Tourist information ✉ Corso Ruggero 77
☎ 0921 421 050 🕐 Mon.–Fri. 8–2:30 and 3:30–8,
Sat. 9–1 and 3:30–8, Sun. 9–1:30 🚢 To Aeolian
Islands
Duomo ✉ Piazza del Duomo ☎ 0921 922 021
🕐 Daily 8–noon and 3:30–8 💲 Free
Museo Mandralisca ✉ Via Mandralisca 13
☎ 0921 421 547 🕐 Daily 9–7 💲 $$

ENNA

The ancient mountain stronghold of
Enna stretches along a 3,000-foot-high
ridge in the hills of inland Sicily. Just
below the highest point stands the castle,
built by Frederick II in the 14th century, a
massive fortress with towers that offer
magnificent views over Enna and the
rugged interior landscape. From here Via
Roma, the main street, runs down the

Sicily and Sardinia

ridge to Piazza Vittorio Emanuele, packed with crowds during the evening *passeggiata*. Enna's Duomo (Cathedral) partly dates from 1307, and you can see its treasures in the Museo Alessi. The nearby Museo Archeologico has some fine Greek vases from the surrounding area. Spend time wandering along the promenade; from here hills stretch out in the distance, with the tumbling ochre-colored village of Calascibetta in the foreground.

➕ D2

Tourist information ✉ Via Roma 413
☎ 0935 528 288 🕐 Mon.–Sat. 9–1 and 3:30–6:30
Duomo ✉ Piazza Mazzini, Via Roma 🕐 Daily 9–1 and 4–7 🎫 Free
Museo Civico Alessi ✉ Piazza Mazzini, Via Roma ☎ 0935 503 165 🕐 Daily 8–8 🎫 $$
Museo Archeologico Varisano ✉ Piazza Mazzini, Via Roma ☎ 0935 528 100 🕐 Daily 9 to 1 hour before dusk 🎫 $

ÉRICE

A twisting road winds up to lovely Érice, a tiny hilltop town with sweeping views over the port of Trápani and its surrounding salt flats to the Isole Égadi (Égadi Islands) off the coast. It's easy to escape the throngs of summer visitors to wander through the pebbled streets and tiny piazzas, pausing to peek at the myriad courtyards bright with flowering tubs. Érice was ancient Eryx; the temple of Aphrodite attracted worshippers from all over the Mediterranean. Succeeding waves of Carthaginian, Roman, Arab and Norman invaders settled here. Visitors can explore Roger II's Castello di Vénere, built on the site of the ancient temple. There are aged walls, towers and gates, some lovely churches, a 14th-century Duomo (Cathedral), a small museum and a wooded public garden, but your chief memories will be of winding alleyways and superb views. Have a drink in the pretty Piazza Umberto, where you also can sample some of the almond-based sweetmeats, *dolce di badia*, for which the town is renowned.

➕ A3

Tourist information ✉ Viale Conte Pepoli 11
☎ 0923 869 388 🕐 Mon.–Fri. 9–1
Castello di Vénere ✉ Via Castello di Vénere
🕐 Daily 8–2 and 3–6:30, but often closed 🎫 Free
Duomo ✉ Piazza Matrice 🕐 Daily 10–noon and 3–6 🎫 Free
Museo Comunale ✉ Piazza Umberto I
☎ 0923 860 048 🕐 Mon.–Fri. 8:30–1:30 (also Mon. and Fri. 2:30–5:30), Sun. 9–2 🎫 Free

Érice's ancient castle perches above the coastal plain

Sicily and Sardinia

MONREALE

Above the slopes of the Conca d'Oro (Golden Shell) valley, some 8 kilometers (5 miles) from Palermo, stand the small town of Monreale and its Norman Duomo (Cathedral). Here you'll find the world's most extraordinary and accomplished Christian mosaics. The cathedral's ceilings and walls glitter with brilliant splendor. It was built from 1174 to 1184 by the Norman King William II as a direct challenge to Palermo's cathedral, which was erected at the same time by William's powerful rival, the archbishop of Palermo. Completed in only 10 years, the result is an astonishingly homogenous building, its mosaics almost certainly the work of Greek and Byzantine craftsmen. The interior is dominated by the great Christ Pantocrator, while the Madonna and Child, angels and saints are ranked beneath this powerful image. The side apses portray St. Peter and St. Paul and their martyrdoms, while the nave and aisles are covered with gloriously detailed mosaics showing scenes from the Old and New Testaments. Outside the cathedral a side entrance leads to the superb Chiostro dei Benedettini (Cloisters), part of William's original Benedictine monastery. The elegant arcades are supported by 216 columns, with no two capitals the same.
➕ B3

Duomo ✉ Piazza del Duomo ☎ 091 640 4413
🕐 Daily 8–noon and 3:30–6:30 🖐 Take plenty of change for the coin-operated light switches and wear modest clothing

Chiostro dei Benedettini ✉ Piazza del Duomo
🕐 Mon.–Sat. 9–noon and 4–7, Sun. 9–12:30 🖐 $

NOTO

In 1693 a severe earthquake devastated much of eastern Sicily, destroying churches, houses and entire communities. The town of Noto was completely flattened, but within weeks construction had started on what was to become one of Sicily's most beguiling baroque townscapes – a new town on a new site. Sicilian-Spanish aristocrat Giuseppe Lanza was in charge of the plan, and it

was his vision that produced today's town.

Noto was deliberately designed so that the political and religious buildings stood apart from the residential streets. The Corso Vittorio Emanuele is the finest of the streets; it's lined with graceful *palazzi* with sumptuously decorated facades. It leads to the Piazza del Municipio, a harmonious tree-shaded square lined with fine buildings. It's also the site of the twin-towered cathedral, much restored since the collapse of its dome in 1996. Stabilization work is ongoing. West of the square is the eccentrically decorated Palazzo Villadorata, with galloping horses and plump cherubs. Spend time wandering the side streets, where you'll find architectural delights on all corners.
➕ E1

Tourist information ✉ Piazza XVI Maggio
☎ 0931 573 779 🕐 Mon.–Sat. 8–2 and 3:30–7, Apr.–Sep.; Mon.–Sat. 9–1:30, rest of year

PIAZZA ARMERINA AND VILLA IMPERIALE

The pleasant town of Piazza Armerina stands in the wooded hills of the southern interior, a mixture of narrow streets and handsome squares with an elegant cathedral and some attractive, if crumbling, churches and palaces. A few miles southwest of town in the hamlet of Casale, a wealthy Roman (possibly Maximianus Herculeus, co-emperor with Diocletian) built a vast and grand villa in the heart of the country. The early fourth-century structure was probably designed as a hunting lodge, a theory borne out by the astounding mosaics that adorn virtually every floor. They show a wide variety of animals and birds, many native to Africa, which tie in with the African-Roman style of the compositions. Around the peristyle (courtyard) is a wide corridor decorated featuring a lively hunting scene with tigers, elephants and sea creatures. The highlight is a pavement adorned with 10 bikini-clad girls engaged in sporting activities; the winner, with her triumphant smirk and laurel wreath, is easy to spot.
➕ D2

Villa Imperiale ☎ 0935 680 036 🕐 Daily 8 or 9–6:30 or 7:30 🍴 Cafeteria and bar open May–Oct. 🖐 $$

Slopes beneath the summit of one of the world's most active volcanoes, Mount Etna

DRIVE: THE SLOPES OF MOUNT ETNA

Duration: 5 to 6 hours

This drive takes you on a tour of 10,902-foot Mount Etna, with an opportunity to ascend as high as possible toward the summit of one of the world's largest and most active volcanoes. You'll drive through countryside graced with groves of citrus and fig trees, forests of chestnut and oak, and wonderful and ever-changing views of the mountain.

For all its grandeur, Mount Etna is little more than 60,000 years old – a mere stripling in geological terms. Its first recorded eruption was in 475 BC. Since then there have been 90 major eruptions, the worst in 1669, when a fissure opened on the mountain's flank and a stream of magma engulfed Catánia, 40 kilometers (25 miles) away. Ash was thrown as far as 100 kilometers (60 miles), and in places the lava took seven years to cool completely. Etna last erupted in 1991 and was

dangerously active during 1992, when streams of lava destroyed local roads and threatened villages. In early 1999 there was enough activity that planes had to change their flight paths, and January 2000 saw another dramatic eruption.

> *Start your drive at Taormina (see page 188) and take the SS114 south toward Catánia. Turn right onto the SS120 (signposted Linguaglossa) at Fiumefreddo di Sicilia.*

Linguaglossa is the main tourist center on Etna's northern slopes. In winter it's packed with skiers who base themselves here to use the lifts at Piano Provenzana, farther up the mountain. In summer it's a quiet and attractive town surrounded by pine forests.

> *Continue on the SS120 to Randazzo, well worth a stop.*

As the crow flies, Randazzo is the town closest to Etna's summit and has been frequently threatened by lava flows, although never engulfed. The 1981 eruption came very close, and you can see the flow on the road near town. Built almost entirely of lava, Randazzo's gloomy medieval heart is, in fact, a reconstruction. The town was one of the

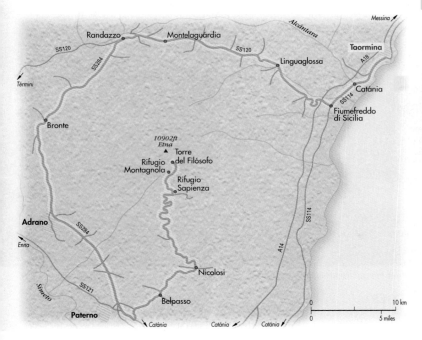

main German defensive positions during their 1943 defense of Sicily against the Allies in World War II and was heavily bombed.

A short distance beyond Randazzo, fork left onto the SS284 toward Bronte.
The road climbs steadily from here, and you'll approach ever closer to the lava flows as you drive through woods of walnut and chestnut trees. Bronte was founded in 1535, and many of its churches date from this time. Today it's surrounded by pistachio-nut plantations; almost 85 percent of Italy's production comes from this vicinity.

Continue on the SS284 to Adrano; the road bypasses the town, but you can detour to visit it.
Founded by the Greeks, Adrano has a solid medieval castle and a clutch of churches (the nicest is the Chiesa Madre, which stands next to the castle).

Continue on the SS284 to the major junction with the SS121 at Paterno. Leave the main road here and take the unclassified road that climbs up Mount Etna, signposted Belpasso and Nicolosi.
Nicolosi, another winter ski resort, marks the start of steeper roads leading up toward the summit. The road climbs up grassy slopes

and through woods before emerging into the weird volcanic landscape. Here the slopes are dotted with spent craters and black-and-gray mounds of volcanic debris. The road ends at Rifugio Sapienza, 4,600 feet below the summit. There's a place here for overnight stays, as well as restaurants and souvenir shops.

You can continue farther up Etna, either by walking on a rough track (six tough hours), or by taking am off-road vehicle. The cable car runs (weather permitting) as far as Rifugio Montagnola, from where jeeps and a guide take you as far as the Torre del Filósofo. Wear sturdy shoes or boots and glasses to keep the flying grit out of your eyes, and take plenty of warm and waterproof clothing. At this height you'll find yourself in a lunar landscape; no vegetation can compete with the folds and craters of black, gray and red lava. Farther up the southeast crater of Etna smokes gently; the main crater is behind it. At this altitude you may see gaseous explosions, rock showers and molten lava.

Nicolosi tourist information ✉ Vittorio Emanuele II 45 ☎ 095 914 488 ◷ Mon.–Sat. 9–1 and 4–7:30, May–Oct.; 8:30–1, rest of year
Etna Park Centre ✉ Via Etnea 107 ☎ 095 821 111

The architectural perfection of the Greek temple at Segesta is like a dream from the classical age

SEGESTA

Standing gloriously alone on a windswept hillside, the luminous Greek temple of Segesta is probably the most evocative of all Sicily's great Hellenistic monuments. The city of Segesta flourished as early as the 12th century BC, became Greek in the fifth century BC and spent the following centuries fighting other Greek settlements and allying itself with Carthage. It was eventually overtaken by the city of Selinus to the south. All that remains is its glorious unfinished temple and hillside theater, although excavation work has been ongoing since 1987. From a distance the temple appears complete, its 36 columns, entablature and pediment all intact. Venture closer and you'll see the columns are unfluted and there's no interior *cella* (the area delineated by the outer columns), while the stone building studs have never been removed. Unfinished and romantic, the haunt of birds and lizards, it embodies the classical dream. On a hillside to the east stands the second-century BC theater, a graceful white shell hewn out of the living rock, with breathtaking views across the hills to the sea.

✚ B3 ☎ 0924 952 356 ⊙ Daily 9–1 hour before dusk 🍴 Bar/cafeteria 🚌 Half-hourly shuttle bus service to theater in summer months 🚹 $$

ℹ️ Segesta stages classical Greek and Roman drama at the theater during the summer. For further details ☎ 0924 950 012

SELINUNTE

The Greek city of Selinus (modern Selinunte), founded in the seventh century BC, reached its peak in the fifth century BC, the era from which the greatest of its temples date. Constantly at loggerheads with its northern neighbor Segesta, it was attacked by Segesta's ally Carthage, which sacked this powerful city in 250 BC. Selinus never really recovered; time and repeated earthquakes did the rest, and today it remains a vast jumble of ruins from which surviving temples soar. Nobody knows to which gods the temples were dedicated, so they are designated by letters. The site is huge, and you'll need comfortable shoes and stamina to explore it thoroughly. Pick up a plan from the tourist office outside the gates of the archeological park before you start. Temples E, F and G stand amid the wild parsley that gave Selinus its name. The reconstructed columns of E shine against the sky, with the sea behind them. A mile or so away and down by the sea lies the acropolis, as well as five additional temples, stretches of well-preserved streets and massive fifth-century BC walls. Climb to temple C at the highest point; from its 14 standing columns you can gaze over this once-mighty city to the sea.

B2

Tourist information ✉ Entrance to Acheological Zone ☎ 0924 46 251 🕐 Daily 8–8, May–Sep.; Mon.–Sat. 9–8, Sun. 9–noon and 3–5, rest of year
Parco Archeologico ☎ 0924 46 277 🕐 Daily 9–1 hour before dusk, May–Sep.; 8–1 hour before dusk, rest of year. Tickets are issued up to two hours before dusk 🎫 $$

SIRACUSA

Ancient and captivating Siracusa (Syracuse) grew up around the eighth century BC on a coastal island with two natural harbors. By the fifth century BC, it had grown to become the most powerful Greek settlement in the Mediterranean. Glorious centuries followed until Syracuse fell to Rome in 214 BC; it later became a prominent early Christian city, only to suffer successive waves of Arab, Norman and Spanish invaders. Much was destroyed in the 1693 earthquake; the subsequent rebuilding has shaped the existing glorious city. The main sights fall neatly into two areas: Ortigia, the old town on the island, linked for centuries to the mainland by a bridge; and the archeological zone, with its excavations and museum.

On Ortigia, head first to the Piazza del Duomo, an exquisite elongated square lined with graceful baroque buildings and dominated by the sumptuous facade of the Duomo (Cathedral). Its interior is unique; embedded in the walls you'll see massive columns, the remains of the original Greek temple around which the cathedral was built. No other building gives a better idea of the weight of Syracuse's history. Head next for the Museo Bellomo, housed in a Renaissance palace; highlights include Antonello da Messina's serene *Annunciation* and a vigorous Caravaggio showing the burial of St. Lucy, Syracuse's patron saint.

Other sights on Ortigia include the massive ruins of the Tempio di Apollo and the Fontana di Aretusa (Arethusa's Fountain), the spring which attracted the first citizens to Ortigia. North of the city center is the Parco Archeologico (Archeological Park); the park's highlight is the Teatro Greco (Greek Theater), the most complete theater in the ancient Greek world. This 15,000-seat auditorium is carved from living rock and has sublime views over the city and sea. Wander through the adjacent *latomia* (pits), the quarries which provided the building stone for the ancient city, now a verdant oasis of olive and lemon trees. Here you'll see the oddly shaped cave known as the Orecchio di Dionisio (Dionysius' Ear), while nearby is the vast Roman amphitheater. Outside the park, take in the Basilica di San Giovanni, from which there is access to an underground catacomb system, where Christians were buried beginning around AD 200. Leave time for the splendid Museo Nazionale Archeologico (National Archeological Museum), where English labels guide you through the superb, if daunting, collections. Don't miss the *Venus Landolina*, a decadent goddess rising from the sea. Also outstanding are some *kouroi*, naked athletes dating from the fifth century BC.

E1

Tourist information ✉ Via San Sebastiano 43 (Archeological Zone) ☎ 0931 67 710 🕐 Mon.–Fri. 8:30–1:30 and 3:30–6:30, Sat. 8:30–1, May–Sep.; Mon.–Sat. 8:30–1:30 (times may be erratic), rest of year ✉ Via Maestranza 33 (Ortigia) ☎ 0931 65 201 🕐 Mon.–Sat. 8:30–2 and 4:30–7:30, Sun. 8:30–2, May–Sep.; Mon.–Sat. 8:30–2 and 4:30–7 (times may be erratic), rest of year
Duomo ✉ Piazza del Duomo 🕐 Daily 8–noon and 4–7 (times may be erratic) 🎫 Free
Museo Bellomo ✉ Via Capodieci 14 ☎ 0931 69 617 🕐 Tue.–Sat. 9–7, Sun. 9–2 🎫 $
Parco Archeologico ✉ Viale Augusto-Largo Paradiso ☎ 0931 66 206 🕐 Daily 9–1 hour before dusk 🍴 Bars and cafeterias outside park entrance 🚌 4, 5, 12 from city center 🎫 $$$
Basilica di San Giovanni ✉ Via San Giovanni 🕐 Daily 9–6, mid-Mar. to mid-Nov. (by guided tour only in English); 9–1 and 3–6, rest of year 🚌 4, 5, 12 from city center 🎫 $$
Museo Nazionale Archeologico ✉ Viale Teocrito 66 ☎ 0931 464 022 🕐 Tue.–Sat. 9–1 and 3–5, Sun. 9–1 🎫 $$

Etna is framed by the stage at the well-preserved Greco-Roman theater at Taormina

TAORMINA

Taormina draws visitors from all over the world, attracted by its sublime location, mild climate and excellent facilities. There are more good hotels here than anywhere else in Sicily, plus elegant shops and good restaurants.

Taormina tumbles down steep cliffs to a clutch of tiny beaches and enchanting islets and headlands, while to the southwest rises the graceful sweep of smoldering Mount Etna, a fitting backdrop for the town's lush subtropical vegetation, palm trees and cascades of bougainvillea. It's the ideal spot for a stopover, a chance to unwind and experience its charm after the tour buses and day excursions have departed.

The main street, Corso Umberto I, runs from one end of the walkable town center to the other. It's lined with 15th- to 19th-century palazzi and punctuated by the cathedral, churches and tiny piazzas. Piazza IX Aprile, at the halfway point, is a good place to pause at an outdoor café and enjoy the splendid views of Etna and the bay. Farther east, the Corso leads to Via Teatro Greco, which offers access to Taormina's main draw, a Greco-Roman theater carved out of the hillside with a superlative backdrop of sea, coast and mountains. The theater dates mainly from first-century Roman adaptations of the original third-century BC Greek construction, and you can climb up and down the tiers of seats and explore the backstage areas.

Down the hill below the theater, don't miss the Villa Comunale (Giardino Trevelyan), a lovely English-inspired park above the sea. Taormina's beaches lie far below the city center in outlying Mazzarò; the best way to reach them is to take the *funivia* (cable car) from Via L Pirandello at the east end of town.

For the energetic, there are some good hikes around town; you could walk up to the medieval castle above Taormina or hike to the tiny hill village of Castelmola.
✚ E2

Tourist information ✉ Palazzo Corvaja, Piazza Vittorio Emanuele II ☎ 0942 23 243; www.gate2taormina.com 🕐 Mon.–Sat. 8:30–2 and 4–7 (also Sun. 9–1, Apr.–Oct.)

Teatro Greco ✉ Via Teatro Greco ☎ 0942 23 220 🕐 Daily 9–1 hour before dusk 🛈 Contact the tourist office for details about Jul. and Aug. festivals

Villa Comunale ✉ Via Bagnoli Croce 🕐 Daily dawn–dusk 🛈 Contact the tourist office for details about summer events

Funivia ✉ Via L Pirandello ☎ 0942 23 906 🕐 Daily 8:30 a.m.–1 a.m., Apr.–Sep.; 8:30–8:15, rest of year

THE MAFIA

As a tourist in Sicily, you will remain untouched by the tentacles of the Mafia. But this mysterious criminal fraternity is inextricably linked with most aspects of Sicilian life; its members are *uomini d'honore* (men of honor) who live by a code of silence (*omertà*).

Top: The code of silence shrouds Mafia killings
Inset: Lucky Luciano

Beginnings

The Mafia goes back hundreds of years to Bourbon times, when ex-bandits were recruited to "police" the interior, taking payments from colleagues and acting as middlemen between landowners and peasants. Bound together by ties of self-interest, they grew rich and powerful and established a semi-formal organization shrouded in secrecy. They filled the gap between Sicilians and authority, whether that authority came from the state, foreign rulers or absentee landowners. "Families" emerged, their members not always blood relations, headed by a *capo* (godfather). Each took its name from the village under its control and formed alliances with other families for the purpose of business.

The 20th Century

During the 1930s, Mussolini was determined to break the power of the Mafia. He might have succeeded but for World War II. Before the Sicilian landings in 1943, the Allies had only one source of intelligence and local support – the American Mafia, formed from among the thousands of Sicilians who had emigrated to America in the early 20th century. American *capi*, such as Lucky Luciano, provided the introductions in Sicily so vitally needed for the invasion, but at the same time succeeded in ensuring the re-emergence of the Mafia as a powerful force in the postwar Allied military government. During the second half of the century, Mafia tentacles spread everywhere – into politics, construction, and arms and drug dealing. Immensely rich, the organization dealt brutally with anyone who stood in its way. In 1982 General della Chiesa was murdered, and in 1992 all Italy was greatly shocked by the killings of Giovane Falcone, a much respected magistrate, and Judge Paolo Borsellino.

The Future

Recent years have seen arrests of leading *capi*, while former Mafia members such as Tommaso Buscetta have fingered politicians, including Giulio Andreotti and prime minister Silvio Berlusconi. The fight continues, as do the murders, with five people gunned down in a Sicilian bar in early 1999. There is hope that as ordinary Sicilians' attitudes change, the change may finally defeat *la piovra* (the octopus).

Mosaics decorate the cathedral at Cágliari

SARDINIA SIGHTS

Key to symbols

⊞ map coordinates refer to the region map on page 171; sights below are highlighted in yellow on the map

⊠ address or location ☎ telephone number

🅾 opening times 🍴 restaurant on site or nearby

⛴ ferry 🎟 admission charge: $$$ more than €6, $$ €3 to €6, $ less than €3 🛈 information

CÁGLIARI

Sardinia's capital is situated in the southern part of the island. The hinterland is a bird-rich network of marshes and lakes, and in the foreground is the busy Golfo di Cágliari. Despite roughly a quarter of a million residents, Cágliari's center is remarkably compact, the Castello district containing all the main sights. This historic area retains its defensive walls; they include the Torre del Elefante (Elephant's Tower), complete with a statue of an elephant on the facade, and the Torre di San Pancrazio (St. Pancras' Tower). Both were erected in 1305 by the Pisans after they captured the city from the Genoese. The best approach to the Castello today is through the Bastione San Remy; this Spanish-built defensive wall was transformed in the 20th century into a wide esplanade, and it's an ideal location to admire views over the city, port and lagoons. Walk from here to Piazza Palazzo, Castello's main square. Here

you'll find the Cattedrale (Cathedral), first built in the 12th century by the Pisans. The pulpits and lions guarding the entrance are Pisan, although the Romanesque-style facade was added in the 1930s. The interior contains the tombs of the princes of the House of Savoy.

Continue north and you'll come to the Cittadella dei Musei, a modern complex converted from an old arsenal, which now houses Cágliari's main museums. The pick of these is the Museo Archeologico (Archeological Museum), where there's plenty of information on the enigmatic Nuraghic culture. This indigenous civilization, traces of which you'll see all over the island, thrived between 1500 and 500 BC. The bronze votive statues depicting warriors, athletes, workers, animals and other subjects are the main source of information about this culture. The nearby Museo Cardu has a quirky collection of Oriental art, mainly from Thailand, presented to the city in 1917 by a Cágliari native who worked at the Siamese court. More appealing is the small Pinacoteca Nazionale (National Gallery), with Italian paintings dating mainly from the 15th and 16th centuries. Outside the Castello district, head for the church of San Saturnino. Recently restored, this is one of Sardinia's oldest Christian buildings, dating from the fifth century and enlarged in the 11th.

Across town are the second-century Anfiteatro Romano (Roman

Amphitheater) and the Orto Botanico (Botanical Garden), a lovely green oasis filled with 500 varieties of trees, shrubs and tropical plants.

➕ B1

Tourist information ✉ Piazza Matteoti 9
☎ 070 669 255 🕐 Mon.–Fri. 8:30–7:30, Sat. 8:30–1:30
Cattedrale ✉ Piazza Palazzo 🕐 Daily 8–noon and 4–7 💰 Free
Museo Archeologico ✉ Cittadella dei Musei
☎ 070 684 000 🕐 Tue.–Sun. 9–8 💰 $$
Museo Civico d'Arte Orientale Stefano Cardu
✉ Cittadella dei Musei ☎ 070 651 888 🕐 Tue.–Sun. 9–1 and 4–8, Apr.–Oct.; Tue.–Sun. 9–1 and 3:30–7:30, rest of year 💰 $
Orto Botanico ✉ Viale Fra Ignazio 13 ☎ 070 675 3501 🕐 Daily 8:30–1 and 3–6:30 💰 $
Pinacoteca Nazionale ✉ Cittadella dei Musei
☎ 070 674 054 🕐 Daily 9–8 💰 $
San Saturnino ✉ Piazza San Cosimo ☎ 070 674 054 🕐 Daily 10–noon 💰 Free

CALA GONONE

Cala Gonone lies on one of Sardinia's loveliest stretches of mountainous coastline. This once secluded tiny village on the east coast has plenty of hotels, villas and restaurants. There's still a feeling of seclusion, though, and it's a good place to enjoy the spectacular beauty of the area. The maquis shrub-covered white cliffs are pitted with grottoes and sea caves, while tiny secluded coves offer lovely swimming. Take a boat trip to visit the most scenic. Cala Luna and Cala Sisine would be good choices, with wonderful views of the deep gorges that cut through the 3,000-foot-high mountains en route. Don't miss a trip to the Grotta del Bue Marino, said to be one of the last refuges of the Mediterranean monk seal. The cave itself, a luminous cavern forested with stalactites and stalagmites, is astonishing.

➕ B2

CASTELSARDO

Castelsardo occupies the hill around the massive castle built in the 13th and 14th centuries by the Genoese, who founded the little town in 1102. Once known as Castelgenovese after its

Elephant Rock, a bizarre natural rock formation

founders, the name was changed again in 1448 to Castelaragonese, after the Spanish conquerors, and then to Castelsardo in 1776.

Visitors are drawn here by the little handicraft and souvenir shops lining the narrow streets – palm-leaf baskets are the local specialty. You can learn more about this traditional handicraft in the Museo dell'Intreccio (Museum of Wickerwork), which occupies the old castle. It's also worth the climb for the lovely views from the terraces, with Corsica visible on a clear day. The town's Cattedrale (Cathedral), perched on the edge of the cliff, dates from the 17th century. Inside you can see the Madonna degli Angeli (Madonna of the Angels), a much-venerated, 15th-century icon created by a local artist. If you're driving, you'll notice a strange rock formation outside town. This is the Roccia dell'Elefante (Elephant Rock), a bizarre formation wind-sculpted over the centuries into the shape of an elephant with its trunk raised.

➕ A3

Tourist information ✉ Pro Loco, Castelsardo
☎ 079 471 500 🕐 Mon.–Sat. 8–noon and 3–6, May–Sep. ℹ The festival *Lunissanti* is held on Easter Mon.
Museo dell'Intreccio ✉ Castella dei Doria, Via Marconi ☎ 079 471 380 🕐 Daily 3–8:30, Jun.–Aug.; 3–7:30, Apr.–May; 3–6:30, Mar. and Oct.; 3–5:30, rest of year (closed Mon., Oct.–Mar.) 💰 $
Cattedrale di Sant'Antonio Abate ✉ Via Seminario
🕐 Daily 8–6 💰 Free

Luxury yachts are an everyday sight from the picturesque streets of the resort of Porto Cervo

COSTA SMERALDA

Until the early 1960s, the northeastern-most corner of Sardinia was a lonely and idyllic stretch of undiscovered coast. In 1962 the Consorzio Costa Smeralda (Emerald Coast Consortium), headed by the Aga Khan, was formed. Its plan was to turn the area into the Mediterranean's smartest playground, complete with luxury hotels, opulent villas, yachting marinas and excellent sporting facilities. Money poured in, hotels, restaurants and designer shops opened, and the rich followed.

Today, the heart of the Emerald Coast is Porto Cervo and Porto Rotondo, two

planned villages centered around marinas, where you'll see some of the world's most expensive yachts. Construction is done with local materials, and the buildings combine different architectural elements found all over the Mediterranean. Each village is surrounded by indigenous trees and draped in cascades of flowering shrubs. Chic, wealthy and tasteful, the development perfectly fulfills its aim, but loses points on charm and local color. If you plan to stay, it's easy to fall into the sybaritic life and fill your day with gentle strolling and crowd-watching, while swimming and perfecting your tan. There's an excellent golf course and a full summer program of sporting events. For shoppers, the trendy boutiques and designer showrooms of Porto Cervo will be a draw, and there are plenty of expensive and tempting bars and restaurants.

Not all this lovely area is developed, however, you'll find wonderful beaches and laid-back resorts farther along the coast at places such as Santa Teresa Gallura, a small 17th-century town with an active fishing fleet, Punta Falcone, Capo Testa and La Marmorata.

Off the northern coast lies the archipelago of La Maddalena, a group of seven islands with fabulous beaches. Giuseppe Garibaldi, who played a key role in Italy's unification, lived for many years on the island of Caprera and is buried there. Maddalena and Caprera are joined by a bridge, and a scenic road runs around Maddalena, with views of the other islands and Corsica.

Farther east, villages like Cannigione, on the Golfo di Arzachena, also are still relatively quiet.

La Maddalena 🔀 B3
Tourist information ✉ Via XX Settembre 24
☎ 0789 736 321 🕐 Daily 8–8, May–Oct.; Mon.–Fri. 8–2, rest of year

GENNARGENTU

The Monti del Gennargentu (Gennargentu Mountains) lie at the heart of Sardinia's rugged interior. Now

preserved within Parco Nazionale del Gennargentu, a huge national wilderness park, the region contains Sardinia's highest peak, Punta La Marmora (6,052 feet), which rises above these lonely and unspoiled uplands.

Small towns are located throughout the area; isolated and self-contained, these farming villages are home to generous people whose pattern of life has scarcely changed over hundreds of years. Feast days and festivals with traditional celebrations are the best places to see traditional dress being worn.

Driving is the only way to explore this fascinating area, basing yourself perhaps at Nuoro, an inland city situated on a plateau beneath Monte Ortobene. From here you can easily reach the wilderness park, which offers excellent hiking and is home to such wildlife as pine martens, wild boar, mouflon, griffon vultures and eagles. 🔀 B2

Nuoro tourist information ✉ Piazza Italia 19
☎ 0784 32 307; www.parks.it 🕐 Daily 9–1 and 4–6:30, May–Oct. 🛈 Further information is available from the World Wildlife Fund office, Piazza Santa Maria delle Neve 8, Nuoro (☎ 0784 328 88)

GIARA DI GESTURI

Strange basalt plateaus, known as *giare*, are found all over Sardinia. The Giara di Gesturi is one of the largest. It's an extensive plain more than 12 kilometers

Despite the development, quiet corners can still be found on the Costa Smeralda

(7 miles) across, and its basalt outcrops, covered in maquis and wildflowers, appear amid huge forests of cork oaks. The plateau is home to a tiny native wild horse, which was once found all over the island.

Marshy areas form after rain, making the Giara a favorite feeding ground in spring for migratory birds. To the southeast lies Su Nuraxi, the most extensive and oldest Nuraghic complex in Sardinia. Built by the indigenous population around 1500 BC, the site comprises a fortress structure surrounded by living areas and defensive walls. It was probably inhabited by the Sards and later the Carthaginians for 2,000 years, until it was covered with earth around the time of the Roman conquest; a rainstorm exposed it in 1949. The excellently preserved buildings include a mill and a bakery.

✚ B2

Tourist information ✉ Via Mameli 97, Cágliari
☎ 070 669 255
Su Nuraxi ✉ 1 kilometer (half a mile) east of Barumini ☎ 070 936 8024 🕐 Daily 9–dusk
🍴 Bar and restaurant nearby 🖐 $$

NORA

Sardinia's most important archeological site is located 40 kilometers (25 miles) south of Cágliari on a narrow spit of land swelling into the sea. Nora was founded by the Phoenicians in the eighth century BC and later settled by the Carthaginians before becoming the Roman capital of Sardinia in AD 238. The city was abandoned around the third century, possibly because of a natural disaster. Some parts are now submerged, and you can see ruins beneath the water, but plenty remains on dry land. The oldest ruin is that of the Carthaginian Temple of Astarte.

Roman remains are plentiful; look for the fourth-century baths decorated with mosaics, the theater, the Forum, and the traces of streets and houses. Many finds from the site are in Cágliari's Archeological Museum (see page 190), including a Punic inscription with the first mention of the name "Sardinia"; other finds are in the museum in nearby

Pula. Close by you'll see the Romanesque church of Sant'Efisio, the site of a famous spring procession from Cágliari. The church backs up to a tempting beach with crystal-clear waters, but it can be horribly crowded in summer.

✚ A1

✉ 40 kilometers (25 miles) south of Cágliari
☎ 070 920 9138 🕐 Daily 9–7, Apr.–Oct.; 9–noon and 2–5, rest of year 🖐 $ 🎉 Festival of Sant'Efisio May 1–4; commemorates the end of the plague in 1656. The saint's statue is carried through the streets of Cágliari, then taken to Nora on a cart drawn by oxen
Museo Civico Archeologico ✉ Corso Vittorio Emanuele II 67 ☎ 070 920 9610 🕐 Daily 9–7 or 8
🖐 $ or $$$ (combined ticket with Archeological Zone)

PORTO CONTE

Near the Spanish-influenced, pleasant old port town of Alghero are a series of beaches collectively known as the Ponte Conte. Embraced by two rocky promontories, the beaches are part of the Riviera del Corallo (Coral Riviera). Much of the coral used in the jewelry on display in Alghero originates from here.

The northern promontory, Capo Caccia, rears up above the sea with stunning views of Alghero to the south. The Capo is best known for the Grotta di Nettuno (Neptune's Grotto), a spectacular sea cave extending for more than a mile. Access is either by boat from Alghero, or by descending 654 steps from the Capo above. The steps were built in 1954 and are aptly known as the Escala del Cabriol (Goat's Stairway). Before the steps were built, the only way down was along a dizzyingly precipitous path. The caves, dramatically lit, have narrow corridors hung with stalactites and stalagmites. The southern promontory of Porto Conte has good beaches and a fine Nuraghi site, the Nuraghi di Palmavera.

✚ A3

Alghero tourist information ✉ Piazza Portaterra 9
☎ 079 979 054 🕐 Mon.–Sat. 8–8, May–Sep. (also Sun. 8–noon, Jul.–Aug.); Mon.–Sat. 8–2, rest of year
Grotta di Nettuno ✉ Capa Caccia 🕐 Daily 9–7, Apr.–Sep.; 10–5, in Oct.; 9–2, rest of year 🚢 Ferries from Alghero several times daily May–Sep. 🖐 $$$

Many visitors are drawn to Sardinia purely for the beauty of its coastline

The waters around Sardinia are among the clearest and cleanest in the Mediterranean, and the beaches attract tens of thousands of visitors who come to enjoy the sun and sea.

THE SARDINIAN COASTLINE

The Beaches

Around the island, beaches range from tiny hidden coves to glorious stretches of golden sands. The Costa Smeralda (the Emerald Coast, see page 192) in the northeast is the most famous stretch, its granite cliffs and turquoise sea providing great diving, snorkeling and sailing. To the south, the Golfo di Orosei is a paradise for those seeking peace and quiet. Many of its idyllic coves, backed by limestone cliffs, are accessible only by boat or on foot. Poetto, outside Cágliari, provides a lively contrast. Packed with locals and visitors, its 6 kilometers (4 miles) of sandy beaches are well stocked with bars and restaurants. In the vicinity of Piscinas, at Sardinia's southwestern corner, are 9 kilometers (6 miles) of sand dunes covered with feathery tamarisk trees, juniper and maquis. Some dunes top 165 feet, the highest in Europe. North of here and south of Alghero, you'll find more sandy beaches and clear sea, which give way to the dramatic cliffs to the north and south of Alghero itself. Windsurfing enthusiasts should head for the northern coast, with its guaranteed steady, strong breezes. Coastal cliffs provide an ideal nesting habitat for bird species. Herring gulls are everywhere, but also look for the rarer Audouin's gull and cormorants fishing from the rocks. Peregrine falcons and kites also use the cliffs as nesting areas.

The Seas

Sardinia's clear azure waters are the least polluted in Italy, with some areas designated international marine reserves. This makes for wonderful diving into waters rich in flora and fauna. Coral grows from 90 to 300 feet down; the mainly red and white Sardinian coral is used in jewelry, while the yellow and white Gorgonian coral can grow to 3 feet in height. Divers will encounter neptune grass, while rocky crevasses make ideal homes for crustaceans and mollusks. If you're offshore, look out for dolphins joyously riding the waves off the northern coast. Sardinia's greatest marine success story is the re-establishment of the monk seal, once thought to be extinct, in the waters of Golfo di Orosei.

HOTELS AND RESTAURANTS

The hotels and restaurants in this book were selected by
local specialists and include establishments in several price
ranges. Since price is often the best indication of the level of
facilities and quality of service, a three-tiered price guide
appears at the beginning of the listings. Because variable
rates will affect the amount of foreign currency that can be
exchanged for dollars (and thus affect the cost of a room or a
meal), price ranges are given in the local currency.

Although price ranges and operating times were
accurate at press time, this information is always subject to
change without notice. If you're interested in a particular
establishment, it is advisable to call ahead to reserve. The larger and more expensive hotels and the better-known restaurants are more likely to have someone who speaks English on
the staff; smaller establishments may not. In such cases it may
be better to inquire by fax or email rather than phone.

Facilities suitable for travelers with disabilities vary greatly,
and you are strongly advised to contact an establishment
directly to determine whether it will be able to meet your
needs. Older buildings may not be adequately designed or
equipped for visitors with limited or impaired mobility.

Accommodations

Accommodations have been selected with two considerations
in mind: a particularly attractive character or sense of local
flavor, or a central location that is convenient for sightseeing.
Remember that centrally located hotels fill up quickly,
especially during busy summer vacation periods; make
reservations well in advance. In-room bathrooms (sometimes
referred to as "en-suite facilities") may not be available in
smaller budget hotels.

Room rates for European hotels normally include a
light breakfast of rolls or croissants and coffee (where this
is not the case, the listing description notes that the rate is
for "room only"). Some hotels offer a price for overnight
accommodations that includes an evening meal.

Eating Out

Listed restaurants range from upscale places suitable for an
elegant evening out to small cafés where you can stop and
take a leisurely break from a busy day of sightseeing.
Some are close to attractions; where this is the case, there
is a cross-reference under the attraction listing. Other
possibilities for getting a bite to eat are the cafeterias and
restaurants on the premises of museums and galleries.

In Italy the different types of restaurants can be
confusing. The terms *ristorante, osteria* and *trattoria* are
fairly interchangable; *tavola calda* and *pizzeria* imply
something a bit more humble.

An elegant Rome hotel – the
choice of good accommodations in
Italian tourist areas is bewildering

The Northwest and Emilia-Romagna

KEY TO SYMBOLS

🏨 hotel
🍽 restaurant
✉ address
☎ telephone number
🕐 days/times closed
Ⓜ nearest subway station
🚌 nearby bus/trolley-bus/tram route(s).
⛴ ferry
AX American Express
CB Carte Blanche
DC Diners Club
MC MasterCard
VI VISA

Hotels
Price guide: double room with breakfast for two people
$ up to €103
$$ €103–€200
$$$ over €200

Restaurants
Price guide: dinner per person, excluding drinks
$ up to €25
$$ €25–€40
$$$ over €40

ROOM FOR TWO

Italian hotels charge for the room, not for each person. The price, by law, is displayed on the back of the room door and may vary according to the season (*alta/bassa stagione*). It may or may not include breakfast. Double beds are far more common than singles; they are generally queen or king size. Single rooms are generally in short supply and cost far more than half that of a double; you are paying for privacy, not space. Many hotels will put another bed in a double room if you request it; the charge for this must also be displayed.

The Northwest and Emilia-Romagna

ALBA

🏨 I Castelli $$
This modern hotel has comfortable rooms, a gym and an excellent restaurant.
✉ Corso Torino 14/1 ☎ 0173 361 978; fax 0173 361 974 AX, CB, DC, MC, VI

🍽 La Libera $
This informal restaurant serves lighter food than many others in town, but does especially good desserts. The decor is modern with marble floors and pale green walls.
✉ Via Pertinace 24/a ☎ 0173 293 155 🕐 Closed Sun., Mon lunch and some weeks in Feb. and May AX, CB, DC, MC, VI

AOSTA

🏨 Europe $$
Room prices vary widely at this traditional hotel, a few minutes' stroll from everything. The elegant rooms are quiet and comfortable.
✉ Piazza Narbonne 8 ☎ 0165 236 363; fax 0165 40566 AX, CB, DC, MC, VI

🍽 Vecchio Ristoro $
Once an old mill, this cozy restaurant offers a good range of seasonal local dishes. Try the *polenta* as a side dish or delicious mushrooms in autumn.
✉ Via Tourneuve 4 ☎ 0165 33 238 🕐 Closed Sun., Mon. lunch and some weeks in Jun. and Nov. AX, CB, MC, VI

ASTI

🍽 Gener Neuv $$$
A well-established Asti institution where you're sure of a friendly welcome. Sample traditional dishes made with the freshest local ingredients. The decor is elegant yet rustic and the wine list formidable.
✉ Lungotanaro Pescatori 4 ☎ 0141 557 270 🕐 Closed Sun., Mon., Aug. and Dec. 24–Jan. 7 AX, CB, DC, MC, VI

🏨 Reale $$
Located next to the venue for Asti's famous Palio, this hotel is a favorite. You'll find well-appointed rooms and a friendly welcome.
✉ Piazza Alfieri 6 ☎ 0141 530 240; fax 0141 34 357 AX, CB, DC, MC, VI

BÉRGAMO

🏨 Agnello d'Oro $
This hotel is housed in a 17th-century building with attractive rooms and a nice restaurant, which spills onto the piazza in summer.
✉ Via Gombito 22 ☎ 035 249 883; fax 035 235 612 AX, CB, DC, MC, VI

🍽 Taverna del Colleoni-dell'Angelo $$
Housed in one of Bérgamo's loveliest palaces, this is the place to enjoy sophisticated cooking of the highest order. Choices include sturgeon, truffles and mushrooms in season, fabulous desserts and a breathtaking wine list. There are tables outside in summer.
✉ Piazza Vecchia 7 ☎ 035 232 596 🕐 Closed Mon. AX, CB, DC, MC, VI

BOLOGNA

🏨 Al Cappello Rosso $$
This wonderful hotel has been in business since the 14th century and still offers a warm welcome, traditional service, and modern comfort and facilities. Conveniently situated in the historic center.
✉ Via de' Fusari 9 ☎ 051 261 891; fax 051 227 179 AX, CB, DC, MC, VI

🍽 Pappagallo $$$
You'll find the best of classical Bolognese cooking at this long-established restaurant in the heart of the old city. Housed in a 14th-century palazzo, the decor and service fully complement the homemade pasta and meat dishes.
✉ Piazza Mercanzia 3 ☎ 051 231 200 🕐 Closed Sun. and Aug. AX, CB, DC, MC, VI

COMO

🏨 Hotel Como $$
This elegant and comfortable hotel is about 15 minutes from the lake and is in the center of town. Its recently refurbished rooms have excellent facilities, and the roof garden has a heated pool.
✉ Via Mentana 28 ☎ 031 266 173; fax 0312 660 20 🕐 Closed Dec. 22–Jan. 13 AX, CB, DC, MC, VI

The Northwest and Emilia-Romagna

¶ Osteria l'Angolo del Silenzio $$

One of the oldest buildings in Como houses this pleasant restaurant offering good local cooking based on fish, mushrooms and game in season. Excellent value. Good wine list.
✉ Viale Lecco 25 ☎ 031 337 2157 ⏰ Closed Mon., Tue. lunch and 2 weeks in Jan. and Aug. AX, CB, DC, MC, VI

CREMONA

⊞ Duomo $

This well-appointed and friendly hotel in the heart of the city offers excellent value, good service, a great location and a restaurant.
✉ Via Gonfalonieri 13 ☎ 0372 35 242; fax 0372 458 392 AX, CB, DC, MC, VI

¶ Osteria la Sosta $$

A welcoming restaurant that specializes in local dishes – don't miss the *mostarda di cremona*, the sweet mustard-spiked fruit that accompanies meat here.
✉ Via Sicardo 9 ☎ 0372 456 656 ⏰ Closed Sun. evening, Mon. and Aug. AX, CB, DC, MC, VI

FERRARA

⊞ Annunziata $$

This elegant and peaceful midsize hotel is wonderfully located in the city center. The rooms are comfortable, and the friendly owners offer free use of bicycles to get around this lovely city.
✉ Piazza Repubblica 5 ☎ 0532 201 111; fax 0532 203 233 ⏰ Closed Ferragosto (August holiday) and Dec. 25 AX, CB, DC, MC, VI

¶ La Provvidenza $$

If you want to experience Ferrarese specialties, head to this pretty restaurant slightly outside the center to sample truffles and mushrooms in season, homemade pasta and delicious desserts. You can eat in the shady courtyard in summer.
✉ Corso Ercole I d'Este 92 ☎ 0532 205 187 ⏰ Closed Mon., Sun. evening and 2 weeks in Aug. AX, CB, DC, MC, VI

GARDA

⊞ Gabbiano $$

This excellent-value hotel overlooks the lake. Each comfortable room has a balcony, making it an excellent summer choice.
✉ Via dei Cipressi 4 ☎ 0457 256 655; fax 0457 255 363 ⏰ Closed Oct.–Mar. CB, MC, VI

¶ Tobago $$

This hotel restaurant is well worth a visit, as much for its pretty location and lovely garden as for the excellent cooking. The menu features a good variety of fish and interesting local dishes.
✉ Via Bellini 1 ☎ 0457 256 340 ⏰ Closed Tue. in winter and Jan. 6 to mid-Feb. AX, CB, DC, MC, VI

GENOA

⊞ City Hotel $$

This modern hotel located in the heart of the city has pleasant bedrooms and good public rooms. It's popular with businesspeople for meetings, so reservations are recommended.
✉ Via S Sebastiano 6 ☎ 010 55 451; fax 010 586 301 AX, CB, DC, MC, VI

¶ Rina $$

Genoa's oldest established restaurant continues to please diners with fresh fish and other high-quality Ligurian dishes. The surroundings are pleasing and the service excellent.
✉ Mura delle Grazie 3/r ☎ 010 246 6475 ⏰ Closed Mon. and Aug. AX, CB, DC, MC, VI

LEVANTO

¶ La Loggia $$

Conveniently located in the center of this coastal town, atttractive La Loggia offers excellent seafood dishes and traditional northern Italian cuisine.
✉ Piazza del Popolo 7 ☎ 0187 808 107 ⏰ Closed Wed. (except Jul.–Sep.) and Feb. AX, DC, MC, VI

⊞ Stella Maris $$

This pretty hotel not far from the sea is located in an 18th-century palazzo. The dining room and some bedrooms have frescoed ceilings and antique furniture. You can relax in the attractive garden.
✉ Via Marconi 4 ☎ 0187 808 258; fax 0187 807 351 ⏰ Closed Nov. AX, CB, DC, MC, VI

MANTOVA

¶ Aquila Nigra $$$

A dining experience in this old palace with frescoed ceilings will be truly memorable. You can enjoy traditional dishes, which vary as the seasons change. Good wine list and professional service.
✉ Vicolo Bonacolsi 4 ☎ 0376 327 180 ⏰ Closed Sun.–Mon., and some weeks in Aug. AX, CB, DC, MC, VI

⊞ San Lorenzo $$$

You'll be within an easy stroll of the Ducal Palace at this lovely hotel in the old center. Antique furnishings blend well with modern comforts, and there is a nice terrace.
✉ Piazza Concordia 14 ☎ 0376 220 500; fax 0376 327 194 AX, CB, DC, MC, VI

MILAN

¶ Il Luogo di Aimo e Nadia $$$

This is one of Italy's top restaurants, where you can enjoy the finest of traditional Milanese cooking using the very best ingredients. Creativity, style and flavor are the keynotes, complemented with impeccable service, elegant surroundings and a superb wine list.
✉ Via Montecuccoli 6 ☎ 02 416 886 ⏰ Closed Sat. lunch, Sun., Aug. and Jan. 1–6 🚇 Bande Nere AX, CB, DC, MC, VI

¶ Bistrot Duomo $$

This restaurant is at the top of the Rinascente building, with superlative views over the cathedral. It offers the best of Lombardy cooking in tasteful surroundings.
✉ Via S Raffaele 2 ☎ 02 877 120 ⏰ Closed Sun.–Mon. lunch and 2 weeks in Aug. 🚇 Duomo AX, CB, DC, MC, VI

⊞ Bristol $$$

This comfortable hotel is aimed at vacationers and has a stylish ambience. The only disadvantage is that it's not right in the center, although transportation is good.
✉ Via Scarlatti 32 ☎ 02 669 4141; fax 02 670 2942 🚇 Lima, Centrale AX, CB, DC, MC, VI

⊞ Lloyd $$

Located in the heart of the city and a short walk from the cathedral, this

The Northwest and Emilia-Romagna

KEY TO SYMBOLS

- 🏨 hotel
- 🍴 restaurant
- ✉ address
- ☎ telephone number
- 🕐 days/times closed
- Ⓜ nearest subway station
- 🚌 nearby bus/trolley-bus/tram route(s).
- ⛴ ferry
- AX American Express
- CB Carte Blanche
- DC Diners Club
- MC MasterCard
- VI VISA

Hotels

Price guide: double room with breakfast for two people

$ up to €103
$$ €103–€200
$$$ over €200

Restaurants

Price guide: dinner per person, excluding drinks

$ up to €25
$$ €25–€40
$$$ over €40

WINE AND WATER

Wine and water are the normal accompaniments to Italian meals, except with pizza, which calls for beer. Water is bottled mineral water, *aqua minerale*, and comes with bubbles, *gassata* or still, *naturale*; it is not expensive. The wine list in cheaper and mid-price restaurants normally has a reasonable selection of local wines, but it's rare to find wine from other Italian areas, let alone foreign wines. All establishments have both red and white carafe wine, *vino della casa*. This may be ordered in one-quarter, one-half or one-liter pitchers. You can order Coke and other soft drinks, although restaurants do not serve milk.

---

hotel has comfortable rooms and every convenience.
✉ Corso di Porta Romana 48
☎ 02 5830 3332; fax 02 5830 3365
🕐 Closed 2 weeks in Aug., Dec 22–Jan 6 Ⓜ Crocceta, Missori
AX, CB, DC, MC, VI

🏨 London $$

Conveniently located in the historic center close to the Castle Sforzesco, this good-value hotel offers comfortable rooms, with attentive service from the English-speaking staff.
✉ Via Rovello 3 ☎ 02 7202 0166; fax 02 805 7037 🕐 Closed Aug. and Dec. 25–Jan. 6 Ⓜ Cadorna, Cairoli CB, MC, VI

🏨 Principe di Savoia $$$

The elegant facade fronts a superbly appointed hotel with excellent service and a good restaurant.
✉ Piazza della Repubblica 17
☎ 02 62 301; fax 02 659 5838
Ⓜ Repubblica AX, CB, DC, MC, VI

🍴 Savini $$$

This huge and bustling restaurant is a Milanese institution, always busy, always convivial. Rich in atmosphere and tradition, the food covers northern cooking at its very best. Try the fixed-price menu for excellent value.
✉ Galleria Vittorio Emanuele II
☎ 02 7200 3433 🕐 Closed Sun., 2 weeks in Aug. and Jan. 1–6
Ⓜ Duomo AX, CB, DC, MC, VI

🍴 Trattoria all'Antica $–$$$

A friendly, warm atmosphere pervades this pleasant restaurant on the edge of the city center, serving hearty portions of Lombardy specialties. Try the homemade gnocchi. Fixed evening menu.
✉ Via Montevideo 4 ☎ 02 837 2849 🕐 Closed Sat. lunch, Sun., Aug. and Dec. 26–Jan 7 Ⓜ S Agostino AX, DC, MC, VI

MODENA

🏨 Centrale $

This is not Módena's smartest hotel, but its location in the old center makes up for a lot. The modernized rooms are comfortable and the service professional.
✉ Via Rismondo 55 ☎ 059 218 808; fax 059 238 201 AX, CB, DC, MC, VI

🍴 Fini $$

First opened in 1912, this Módena institution is today an elegant, restrained and upscale restaurant. Enjoy homemade pasta, *fritto misto* and delicious vegetables, all cooked with flair and served with professionalism.
✉ Rua Frati Minori 54 ☎ 059 223 314 🕐 Closed Mon.–Tue., end of Jul., Aug. and Dec. 22–Jan. 5 AX, CB, DC, MC, VI

MONTEROSSO

🍴 MIKY $$

This friendly, lively restaurant offers everything you'd expect – good pasta dishes, fresh fish, traditional specialties and pizza, which you can enjoy outside on a terrace overlooking the sea.
✉ Via Fegina 104 ☎ 0187 817 608
🕐 Closed Tue. (except in Aug.) and mid-Nov. to mid-Mar. AX, CB, MC, VI

🏨 Pasquale $$

This is a family-run, small hotel right beside the sea, with pleasant and nicely furnished rooms.
✉ Via Fegina 4 ☎ 0187 817 550; fax 0187 817 056 AX, CB, MC, VI

PARMA

🍴 La Greppia $$

This pleasant and welcoming family-run restaurant in the heart of the historic center is a good choice for classic Parma cooking, with home-made pasta and wonderful desserts.
✉ Strada Garibaldi 39/a ☎ 0521 233 686 🕐 Closed Mon.–Tue., Jul. and Dec. 23–Jan. 14 AX, CB, DC, MC, VI

🏨 Verdi $$

Parma's high standard of living is reflected in this elegant hotel overlooking the Parco Ducale. You'll be looked after impeccably. The building dates from the 19th century.
✉ Via Pasini 18 ☎ 0521 293 539; fax 0521 293 559 🕐 Closed 2 weeks in Aug. and Dec. 24–Jan. 10 AX, CB, DC, MC, VI

PAVIA

🏨 Ariston $$

This peaceful hotel, within a short stroll of the lovely city center, has been run for many years by the same

The Northeast

family. Rooms are simple, functional and comfortable. Restaurant.
✉ Via A Scopoli 10/d ☎ 0382 34 334; fax 0382 25 667 ⏲ Closed Dec. 25 –Jan. 6 AX, CB, DC, MC, VI

🍴 Locanda Vecchia Pavia $$–$$$
Relocated to a renovated mill, this restaurant continues to offer excellent traditional cuisine with creative variations. Reservations essential.
✉ Via al Monumento 5, Certosa di Pavia ☎ 0382 925 894 ⏲ Closed Mon., Wed. lunch and 2 weeks in Jan. and Aug. AX, CB, DC, MC, VI

PIACENZA

🍴 Antica Osteria del Teatro $$$
Food guides rate this among the top restaurants in Italy, an elegant place housed in a 15th-century palazzo. The menu has sophisticated interpretations of classic Emilian cooking and international dishes; service is attentive and professional.
✉ Via Verdi 16 ☎ 0523 323 777 ⏲ Closed Sun.–Mon., Jan. 1–7 and 3 weeks in Aug. AX, CB, DC, MC, VI

🏨 Nazionale $$
This makes a good stopping point. Rooms are well-equipped and comfortable, and it's a 15-minute walk to the city center.
✉ Via Genova 33 ☎ 0523 712 000; fax 0523 456 013 AX, CB, DC, MC, VI

🏨 Piccolo Hotel $$$
This charming hotel has access to a private beach. The pretty rooms have balconies facing the sea.
✉ Via Duca degli Abruzzi 31 ☎ 0185 269 015; fax 0185 269 621 ⏲ Closed Nov. and Dec. AX, CB, DC, MC, VI

🍴 Vecchia Piacenza $$
This traditional restaurant is charmingly decorated with frescoes. The menu includes imaginative and regional dishes. Reserve ahead.
✉ Via C.ne San Bernardo 1 ☎ 0523 305 462 ⏲ Closed Sun. and Jul. 1–15 DC, MC, VI

RAVENNA

🍴 Antica Trattoria al Gallo $$
Diners have been well-fed here since 1909, and you'll enjoy the simple excellence of the well-presented dishes. The emphasis is on fresh local produce, with a good range of vegetarian dishes and a comprehensive wine list.
✉ Via Maggiore 87 ☎ 0544 213 775 ⏲ Closed Sun. evening, Mon.–Tue., Easter and Dec. 20–Jan. 10 AX, CB, DC, MC, VI

🏨 Centrale Byron $$
This welcoming and well-furnished hotel is housed in an old palace only a short stroll from the heart of historic Ravenna and the main sights. The rooms are large and airy.
✉ Via IV Novembre 14 ☎ 0544 212 225; fax 0544 34 114 ⏲ Closed during Christmas period AX, CB, DC, MC, VI

RIMINI

🍴 Acero Rosso $$
This popular restaurant has a wide range of dishes using meat, fish and vegetables as a base for light and tasty meals. Desserts are homemade, and the wine list is good.
✉ Viale Tiberio 11 ☎ 0541 53 577 ⏲ Closed Mon., Tue.–Sat. lunch, Sun. dinner in winter and some weeks in Aug. and Jan. AX, CB, DC, MC, VI

🏨 Ambasciatori $$–$$$
Room prices vary tremendously at this mid-size hotel a few hundred yards from the beach. It has a pool, access to a private beach and a rooftop terrace.
✉ Viale Vespucci 22 ☎ 0541 55 561; fax 0541 23 790 AX, CB, DC, MC, VI

STRESA

🏨 Astoria $$
This family-run hotel beside the lake has modern rooms, a pool and a pleasant terrace restaurant for summer dining.
✉ Corso Umberto I 31 ☎ 0323 32 566; fax 0323 933 785 ⏲ Closed mid-Oct. to Mar. 31 AX, CB, DC, MC, VI

🍴 Piemontese $$
A pretty and friendly restaurant with a pergola in the garden for summer dining. Sample the wide range of dishes on the *menu degustazione*.
✉ Via Mazzini 25 ☎ 0323 30 235 ⏲ Closed Mon., Sun. evening Oct.–Nov. and Feb.–Mar., and Dec.–Jan. AX, CB, MC, VI

TURIN

🏨 Conte Biancamano $$
This small and centrally located hotel is housed in an old palace. Many of its well-equipped rooms have wood paneling, and there's a friendly and professional welcome from its owners.
✉ Corso Vittorio Emanuele II 73 ☎ 011 562 3281; fax 011 562 3789 ⏲ Closed Dec. 25 –Jan. 1 and Aug. AX, CB, DC, MC, VI

🍴 Del Cambio $$$
To enjoy Piedmont cooking at its best, head for this very good restaurant in an 18th-century building. High-quality meat is used in the cooking, the wine list is excellent, and the service is professional and attentive.
✉ Piazza Carignano 2 ☎ 011 543 760 ⏲ Closed Sun. and Aug. AX, CB, DC, MC, VI

The Northeast

AQUILEIA

🍴 Colombara $$
This restaurant, popular with local business types, is a good place to find local dishes, with the emphasis on fish. Its two rooms are classically styled and comfortable.
✉ Via S Zilli 42 ☎ 0431 91513 ⏲ Closed Mon. AX, CB, DC, MC, VI

🏨 Patriarchi $$
This comfortable hotel will give you a warm welcome and a real sense of personal service.
✉ Via Giulia Augusta 12 ☎ 0431 919 595; fax 0431 919 596 ⏲ Closed 2 weeks in Nov. AX, CB, DC, MC, VI

ASOLO

🍴 Ai Due Archi $$
This elegant restaurant has wood-paneled walls and antique furniture. Light and refined cooking and gracious service.
✉ Via Roma 55 ☎ 0423 952 201 ⏲ Closed Wed. evening, Thu. (Jun.–Oct.) and 2 weeks in Jan. AX, CB, DC, MC, VI

🏨 Villa Cipriani $$$
This is a truly world-class luxury hotel housed in a beautiful 16th-century

The Northeast

KEY TO SYMBOLS

⊞ hotel
🍴 restaurant
✉ address
☎ telephone number
🕐 days/times closed
Ⓜ nearest subway station
🚍 nearby bus/trolley-bus/tram route(s)
⛴ ferry
AX American Express
CB Carte Blanche
DC Diners Club
MC MasterCard
VI VISA

Hotels

Price guide: double room with breakfast for two people
$ up to €103
$$ €103–€200
$$$ over €200

Restaurants

Price guide: dinner per person, excluding drinks
$ up to €25
$$ €25–€40
$$$ over €40

SHOWERS OR TUBS

Unless your hotel is extremely simple, there will be a private bathroom. It will contain a sink, flush toilet, bidet and bathtub or shower. In much of Italy, showers are far more common than tubs, due to the scarcity and expense of water. Italian showers are often not enclosed in stalls; instead, water drains directly through a hole in the center of the room. Water pressure is far below that in the United States. You will notice a cord in the bathroom; this is a legal requirement for emergencies and summons help when pulled.

---

villa with lovely views over the hills. The clientele is cosmopolitan and often famous, and the level of service reflects that.
✉ Via Canova 298 ☎ 0423 523 411; fax 0423 952 095 AX, CB, DC, MC, VI

BOLZANO

⊞ Pircher $$
This friendly and comfortable hotel makes an excellent base for exploring Bolzano's mountains and wine routes. Rooms are well-equipped, and there's a welcome pool on the grounds.
✉ Via Merano 52 ☎ 0471 917 513; fax 0471 202 433 AX, CB, DC, MC, VI

🍴 Restaurant Pircher $$
Located in the friendly Hotel Pircher, the cuisine here is homemade and features traditional regional cooking. Comfortable surroundings and attentive service.
✉ Via Merano 52 ☎ 0471 917 513 🕐 Closed Sat. evening, Sun. and Jul. 1–15 AX, DC, MC, VI

CIVIDALE DEL FRIULI

🍴 Alla Frasca $$
This is a traditional trattoria, with good home cooking and friendly service from attentive staff. It is possible to eat outside during the summer.
✉ Via de Rubeis 8/a ☎ 0432 731 270 🕐 Closed Mon. and 2 weeks in Jan. AX, CB, MC, VI

⊞ Locanda al Castello $$
This lovely hotel was converted from a convent. Verdant grounds and superb views make up for its location just outside town. Excellent restaurant.
✉ Via del Castello 20 ☎ 0432 733 242; fax 0432 700 901 AX, CB, DC, MC, VI

MERANO

🍴 Maria-Theresia $$
Elegant and comfortable restaurant located in the spa resort Palace Hotel Schloss Maur. Good hospitality complements the regional dishes.
✉ Albergo Palace, Via Cavour 2/4 ☎ 0473 271 000 AX, CB, DC, MC, VI

⊞ Meranerhof $$
This hotel opposite the thermal baths has been run by the same family for 40 years. They pride themselves on their welcome to regulars, international visitors and families. Garden with heated pool.
✉ Via Manzoni 1 ☎ 0473 230 230; fax 0473 233 312 🕐 Closed Jan. 14–Mar. 7 AX, CB, DC, MC, VI

PADUA

🍴 Antico Brolo $$
A 15th-century building houses this elegant restaurant, serving interesting local dishes with an accent on fish. The wine cellar houses a lively pizzeria, and there's a pretty garden for outside dining.
✉ Corso Milano 22 ☎ 049 664 555 🕐 Closed Mon. AX, CB, DC, MC, VI

⊞ Toscanelli $$
The tranquility is more than you'd expect at this smallish hotel in the historic center of town. Reservations are recommended.
✉ Via dell'Arco 2 ☎ 049 875 0814; fax 049 875 6184 AX, CB, DC, MC, VI

TREVISO

🍴 Beccherie $$
One of Treviso's oldest restaurants, the Beccherie is housed in a Venetian-style building with elegant period furniture. Sample the risotto with radicchio, one of Treviso's greatest specialties.
✉ Piazza Ancillotto 10 ☎ 0422 540 871 🕐 Closed Sun. evening, Mon. and part of Jul. AX, CB, DC MC, VI

⊞ Carlton $$
This renovated hotel at the old city walls has good-size rooms, pleasing decor and good service.
✉ Largo Porta Altinia 15 ☎ 0422 411 661; fax 0422 411 620 AX, CB, DC, MC, VI

TRIESTE

🍴 Antica Trattoria Suban $$
Founded in 1865, this restaurant is still run by the Suban family, who bring the art of Trieste's central European cooking style to great heights with old recipes and traditional flavors.
✉ Via Comici 2 ☎ 040 54 368

Ⓘ Closed Mon.–Tue. lunch, 2 weeks in Jan. and 2 weeks in Aug. AX, CB, DC, MC, VI

🏨 Grand Hotel Duchi d'Aosta $$

The style and atmosphere of this impeccably run hotel encapsulate Trieste's central European atmosphere – somber and restrained elegance with modern comforts.
✉ Piazza Unità d'Italia 2 ☎ 040 760 0011; fax 040 366 092 AX, CB, DC, MC, VI

VENICE

🏨 Agli Alboretti $$

This charming hotel, with a pretty courtyard for breakfast, is on a tree-lined street between the Accademia and the Záttere. It's popular with visitors from all over the world, so it makes sense to reserve well ahead.
✉ Rio Terrà Foscarini, Accademia 884 ☎ 041 523 0058; fax 041 521 0158 🛏 1, 41, 42 Ⓘ Closed 2 weeks in Jan. AX, CB, DC, MC, VI

🏨 Al Gatto Nero da Ruggero $$

This family-run, traditional trattoria is the best place in Burano for simple, reasonably priced seafood. You can sit outside by the canal, close to the old fish market. ·
✉ Calle Sitivallo-Fondamenta Giudecca, Burano 88 ☎ 041 730 120 Ⓘ Closed Mon., Jan. 15–31 and Nov. 15–30 🛏 14 AX, DC, MC, VI

🏨 Cipriani $$$

This is one of the world's most famous luxury hotels, with every comfort and impeccable service, beautifully situated amid gardens on the Giudecca. Every room and suite is different. There's a sense of space you'll find nowhere else in the city.
✉ Fondamenta San Giovanni, Giudecca 10 ☎ 041 520 7744; fax 041 520 3930 🛏 82 (or use hotel's private launch service) AX, CB, DC, MC, VI

🍴 Corte Sconta $$

A famous Venetian fish restaurant tucked away near the Arsenale, with a garden for summer dining. Recipes are truly Venetian, using whatever fish is best at the Rialto market that day. Reservations are essential.
✉ Calle del Pestrin, Castello 3886 ☎ 041 522 7024 Ⓘ Closed Sun.–Mon. 🛏 82 AX, MC, VI

🏨 Danieli $$$

Generally considered Venice's finest hotel, the Danieli has style, elegance and class, with the advantage of its location in the heart of the city. Be sure to reserve a room in the older part.
✉ Riva degli Schiavoni, Castello 4196 ☎ 041 522 6480; fax 041 520 0208 🛏 1 AX, CB, DC, MC, VI

🍴 Harry's Dolci $$$

This offshoot of the famous Harry's Bar offers equally good food and service, with a waterfront terrace for summer dining. All the famous specialties are on the menu, with particularly excellent desserts as a bonus. Reservations are essential.
✉ Fondamenta San Biagio, Giudecca 773 ☎ 041 522 4844 Ⓘ Closed Tue. and mid-Nov. to Mar. 31 🛏 82 AX, CB, DC, MC, VI

🏨 Paganelli $$

Rooms in this quiet, clean and family-run hotel are on the waterfront overlooking St. Mark's Basin – a bonus that other hotels would charge double for.
✉ Riva degli Schiavoni, Castello 4182 ☎ 041 522 4324; fax 041 523 9267 🛏 1, 41, 42 AX, CB, MC, VI

🍴 Trattoria alla Madonna $$

This big, noisy fish restaurant, one of the most traditional in Venice, is hugely popular with Venetians and tourists. Service can be slow when they're busy, but the standard of cooking is consistently high.
✉ Calle della Madonna, San Polo 594 ☎ 041 522 3824 Ⓘ Closed Wed. and 2 weeks in Jan. and Aug. 🛏 1, 82 AX, MC, VI

🏨 Westin Europa e Regina $$$

This is probably the best value among Venice's luxury hotels; it's right on the Grand Canal, a stone's throw from St. Mark's, and has spacious rooms and a waterside terrace dining area.
✉ Calle Larga XXII Marzo, San Marco 2159 ☎ 041 240 0001; fax 041 523 1533 🛏 1 AX, CB, MC, VI

VERONA

🍴 Il Desco $$$

Verona's best restaurant has everything: service, comfort, antique decor, a superb wine list and attention to every detail. The cooking is light and creative, using the best seasonal ingredients.
✉ Via Dietro S. Sebastiano 7 ☎ 045 595 358 Ⓘ Closed Sun., Dec. 25–Jan. 6 and 2 weeks in Jun. AX, CB, DC, MC, VI

🏨 Torcolo $$

This friendly hotel is one of the most popular in Verona, so make reservations. It's less than a hundred yards from the Arena.
✉ Vicolo Listone 3 ☎ 045 800 7512; fax 045 800 4058 AX, CB, MC, VI

VICENZA

🏨 Campo Marzio $$

Many of Vicenza's more comfortable hotels are outside the center; this is an exception, with good modern rooms and facilities and within an easy stroll of the cathedral.
✉ Viale Roma 21 ☎ 0444 545 700; fax 0444 320 495 AX, CB, DC, MC, VI

🍴 Tre Visi Vecchio Roma $$

It's worth eating here for the series of beautifully furnished 15th-century dining rooms alone. The food is local, with game, mushrooms and mouthwatering desserts.
✉ Corso Palladio 25 ☎ 0444 324 868 Ⓘ Closed Sun. evening, Mon. and Jan. 20–Feb. 10 AX, CB, DC, MC, VI

Tuscany, Umbria and the Marche

AREZZO

🍴 Buca di San Francesco $$

Housed in a 14th-century palazzo with original Etruscan paving, this great restaurant follows three rules in its cooking – simplicity, flavor and genuine ingredients.
✉ Via San Francesco 1 ☎ 0575 23 271 Ⓘ Closed Mon. evening, Tue. and 2 weeks in Jul. AX, CB, DC, MC, VI

🏨 Continentale $$

This spacious and comfortable hotel at the foot of the old center of Arezzo is within easy walking distance of all you'll want to see. Well-furnished rooms and a friendly, professional staff.

Tuscany, Umbria and the Marche

Tuscany, Umbria and the Marche

KEY TO SYMBOLS

- ⊞ hotel
- �¶ restaurant
- ✉ address
- ☎ telephone number
- ⊙ days/times closed
- Ⓜ nearest subway station
- 🚌 nearby bus/trolley-bus/tram route(s).
- ⛴ ferry
- AX American Express
- CB Carte Blanche
- DC Diners Club
- MC MasterCard
- VI VISA

Hotels

Price guide: double room with breakfast for two people
- **$** up to €103
- **$$** €103–€200
- **$$$** over €200

Restaurants

Price guide: dinner per person, excluding drinks
- **$** up to €25
- **$$** €25–€40
- **$$$** over €40

COFFEE

Italian coffee, *caffè*, comes freshly made and very, very strong. It is perceived as a stimulant, not a drink, hence the tiny cups less than half full – a shot in the arm. For breakfast it is drunk with milk, either as a *cappuccino* or *caffè latte*. For the rest of the day, Italians drink an espresso, known in Italy as *un caffè*. It may have a drop of milk to make it *macchiato* (stained) or a shot of liquor for an extra kick, *caffè corretto*. Decaffeinated coffee is *caffè Hag*. To get anything remotely approaching American coffee, ask for *un caffè americano*, which will be weak and watery.

✉ Piazza Guido Monaco 7
☎ 0575 20 251; fax 0575 350 485
AX, CB, DC, MC, VI

ASCOLI PICENO

⊞ Gioli $$

This is a modern and functional hotel within the old walled center of Ascoli. Warm and welcoming.
✉ Viale De Gasperi 14 ☎ 0736 255 550; fax 0736 255 550
⊙ Closed Dec. 23–Jan. 3 AX, CB, DC, MC, VI

¶ Tornasacco $

This lovely restaurant, on the first floor of an old palazzo in the heart of town, serves typical dishes from the area, served with homemade pasta.
✉ Piazza del Popolo 36 ☎ 0736 254 151 ⊙ Closed Fri., 2 weeks in Jul. and Dec. 25–26 AX, CB, DC, MC, VI

ASSISI

¶ Buca di San Francesco $$

You can enjoy some of Assisi's most delicious pasta dishes and a wide variety of other local specialties in this excellent, rustically elegant restaurant housed in a medieval building in the center of town.
✉ Via E Brizi 1 ☎ 075 812 204
⊙ Closed Mon. and Jul. AX, CB, DC, MC, VI

⊞ Subasio $$$

This old-fashioned and historic hotel is within a stone's throw of the Basilica; many famous names have stayed here. The rooms have superb views. Reservations are essential.
✉ Via Frate Elia 2 ☎ 075 812 206; fax 075 816 691 AX, CB, DC, MC, VI

FLORENCE

⊞ Aprile $$

This peaceful hotel is housed in a Medici palace with a quiet garden. The bedrooms, with frescoed ceilings and old paintings, have every modern amenity.
✉ Via della Scala 6 ☎ 055 216 237; fax 055 280 947 🚌 2, 17, 22
AX, CB, MC, VI

⊞ Brunelleschi $$$

Reserve ahead to stay in this comfortable hotel in the heart of Florence. A real sense of tradition and history.

✉ Piazza Sta Elisabetta 3 ☎ 055 27 370; fax 055 219 653 🚌 In the pedestrian zone AX, CB, DIC MC, VI

¶ Cantinetta Antinori $$

Enjoy Tuscan food with superb wine in the 15th-century Palazzo Antinori, the Florence home of this great wine-producing family. The restaurant is furnished with simple elegance in the Florentine style.
✉ Piazza Antinori 3 ☎ 055 292 234 ⊙ Closed Sat.–Sun., Dec. 25–Jan. 6 and 2 weeks in Aug.
🚌 6, 11, 31 AX, CB, DC, MC, VI

¶ Dino $$

This uncluttered restaurant, housed in three separate rooms in a 14th-century palazzo, serves simple food inspired by centuries-old recipes.
✉ Via Ghibellina 51/r ☎ 055 241 452 ⊙ Closed Sun. evening, Mon. and 2 weeks in Aug. 🚌 14 AX, CB, DC, MC, VI

¶ Enoteca Pinchiorri $$$

Considered one of the top five restaurants in Italy, this establishment is set in a 16th-century palazzo with a garden for summer dining. Outstanding and imaginative food, and worth a visit for the wines alone.
✉ Via Ghibellina 87 ☎ 055 242 777 ⊙ Closed Sun.–Mon., Tue.–Wed. lunch, and Aug. 🚌 14 AX, CB, DC, MC, VI

⊞ Hermitage $$

You can see the Ponte Vecchio from the fifth-floor public rooms and garden of this comfortable hotel. The well-appointed bedrooms occupy the lower floors.
✉ Vicolo Marzio I, ang. Piazza del Pesce ☎ 055 287 216; fax 055 212 208 🚌 In the pedestrian zone
CB, MC, VI

¶ Osteria de'Benci $

A genuine Florentine *osteria*. Start with *crostini* (Tuscan *bruschetta* – toasted bread served with spreads, cheeses and cold meats), then choose from the day's menu that often includes spaghetti in red wine.
✉ Via d'Benci ☎ 055 234 4923
⊙ Closed Mon. 🚌 In the pedestrian zone AX, DC, MC, VI

⊞ Westin Excelsior $$$

One of Florence's smartest and most elegant hotels, in a Renaissance-style palazzo in the heart of the historic center, offers every comfort, exceptional service and a roof terrace.

✉ Piazza Ognissanti 3 ☎ 055 264 201; fax 055 210 278 🖥 C, 9 AX, CB, DC, MC, VI

GREVE IN CHIANTI

🏨 Giovanni da Verrazzano $$
This hotel, housed in an old building on the square of this popular Chianti village, has well-kept and well-equipped rooms.

✉ Piazza Matteotti 28 ☎ 055 853 189; fax 055 853 648 ⏰ Closed mid-Jan. to mid-Feb. AX, CB, DC, MC, VI

🍴 Villa Sangiovese $$
It's worth driving the few miles to Panzano to find this panoramic garden terrace at the Hotel Villa Sangiovese. This is the perfect place to sample a Tuscan meal in a picturesque vineyard setting.

✉ Piazza Bucciarelli 5, Panzano ☎ 055 852 461 ⏰ Closed Dec. 25 through Feb. MC, VI

GUBBIO

🏨 Gattapone $$
This medieval building in the heart of old Gúbbio has been tastefully converted into a comfortable hotel. Its antique furniture and pretty grounds are bonuses.

✉ Via Beni 11 ☎ 075 927 2489; fax 075 927 2417 ⏰ Closed Jan. 8–Feb. 8 AX, CB, DC, MC, VI

🍴 Taverna del Lupo $$
This big, busy restaurant offers delicious dishes, good service and a friendly and relaxed atmosphere.

✉ Via Ansidei 6 ☎ 075 927 4368 ⏰ Closed Mon. (except Aug.–Sep.) AX, CB, DC, MC, VI

LUCCA

🍴 Buca di Sant'Antonio $$
A series of cozy rooms gives this restaurant its special atmosphere. Superb food and good service make it one of Tuscany's top establishments, where traditional dishes are served with a modern twist.

✉ Via della Cervia 1/5 ☎ 0583 55 881 ⏰ Closed Sun. evening, Mon., Jan. 13–28 and 2 weeks in Jul. AX, CB, DC, MC, VI

🏨 La Luna $$
One of the very few hotels within the city walls of Lucca. Comfortable rooms; within walking distance of the Piazza Anfiteatro.

✉ Via Fillungo, ang. Corte Compagni 12 ☎ 0583 493 634; 0583 490 021 ⏰ Closed Jan. 7–Feb. 7 AX, CB, DC, MC, VI

MONTALCINO

🏨 Hotel dei Capitani $$
This well-converted hotel is in the heart of town. Many of the pretty rooms have lovely views, and there's a small pool.

✉ Via Lapini 6 ☎ 0577 847 227; fax 0577 847 239 ⏰ Closed mid-Jan. through Feb. AX, CB, DC, MC, VI

🍴 Taverna dei Barbi $$
Drive out to one of Montalcino's finest wine producers to enjoy local specialties served in a converted old farm building. Homemade pasta and game in season.

✉ 5 kilometers (3 miles) from Montalcino at Podernovi ☎ 0577 841 200 ⏰ Closed Tue. evening, Wed. (except in Aug.) and 3 weeks in Jan. AX, CB, DC, MC, VI

MONTEPULCIANO

🍴 La Grotta $$
A stroll downhill brings you to this elegantly pretty restaurant on the edge of town. The building was once the home of Sangallo, a Renaissance architect.

✉ Località San Biagio 16 ☎ 0578 757 479 ⏰ Closed Wed. and Jan. 6–end Feb. AX, CB, MC, VI

🏨 Hotel il Marzocco $$
Housed in a 16th-century building, this comfortable hotel just off the main street has been run by the same family for more than 150 years.

✉ Piazza Savonarola 18 ☎ 0578 757 262; fax 0578 757 530 ⏰ Closed mid-Jan. to mid-Feb. AX, CB, DC, MC, VI

NORCIA

🍴 Granaro del Monte $$
Nórcia's best restaurant, where you can eat truffle dishes, game in season and meat cooked over a huge open fire. Busy but friendly.

✉ Via Alfieri 12 ☎ 0743 816 513 AX, CB, DC, MC, VI

ORVIETO

🏨 Maitani $$$
Less than 200 yards from the cathedral, this elegant and comfortable hotel in a historic building has good-size rooms.

✉ Via Maitani 5 ☎ 0763 342 011; ⏰ Closed 3 weeks in Jan. AE, CB, DI, MC, VI

🍴 Tipica Trattoria Etrusca $$
This upscale restaurant in a medieval building is a few paces from the cathedral. Truffles, game and traditional local dishes are featured, and you can visit the wine vaults, carved from tufa rock, beneath the dining room.

✉ Via Maitani 10 ☎ 0763 344 016 ⏰ Closed Mon. AX, CB, DC, MC, VI

PASSIGNANO

🏨 Lido $$
Right on the edge of Lake Trasimeno, this hotel has airy and spacious rooms and a pretty garden.

✉ Via Roma 1 ☎ 075 827 219; fax 075 827 251 ⏰ Closed Dec.–Mar. AX, CB, DC, MC, VI

PERUGIA

🍴 Falchetto $$
This long-established restaurant has kept a tradition of unsophisticated elegance. The cooking is special and features traditional dishes with a modern slant.

✉ Via Bartolo 20 ☎ 075 573 1775 ⏰ Closed Mon. AX, CB, DC, MC, VI

🏨 Locanda della Posta $$$
If you want to be in the heart of Perúgia, this is an ideal choice. The excellent rooms are in an old palazzo overlooking the town's main street.

✉ Corso Vannucci 97 ☎ 075 572 8925; fax 075 573 2562 AX, CB, DC, MC, VI

PIENZA

🍴 Buca delle Fate $
This big, buzzing restaurant is housed in a 16th-century palazzo and serves straightforward Tuscan cooking, backed up by fine local wines.

✉ Corso Rossellino 38/a ☎ 0578 748 272 ⏰ Closed Mon., 3 weeks in Jan. and Jun. AX, CB, DC MC, VI

Tuscany, Umbria and the Marche

KEY TO SYMBOLS

- ▦ hotel
- 🍴 restaurant
- ✉ address
- ☎ telephone number
- ⊘ days/times closed
- Ⓜ nearest subway station
- 🚌 nearby bus/trolley-bus/tram route(s).
- ⛴ ferry
- AX American Express
- CB Carte Blanche
- DC Diners Club
- MC MasterCard
- VI VISA

Hotels

Price guide: double room with breakfast for two people
$ up to €103
$$ €103–€200
$$$ over €200

Restaurants

Price guide: dinner per person, excluding drinks
$ up to €25
$$ €25–€40
$$$ over €40

AGRITURISMO

Agriturismo is a term referring to accommodations on functioning farms or agricultural estates, giving guests the chance to enjoy local cooking at its place of origin. The concept began as a means of restoring old, unused rural properties and agricultural buildings, as well as encouraging traditional crafts and food production methods. Hundreds of lovely old structures have been converted to holiday accommodations – some on a room-only basis, others with simple rooms and dining facilities, and some as smart as a good hotel.

▦ Relais il Chiostro di Pienza $$$
Converted from a 15th-century convent, this is the only hotel within the old town. Frescoed rooms, vaulted ceilings, a garden with a view and a shady cloister.
✉ Corso Rossellino 26 ☎ 0578 748 400; fax 0578 748 440 ⊘ Closed Jan. 1 to mid-Mar. AX, CB, DC, MC, VI

PISA

🍴 Ristoro dei Vecchi Macelli $$
You'll find good local cooking and a friendly welcome at this stylish, modern restaurant. Fish is recommended, and there are interesting vegetable dishes.
✉ Via Volturno 49 ☎ 050 20 424; fax 050 506 008 ⊘ Closed Wed., Sun. lunch CB, VI

▦ Verdi $$
An old palace houses this recently renovated hotel in the heart of the Old Town, within easy reach of the Piazza dei Miracoli.
✉ Piazza Repubblica 5 ☎ 050 598 947; fax 050 598 944 ⊘ Closed Jan. 2–30 AX, CB, DC, MC, VI

RADDA IN CHIANTI

▦ Relais Fattoria Vignale $$$
This 18th-century villa has been transformed into one of Tuscany's luxury hotels. Frescoed ceilings and lovely stonework offset the antique furnishings. There's an excellent restaurant, pool and gardens.
✉ Via Pianigiani 9 ☎ 0577 738 300; fax 0577 738 592 ⊘ Closed Jan. 7 to mid-Mar. and Dec. 1–24 AX, CB, DC, MC, VI

🍴 Vignale $$$
This rustic restaurant housed in an old agricultural building serves local dishes with a twist. It's popular with residents and visitors.
✉ Via XX Settembre 23 ☎ 0577 738 094 ⊘ Closed Thu. and Jan. 6 to mid-Mar. AX, CB, DC, MC, VI

SAN GIMIGNANO

🍴 La Griglia $$
You can enjoy eating on the terrace at this well-known restaurant in the heart of San Gimignano. There are plenty of local specialties, many of them grilled on an open fire, from

which the restaurant gets its name.
✉ Via San Matteo 34/36 ☎ 0577 940 005 ⊘ Closed Thu. and mid-Dec. through Feb. AX, CB, DC, MC, VI

▦ Leon Bianco $$
This tastefully converted, family-run hotel on the town's main square has spacious rooms, lofty vaulted ceilings and a pretty breakfast terrace.
✉ Piazza della Cisterna 13 ☎ 0577 941 294; fax 0577 942 123 ⊘ Closed mid-Jan. through Feb. AX, CB, DC, MC, VI

SIENA

🍴 Al Marsili $$$
Impeccable service, a wide-ranging wine list and interesting dishes all feature in the vaulted elegance of this upscale restaurant.
✉ Via del Castoro 3 ☎ 0577 47 154 ⊘ Closed Mon. AX, CB, DC, MC, VI

▦ Athena $$$
This is a big, modern hotel inside the walls of the old city and 15 minutes from the Campo. Comfortable rooms and professional service.
✉ Via Mascagni 55 ☎ 0577 286 313; fax 0577 48 153 AX, CB, DC, MC, VI

🍴 Osteria Le Logge $$
This restaurant occupies a former medieval apothecary's shop. The cooking is good, with plenty of Sienese dishes and wonderful *porcini* (mushrooms) in autumn.
✉ Via del Porrione 33 ☎ 0577 48 013; fax 0577 224 797 ⊘ Closed Sun. and Jan. AX, CB, DC, MC, VI

SPELLO

🍴 Cacciatore $$
If you're looking for perfect terrace dining with a view, head for this restaurant at the top end of town. Umbrian food and good local wines are served in the cozy dining room or under the stars.
✉ Via Giulia 42 ☎ 0742 651 141; fax 0742 301 603 ⊘ Closed 2 weeks in Jul. AX, CB, DC, MC, VI

▦ Palazzo Bocci $$
This 17th-century palazzo was transformed in the mid-1990s into a luxury hotel with a high level of service and comfort. Vaulted

Central Italy

ceilings, terraces and frescoes complete the stylish ambience.
✉ Via Cavour 17 ☎ 0742 301 021; fax 0742 301 464 AX, CB, DC, MC, VI

SPOLETO

🏨 Gattapone $$$
Every room has a view of the gorge and the Ponte delle Torri at this elegant hotel. Good public areas and pretty terraces complete the picture.
✉ Via del Ponte 6 ☎ 0743 223 447; 0743 223 448 AX, CB, DC, MC, VI

🍴 Sabatini $$
Among Spoleto's many excellent restaurants, Sabatini stands out for its lovely garden, where you can enjoy imaginative dishes using superb local ingredients. Be sure to try the *antipasto*.
✉ Corso Mazzini 52/54 ☎ 0743 221 831 ⏰ Closed Mon. and 2 weeks in Aug. AX, CB, DC, MC, VI

TODI

🏨 Fonte Cesia $$
In the heart of the historic center of Todi, this 18th-century building still has original features, but the charming rooms are furnished in contemporary style.
✉ Via L Leony 3 ☎ 075 894 3737; fax 075 894 4677 AX, CB, DC, MC, VI

🍴 Umbria $$
You can enjoy a warm welcome and excellent home cooking at this restaurant. Enjoy such specialties as truffle dishes and wild boar on the summer terrace, which offers superb views. Reservations suggested.
✉ Via S Bonaventura 13 ☎ 075 894 2737 ⏰ Closed Tue. AX, CB, DC, MC, VI

URBINO

🏨 Bonconte $$
This comfortable hotel is just inside the city walls, a short walk from the Palazzo Ducale. Avoid the smaller rooms on the top floor.
✉ Via delle Mura 28 ☎ 0722 2463; fax 0722 4782 AX, CB, DC, MC, VI

🍴 Vecchia Urbino $$
A family-run restaurant in the heart of the historic center where you can enjoy truffles, mushrooms and a

superb range of olive oils, all in elegant surroundings.
✉ Via dei Vasari 3/5 ☎ 0722 44 47 ⏰ Closed Tue. AX, CB, DC, MC, VI

VOLTERRA

🏨 San Lino $$
This comfortable hotel located within the city's walls was once a convent. It has spacious rooms, and there's a pretty terrace and pool behind the main building.
✉ Via S Lino 26 ☎ 0588 85 250; fax 0588 80 620 ⏰ Closed Nov. AX, CB, DC, MC, VI

🍴 Trattoria del Sacco Fiorentino $$
This attractive and friendly restaurant run by an enthusiastic young chef serves Tuscan dishes and some interesting historic recipes rarely found in restaurants.
✉ Piazza XX Settembre 18 ☎ 0588 88 537 ⏰ Closed Wed. and Jan. 10–Mar. 1 AX, CB, DC, MC, VI

Central Italy

L'AQUILA

🏨 Duomo $$
A converted 19th-century building houses this comfortable hotel. The rooms are functional and it has a good location.
✉ Via Dragonetti 10 ☎ 0862 410 893; fax 0862 413 058 AX, CB, MC, VI

🍴 Tre Marie $
This restaurant has been run by five generations of the same family. The relaxed and cozy atmosphere makes it an ideal place to sample true Abruzzo dishes.
✉ Via Tre Marie 3 ☎ 0862 413 191 ⏰ Closed Sun. evening, Mon. (except Aug.) and Dec. 24–31 V1

MONTECASSINO

🏨 Alba $$
This hotel in the town of Cassino is modern and comfortable. It makes a good stopping point if you want to spend some time visiting the monastery.
✉ Via G Di Biasio 53 ☎ 0776 21 873; fax 0776 21 873; fax 0776 270 000 AX, CB, DC, MC, VI

🏨 Villa della Meridiana $$
An early 20th-century building houses this pleasant restaurant, where you'll find a good choice of local favorites and plenty of local diners. The garden is lovely for summer dining.
✉ Via S Pasquale 125 ☎ 0776 312 846 ⏰ Closed Mon., Ferragosto (August public holiday) and Dec. 25 AX, CB, DC, MC, VI

ROME

🍴 Agata e Romeo $$
This upscale, welcoming restaurant near Santa Maria Maggiore offers a wide range of fish dishes in elegant surroundings.
✉ Via Carlo Alberto 45 ☎ 06 446 6115; fax 06 446 5842 ⏰ Closed Sat.–Sun. and 2 weeks in Jan. and Aug. 🚌 27, 70, 93 AX, CB, DC, MC, VI

🍴 Alberto Ciarla $$$
One of Rome's finest restaurants, with an elegant atmosphere and fine fish dishes. Family-run, with excellent service and a huge and distinguished wine list.
✉ Piazza San Cosimato 40 ☎ 06 581 8668; fax 06 588 4377 ⏰ Closed Sun. lunch 🚌 44, 75, 170 AX, CB, DC, MC, VI

🍴 Al Moro $$
This friendly, traditional neighborhood restaurant is tucked away in an alley near the Fontana di Trevi. More sophisticated than it first appears, it's extremely popular and reservations are essential.
✉ Vicolo delle Bollette 13 ☎ 06 678 3495 ⏰ Closed Sun. and Aug. 🚌 56, 60, 85 VI

🍴 Checchino dal 1887 $$
A long-established restaurant specializing in traditional Roman dishes – this is the place to try tripe, brains and offal, as well as delicate ricotta and fruit tarts. The decor is cozy and there's an open fire. The wine list is long and interesting.
✉ Via Monte Testaccio 30 ☎ 06 574 6318 ⏰ Closed Sun.–Mon., Dec. 25–Jan. 1 and Aug. 🚌 13, 23, 57 AX, CB, DC, MC, VI

🏨 Columbus $$
This hotel is just a stone's throw from St. Peter's and is housed in a former monastery, with many of the original

The South

KEY TO SYMBOLS

🏨	hotel
🍴	restaurant
✉	address
☎	telephone number
🕐	days/times closed
Ⓜ	nearest subway station(s)
🚌	nearby bus/trolley-bus/tram route(s).
⛴	ferry
AX	American Express
CB	Carte Blanche
DC	Diners Club
MC	MasteCard
VI	VISA

Hotels

Price guide: double room with breakfast for two people

$	up to €103
$$	€103–€200
$$$	over €200

Restaurants

Price guide: dinner per person, excluding drinks

$	up to €25
$$	€25–€40
$$$	over €40

BARS

Brightly lit and sparklingly clean, bars are open from 6 a.m. until late at night and serve everything from soft drinks, coffee and tea to beer, wine and scotch. You'll usually find a good selection of snack foods and sandwiches, while many double up as *pasticcerie* (pastry shops) or *gelaterie* (ice cream parlors). If you sit down for waiter service you will pay a premium, whether inside or out. The normal procedure is to pay for what you want first at the cash-desk *(la cassa)*, then take the receipt *(lo scontrino)* to the bar and repeat your order. All bars have bathrooms — you may have to ask for the key from the bartender — and provide daily newspapers.

decorative features. The perfect pilgrimage hotel, it's a favorite with visiting prelates.

✉ Via della Conciliazione 33
☎ 06 686 5435; fax 06 686 4874
🚌 23, 64   AX, CB, DC, MC, VI

🍴 El Toulà $$$

Many people consider this elegant restaurant Rome's best. Impeccable service, a menu that includes Venetian international cooking at its best, plus a good wine list make an evening here truly memorable.

✉ Via della Lupa 29/b ☎ 06 687 3498 🕐 Closed Sun., Mon. and Sat. lunch, Aug. and Dec. 24–26
🚌 81, 90   AX, CB, DC, MC, VI

🏨 Hotel d'Inghilterra $$$

A short walk from the Spanish Steps in the heart of an upscale shopping area, the comfortable rooms of this historic hotel have antique furniture. Excellent service.

✉ Via Bocca di Leone 14 ☎ 06 69 981; fax 06 6992 2243 Ⓜ Spagna
🚌 119, 52, 61   AX, CB, DC, MC, VI

🏨 Portoghesi $$

You'll be within a short walk of Piazza Navona at this old-fashioned and well-known hotel, tucked away on a cobbled street. The rooms have been refurbished, and there's a pretty roof terrace.

✉ Via dei Portoghesi 1 ☎ 06 686 4231; fax 06 687 6976 🚌 70, 81 90 CB, MC, VI

🏨 Westin Excelsior $$$

If you want the best European hotels have to offer, stay at this world-class luxury hotel. Its opulent decor and high standard of service make a few days here one of Rome's most sybaritic experiences.

✉ Via Vittorio Veneto 125 ☎ 06 47 081; fax 06 482 6205
Ⓜ Barberini 🚌 52, 53, 95   AX, CB, DC, MC, VI

TARQUINIA

🍴 Bersagliere $$

A big, busy restaurant popular with locals and tourists, where you can eat fish dishes as well as good local Lazio cooking. Comfortable but noisy and bustling.

✉ Via B Croce 2 ☎ 0766 856 047
🕐 Closed Mon., Sun. evening, Dec. 25–Jan. 6 and 2 weeks in Jul.
AX CB, DC, MC, VI

🏨 Tarconte $$

This hotel is good for visiting this historic Etruscan city. It has friendly and professional service and bright and comfortable rooms.

✉ Via della Tuscia 19 ☎ 0766 856 141; fax 0766 856 585   AX, CB, DC, MC, VI

TIVOLI

🍴 Cinque Statue $

This big restaurant, with many outside tables, attracts Romans visiting Tivoli for the day as well as visitors staying in town. The cooking is simple and robust, with an emphasis on freshness.

✉ Largo S Angelo 1 ☎ 0774 335 366 🕐 Closed Fri., Sun. evening and 2 weeks between Aug. and Sep. AC, CB, DC, MC, VI

🏨 Torre Sant'Angelo $$

You'll find every modern comfort in this beautifully located hotel. It's small enough for truly personal service, but with the facilities of many larger hotels, including a restaurant and pool.

✉ Via Quintilio Varo ☎ 0774 332 533; fax 0774 332 533   AX, CB, DC, MC, VI

VITERBO

🍴 Il Portico $–$$

Located in the historic center of the village, this country-style restaurant, with terra-cotta floors and original fireplace, serves Viterbo-style dishes and fish specialties.

✉ Piazza Don Mario Gargiuli 11 ☎ 0761 328 021 🕐 Closed Mon. AX, DC, MC, VI

🏨 Tuscia $$

This family-run hotel is near the medieval city center and within an easy stroll of the commercial area and shops. Rooms are pleasant and comfortable. Good value.

✉ Via Cairoli 41 ☎ 0761 344 400; fax 0761 345 976   AX, CB, DC, MC, VI

The South

ALBEROBELLO

🍴 Il Poeta Contadino $$$

It's worth the journey to Alberobello to sample the food and outstanding wine list at this pretty restaurant. ✉ Via Indipendenza 21 ☎ 080 4321 917 🕐 Closed Mon. (except Jul.–Aug.) and Jan. AX, CB, DC, MC, VI

🏨 Hotel dei Trulli $$
A peaceful hotel with a nice garden, friendly owners and very comfortable rooms.
✉ Via Cadore 28 ☎ 080 432 3555; fax 080 432 3560 AX, CB, MC, VI

AMALFI

🏨 La Bussola $$
In the heart of Amalfi, this excellent-value hotel has traditional decor, airy rooms and is located beside the sea.
✉ Lungomare dei Cavalieri 16, ☎ 089 871 533; fax 089 871 369 AX, CB, DC, MC, VI

🍴 Da Gemma $$
You can enjoy traditional dishes on a terrace overlooking Amalfi's main square in one of the coast's most popular and best-known restaurants.
✉ Via Fra' Gerardo Sasso 10 ☎ 089 871 345 🕐 Closed Wed. (except Jul.–Aug.) and mid-Jan. to mid-Feb. AX, CB, MC, VI

BARI

🍴 Ai 2 Ghiottoni $$
This rustic-style restaurant puts the emphasis firmly on local dishes, with an interesting wine list heavily weighted with Puglian wines.
✉ Via Putignani 11 ☎ 080 523 2240 🕐 Closed Sun. AX, CB, DC, MC, VI

🏨 Boston $$
A good mid-range hotel within easy reach of both the historic center and the railroad station. Comfortable and professionally run.
✉ Via Piccinni 155 ☎ 080 521 6633; fax 080 524 6802 AX, CB, DC, MC, VI

CAPRI

🍴 Capannina $$
You can eat either in the pretty dining room or on the green terrace of this well-known establishment, where specialties include imaginative use of fish and vegetable combinations.
✉ Via delle Botteghe 12 bis ☎ 081 837 0732; fax 081 837 6990

🕐 Closed mid-Nov. to mid-Mar. (except one week at New Year's) AX, CB, DC, MC, VI

🍴 Da Paolino $$
Try the delicious *antipasto* buffet in this restaurant serving local dishes, where you can eat outside in the shade of a lemon-tree pergola.
✉ Via Palazzo a Mare 11, Marina Grande ☎ 081 837 6102; fax 081 837 5611 🕐 Closed Nov.–Mar., and lunch Jun.–Sep. and in Aug. AX, CB, DC, MC, VI

🏨 Palatium $$$
An exclusive hotel by the water's edge, this is the only Capri hotel to have access to a beach, with gardens, terrace, salt-water pool, and a good restaurant.
✉ Via Provinciale, Marina Grande 225 ☎ 081 837 6144; fax 081 838 4111 AX, CB, DC, MC, VI

🏨 Syrene $$$
This luxurious and pretty hotel is built in Mediterranean style. The terrace overlooks the cliffs, and the pool stands amid lemon trees.
✉ Via Camerelle 51 ☎ 081 837 0522; fax 081 837 0957 🕐 Closed Nov.–Apr. AX, CB, DC, MC, VI

LECCE

🏨 Grand Hotel $$
This splendidly old-fashioned and elegant hotel offers marvelous decor and stucco ceilings. Rooms are simple and comfortable and there's a roof garden and restaurant.
✉ Via O Quarta 28 ☎ 0832 309 405; fax 0832 309 891 AX, CB, DC, MC, VI

🍴 Trattoria Casareccia $
Exceptional value for delicious home cooking in a homey atmosphere. Great welcome and some interesting Puglian cuisine.
✉ Via Costadura 19 ☎ 0832 245 178 🕐 Closed Mon., Sun. evening, Dec. 24–Jan. 6 and Aug. 30–Sep.15 VI

MARATÈA

🏨 Villa del Mare $$
Perched on a rocky headland, this perfect vacation hotel has nice rooms, a pretty terrace and a private elevator down to the hotel's beach.
✉ Strada Statale Sud 18,

Acquafredda ☎ 0973 878 007; fax 0973 878 102 🕐 Closed Nov. to mid-Apr. AX, CB, DC, MC, VI

🍴 Zà Mariuccia $$
A long-established restaurant in a pretty location, run by the same family for three generations. You can choose your fish from the tank while it's still alive.
✉ Via Grotte 2 ☎ 0973 876 163 🕐 Closed Nov.–Feb., lunch Jun. and Aug. and Thu. (except in Aug.) AX, CB, DC, MC, VI

MATERA

🏨 Italia $$
This comfortable hotel in a historic building has a good restaurant and great views over the *sassi* quarter of town.
✉ Via Ridola 5 ☎ 0835 333 561; fax 0835 330 087 AX, CB, DC, MC, VI

🍴 Trattoria Lucana $
Local specialties and excellent vegetarian options are served in an informal atmosphere.
✉ Via Lucana 48 ☎ 0835 336 117 🕐 Closed Sun. and Sep. 10–25 AX, DC, MC, VI

NAPLES

🏨 Britannique $$
This comfortable hotel in a 19th-century villa has lovely views over the Bay of Naples, a secluded garden and a restaurant.
✉ Corso Vittorio Emanuele II 133 ☎ 081 761 4145; fax 081 660 457 🚇 V1 AX, CB, DC, MC, VI

🍴 La Cantinella $$$
This seafront restaurant specializes in creative fish preparations, which you can enjoy on the terrace.
✉ Via Cuma 42 ☎ 081 764 8684; fax 081 764 8769 🕐 Closed Sun. (except Nov.–May) and 2 weeks in Aug. 🚇 R3 AX, CB, DC, MC, VI

🍴 Don Salvatore $$
You'll find very good cooking using the freshest fish and other ingredients at this traditional restaurant, which also doubles as a pizzeria. Excellent desserts.
✉ Strada Mergellina 4A ☎ 081 681 817 🕐 Closed Wed. 🚇 Mergellina 🚇 R3, C21 AX, CB, DC, MC, VI

KEY TO SYMBOLS

- ⊞ hotel
- ⬛ restaurant
- ✉ address
- ☎ telephone number
- ⊕ days/times closed
- Ⓜ nearest subway station
- 🚍 nearby bus/trolley-bus/tram route(s).
- ⛴ ferry
- AX American Express
- CB Carte Blanche
- DC Diners Club
- MC MasterCard
- VI VISA

Hotels

Price guide: double room with breakfast for two people

- $ up to €103
- $$ €103–€200
- $$$ over €200

Restaurants

Price guide: dinner per person, excluding drinks

- $ up to €25
- $$ €25–€40
- $$$ over €40

HOTEL FACILITIES

Outside resorts, mid-range Italian hotels are essentially places to sleep. Top-quality hotels have everything you'd expect, but smaller ones will not have every amenity. Many hotels have neither restaurant nor bar, and are unlikely to have lounge areas or other public rooms. Some do not offer breakfast. Rooms will be simple and functional, with tiled floors, limited cupboard space and no easy chairs. Satellite TV is increasing in the north, but is generally limited to hotels catering to business travelers. It is quite normal to ask to see the room before you accept it.

⊞ Excelsior $$$
One of Naples' grandest establishments, located in the elegant Chiaia district. The hotel has period-style rooms and superb views over the bay to Capri.
✉ Via Partenope 48 ☎ 081 764 0111; fax 081 764 9743 🚍 R3 AX, CB, DC, MC, VI

⊞ Grand Hotel Parker's $$
Nineteenth-century decor combines with 21st-century comforts at this elegant hotel located west of the center. There are lovely views over the city, and the popular rooftop restaurant serves Neapolitan specialties.
✉ Corso Vittorio Emanuele II 135 ☎ 081 761 2474; fax 081 663 527 🚍 V1 AX, CB, DC, MC, VI

⬛ Mimì alla Ferrovia $$
A typical Naples restaurant, buzzing and chaotic, where you can enjoy delicious dishes using the freshest ingredients. A local favorite.
✉ Via Alfonso d'Aragona 21 ☎ 081 553 8525; fax 081 289 004 ⊕ Closed Sun. and 2 weeks in Aug. 🚍 42, 47, 110 AX, CB, DC, MC, VI

⬛ Taverna dell'Arte $
This characteristic Neapolitan restaurant, with an outside terrace for summer dining, offers traditional dishes made with attention to detail.
✉ Rampe San Giovanni Maggiore 1/A ☎ 081 552 7558 ⊕ Closed lunch, Sun. and 2 weeks in Aug. 🚍 R1, 42, 47 VI

⊞ Villa Capodimonte $$
This lovely hotel opened in 1995. It's near the park surrounding Capodimonte and offers modern comforts, traditional service and style, a warm welcome and peace and quiet.
✉ Via Moiariello 66 ☎ 081 459 000; fax 081 299 344 🚍 R4, 24 AX, CB, DC, MC, VI

POSITANO

⊞ Buca di Bacco $$
This friendly, family-run hotel offers wonderful sea views, comfortable rooms and the bonus of no vehicle access. The hotel will help with your luggage. Excellent restaurant.
✉ Via Rampa Teglia 4 ☎ 089 875 699; fax 089 875 731 ⊕ Closed Nov.–Apr. AX, CB, DC, MC, VI

⬛ Cambusa $$
You can eat right on the main beach on the terrace of this lovely restaurant. The interior decor has a nautical theme.
✉ Piazza A Vespucci 4 ☎ 089 812 051; fax 089 875 432 ⊕ Closed 3 weeks in Jan. and Wed. in winter AX, CB, DC, MC, VI

REGGIO DI CALABRIA

⬛ Baylik $$
This friendly restaurant is near the harbor and offers imaginative seafood dishes.
✉ Vico Leone 1 ☎ 0965 48 624; fax 0965 45 525 ⊕ Closed Thu. and 2 weeks in Aug. AX, CB, DC, MC, VI

⊞ Grand Hotel Excelsior $$
Close to the Museo Nazionale and not far from the ferry port. The rooms offer old-fashioned elegance, modern comforts and good views across the Straits of Messina.
✉ Via Vittorio Veneto 66 ☎ 0965 812 211; fax 0965 893 084 AX, CB, DC, MC, VI

SORRENTO

⬛ Caruso $$$
An elegant, refined and award-winning restaurant with imaginative fish dishes and over 300 wines.
✉ Via Sant'Antonino 12 ☎ 081 807 3156 AX, CB, DC, MC, VI

⊞ Grand H. Excelsior Vittoria $$$
An elegant Edwardian hotel at a fine location, with modern comforts. An elevator in the garden takes guests to the beach and harbor.
✉ Piazza T Tasso 34 ☎ 081 807 1044; fax 081 877 1206 AX, CB, DC, MC, VI

TROPEA

⬛ Pimm's $
This friendly, good-value restaurant overlooking the sea serves Calabrian dishes and fish grills.
✉ Largo Migliarese 2 ☎ 0963 666 105 ⊕ Closed Mon. (except Jul.–Aug.) and 3 weeks in Jan. DC, MC, VI

⊞ Rocca Nettuno $$
Many rooms in this big hotel are individual bungalows offering perfect privacy. There's an elevator down to the beach.

✉ Via Annunziata ☎ 0963 998 111; fax 0963 603 513 🕐 Closed Nov.–May AX, CB, DC, MC, VI

VIESTE

🍴 A Dragone $$
Set in a natural cave, this friendly restaurant is in the heart of the old town. Excellent wine list and fish dishes of all sorts.
✉ Via Duomo 8 ☎ 0884 701 212 🕐 Closed Oct. to mid-Apr. and Tue. from mid-Apr. through May AX, CB, DC, MC, VI

🏨 Seggio $$
A friendly family-run hotel in the heart of the old center, with an excellent restaurant, pool, terrace and steps down to a private beach.
✉ Via Veste 7 ☎ 0884 708 123; fax 0884 708 727 🕐 Closed Nov.–Apr. AX, CB, DC, MC, VI

Sicily

AGRIGENTO

🍴 Baglio della Luna $$
This restaurant is located in a hotel converted from a lookout tower. Set in lovely gardens, it overlooks the Valley of the Temples. Regional cuisine utilizes fresh ingredients and traditional recipes.
✉ Contra Maddalusa ☎ 0922 511 061 🕐 Closed Mon. lunch AX, DC, MC, VI

🏨 Jolly Hotel della Valle $$
This modern hotel overlooks the archeological zone but is close to the city center. It has comfortable rooms and a swimming pool.
✉ Via Ugo La Malfa 3 ☎ 0922 26 966; fax 0922 26 412 AX, CB, DC, MC, VI

CEFALU

🏨 Kalura $$
This clifftop hotel has comfortable rooms overlooking lovely gardens. There are steps running down to the hotel's private beach.
✉ Via V Cavallaro 13 ☎ 0921 421 354; fax 0921 423 122 AX, CB, DC, MC, VI

🍴 Ostaria del Duomo $$
You can eat outside in the piazza overlooking the cathedral at this restaurant, which specializes in Sicilian dishes. Good wine list.
✉ Via Seminario 5 ☎ 0921 421 838 🕐 Closed Mon. (except Jun.–Sep.) and mid-Nov. to mid-Feb. AX, CB, DC, MC, VI

ENNA

🏨 Albergo Sicilia $$
Enna's only hotel stands in the heart of the historic center. The interior belies its somewhat soulless appearance, with comfortable bedrooms and good reception and lounge areas. Friendly staff.
✉ Piazza Colaianni 7 ☎ 0935 500 850 AX, CB, DC, MC, VI

🍴 Centrale $$
This family-run restaurant in the old town serves Sicilian specialties. Try the buffet-style vegetable *antipasto*.
✉ Piazza VI Dicembre 9 ☎ 0935 500 963 🕐 Closed Sat. (except Jun.–Sep.) AX, CB, DC, MC, VI

ERICE

🏨 Moderno $$
Located on one of Érice's prettiest streets, this cozy hotel, housed in an 18th-century building, has an excellent restaurant and attractive terrace.
✉ Via Vittorio Emanuele II 63 ☎ 0923 869 300; fax 0923 869 139 AX, CB, DC, MC, VI

🍴 Monte San Giuliano $$
The garden terrace provides a lovely setting for this typically Sicilian restaurant with a wide range of traditional dishes on the menu. Reservations required.
✉ Vicolo San Rocco 7 ☎ 0923 869 595 🕐 Closed Mon., Jan. 7–25 and Nov. 5–23 AX, CB, DC, MC, VI

PALERMO

🍴 'A Cuccagna $
In the heart of the city, this friendly trattoria, with its cozy ambience, offers classic Sicilian cooking.
✉ Via Principe Granatelli 21/A ☎ 091 587 267 🕐 Closed 2 weeks in Aug. AX, CB, DC, MC, VI

🏨 Excelsior Palace $$$
A top-quality hotel with gracious and spacious surroundings and period furnishings, located within easy reach of Palermo's most popular sights.
✉ Via Marchese Ugo 3 ☎ 091 625 6176; fax 091 342 139 AX, DC, MC, VI

🍴 Friend's Bar $$
You'll find creative Sicilian cooking and excellent fish dishes served at this pretty restaurant with an outdoor seating area for summer dining.
✉ Via Brunelleschi 138 ☎ 091 201 401; fax 091 201 066 🕐 Closed Mon. and 2 weeks in Aug. AX, DC, VI

🏨 Jolly Hotel $$
Standing in the Villa Giulia gardens, this comfortable hotel has high standards of service. The rooms are everything you'd expect from this reputable nationwide chain. Pool.
✉ Foro Italico 22 ☎ 091 616 5090; fax 091 616 1441 AX, CB, DC, MC, VI

🏨 Letizia $$
A friendly welcome awaits at this comfortable hotel located in the heart of the artistic district. The rooms are tastefully furnished with added personal touches from the owners. A great place to stay if you want to be near the city's cultural attractions.
✉ Via Bottai 30 ☎ 091 589 110 AX, DC, MC, VI

🍴 Regine $$
The wonderful display of fish at the entrance gives an idea of the delights that lie in store at this friendly establishment.
✉ Via Trapani 4/a ☎ 091 586 566 🕐 Closed Sun. and Aug. AX, CB, DC, MC, VI

🏨 San Paolo Palace $$
This modern seafront hotel is an ideal choice to escape city noise and confusion. An elevator takes you to the rooftop pool and restaurant.
✉ Via Messina Marine 91 ☎ 091 621 1112; fax 091 621 5300 AX, DC, VI

🍴 Santandrea $
Ingredients at this popular restaurant come from the nearby Vucceria market. There's no menu, but you can't go wrong from the list the server gives you.
✉ Piazza S. Andrea 4 ☎ 091 334 999 🕐 Closed Tue., Sun. in Jul. and Aug., and 2 weeks in Jan. AX, CB, DC, MC, VI

Sardinia

KEY TO SYMBOLS

🏨 hotel
🍴 restaurant
✉ address
☎ telephone number
🕐 days/times closed
Ⓜ nearest subway station
🚌 nearby bus/trolley-bus/tram route(s).
⛴ ferry
AX   American Express
CB   Carte Blanche
DC   Diners Club
MC   MasterCard
VI   VISA

Hotels

Price guide: double room with breakfast for two people

$ up to €103
$$ €103–€200
$$$ over €200

Restaurants

Price guide: dinner per person, excluding drinks

$ up to €25
$$ €25–€40
$$$ over €40

TYPES OF RESTAURANTS

There are many different types of restaurants in Italy, the distinctions between them subtle. A *trattoria, osteria* and *ristorante* are pretty similar in terms of price, atmosphere and cuisine, although originally *ristorante* were far smarter than the homely *trattorie*. Less expensive choices might be a *pizzeria* (which often serves simple pasta and meat dishes as well as pizza) or a *birreria*. Other options include a *tavola calda* (hot table), a type of lunch bar, or a *rosticceria*, which is similar but also offers food to go.

🏨 **Villa Igiea Grand Hotel $$$**
This hotel has an old-fashioned atmosphere and high standards of comfort and service. It stands in a beautiful seafront garden with tennis courts and swimming pool. Considered among Sicily's top hotels.
✉ Salita Belmonte 43   ☎ 091 543 744; fax 091 547 654   AX, DC, MC, VI

SELINUNTE

🏨 **Alceste $$**
This modern hotel is an ideal choice if you want to stay near the classical site; cool, airy rooms and a pretty terrace overlooking the sea.
✉ Via Alceste 21   ☎ 0924 46 184; fax 0924 46 143   🕐 Closed mid-Jan. to mid-Feb. and mid-Nov. to mid-Dec.   AX, CB, DC, MC, VI

🍴 **Pierrot $$**
This Mediterranean-style restaurant has wonderful views of the sea and temples, which you can enjoy while sampling freshly caught seafood.
✉ Via Marco Polo 108   ☎ 0924 46 205   🕐 Closed Tue. in winter and Jan. 6–Mar. 31   AX, CB, DC, MC, VI

SIRACUSA

🏨 **Grand Hotel $$$**
This luxurious old hotel, on Ortigia in the heart of the old city, has been renovated to include contemporary design. Lovely sea views, excellent service and a rooftop restaurant.
✉ Viale Mazzini 12   ☎ 0931 464 600; fax 0931 464 611   AX, CB, DC, MC, VI

🍴 **Minosse $**
A popular restaurant in classic surroundings; known for its pasta with prawns and sweet cherry tomatoes. Fast service.
✉ Via Mirabella 6   ☎ 0931 66 366   🕐 Closed Mon.   AX, DC, MC, VI

TAORMINA

🍴 **Il Baccanale $**
Dine on typical Italian fare outside in the square or indoors in a simple atmosphere with rustic charm.
✉ Piazzetta Filea 1   ☎ 0942 625 390   MC, VI

🏨 **San Domenico Palace $$$**
A 15th-century convent houses Taormina's most luxurious hotel. Its elegant rooms, impeccable facilities and superb service perfectly complement the stunning views.
✉ Piazza S. Domenico 5   ☎ 0942 23 701; fax 0942 625 506   AX, CB, DC, MC, VI

🏨 **Villa Belvedere $$**
There are lovely views of Etna and the sea from this pretty hotel set amid palm and olive trees. Traditional furnishings and a poolside restaurant add to its charm.
✉ Via Bagnoli Croci 79, Messina 98039   ☎ 0942 23 791; fax 0942 625 830   🕐 Closed late Nov. to Dec. 20 and Jan. 10–Mar.10   AX, CB, DC, MC, VI

Sardinia

CAGLIARI

🍴 **Dal Corsaro $$**
This restaurant is a real institution in Cágliari and offers Sardinian dishes, with an emphasis on fish, welcoming surroundings and an excellent wine list.
✉ Viale Regina Margherita 28   ☎ 070 664 318; fax 070 653 439   🕐 Closed Sun., 2 weeks in Aug. and Dec. 23–Jan. 6   AX CB, DC, MC, VI

🏨 **Sardegna $$**
A quiet and comfortable hotel with good facilities and a restaurant.
✉ Via Lunigiana 50   ☎ 070 286 245; fax 070 290 469   AX, CB, DC, MC, VI

COSTA SMERALDA

🍴 **Gianni Pedrinelli $$$**
This is a popular seafood restaurant so it is best to reserve in advance. Pleasant terrace for summer dining.
✉ Strada provinciale bivio Pevero Sud   ☎ 0789 92 436   🕐 Closed Nov.–Feb. and for lunch from Jun.15–Sep. 15   AX, DC, MC, VI

🏨 **Green Park $$$**
Located in Porto Rotondo, this is one of the best values on the Costa Smeralda. The hotel offers good service and high levels of comfort, and there are lovely sea views from the terraces.
✉ Località Aldia Manna, Porto Rotondo 07020   ☎ 0789 380 100; fax 0789 380 043   🕐 Closed Nov.–May   CB, MC, VI

ESSENTIAL INFORMATION

"P LANNING advice and practical travel tips "

The information in this guide has been compiled for U.S. citizens traveling as tourists.

Travelers who are not U.S. citizens, or who are traveling on business, should check with their embassies and tourist offices for information on the countries they wish to visit.

Entry requirements are subject to change at short notice, and travelers are advised to check the current situation before they travel.

Italy – Essential Information

ESSENTIAL FOR TRAVELERS

	● Required	● Recommended	○ Not required
Passport			●
Visa			○
Travel, medical insurance		●	
Round-trip or onward airline ticket		●	
Local currency		●	
Traveler's checks		●	
Credit cards		●	
First-aid kit and medicines		●	
Health inoculations	○		

ESSENTIAL FOR DRIVERS

	● Required	● Recommended	○ Not required
Driver's license	●		
International Driving Permit	●		
Car insurance (for private cars)	●		
Car registration (for private cars)	●		

*see also DRIVING section

BEFORE YOU GO
PASSPORTS
Passport application forms can be obtained by contacting any federal or state court or post office authorized to accept passport applications. U.S. passport agencies have offices in most major cities. You can also request an application form by calling the National Passport Information Center at 1-877-487-2778). Comprehensive passport information and application forms are available on the U.S. State Department internet site at www.travel.state.gov.

Apply for your passport in good time as processing can take several months from the time of application until it arrives. Rush service is available for an extra charge. Before departure, make sure your passport is valid for at least six months after you are due to travel: some European countries require this.

You may be required to leave your passport with the hotel when you check in; this is to satisfy regulations requiring the hotel to register all foreign visitors with local police authorities. Also, you must show your passport whenever you cash a traveler's check. Passports need to be shown whenever national borders are crossed, although in practice border controls have been relaxed between many European Union (E.U.) member countries.

In addition to a passport, some countries require a visa. Travel visas are not necessary to visit Italy, but if you'll be traveling to other nations, check their entry requirements before you leave home.

WHEN TO GO
Despite its basically mild winters and warm summers, Italy has a varied and extreme climate. In winter, Venice, Turin and Milan can be quite chilly, and you can ski in parts of the country in September. The best months for sightseeing are April, May, June, September and October, although rain and cold linger in northern and mountain areas throughout spring and autumn. July and August are the hottest months everywhere. Winters can be severe, particularly in the Alps and fogbound plains of Lombardy and Emilia-Romagna. European school vacations are another factor in planning when to schedule your trip. Schools in Italy are normally in session from September until early July This makes May and June good months to visit, both from a weather standpoint and the fact that there are likely to be fewer crowds at major attractions.

TRAVEL INSURANCE
Before departing, make sure you are covered by insurance that will reimburse travel expenses if you need to cancel or cut short your trip due to unforeseen circumstances. You'll also need coverage for property loss or theft, emergency health or dental treatment, and emergency evacuation if necessary. Before taking out additional insurance, check to see if your current homeowners or medical coverage already covers you for travel abroad. If you make a claim, your insurance company will need proof of the incident or expenditure. Keep copies of any police report and related documents, or medical bills or statements, to submit with your insurance claim.

IMPORTANT ADDRESSES
Italian Government Tourist Office
630 Fifth Avenue
Suite 1565 Rockefeller Center
New York, NY 10111
☎ (212) 245-4822 or (212) 245–5618
Fax (212) 586-9249; www.italiantourism.com

Italian State Tourist Board
Via Marghera 2
00185 Rome, Italy
☎ 06 49711
Fax 06 446 3379; www.enit.it

American Embassy
Via Vittorio Veneto 119a
00187 Rome, Italy
☎ 06 4674 2382 or 06 46741
Fax 06 488 2672; www.usembassy.it
Open Mon.– Fri. 8:30–1 and 2–5:30

TIME ZONES

ROME 12:00 noon | **NEW YORK** 6 hours behind Italy | **CHICAGO** 7 hours behind Italy | **DENVER** 8 hours behind Italy | **SAN FRANCISCO** 9 hours behind Italy

215

CUSTOMS

YES

Goods brought into Italy from non-European Union countries limited to: 200 cigarettes or 100 cigarillos or 50 cigars or 250 g. tobacco; 2 L. wine; 1 L. alcohol over 22% volume; 2 L. alcohol under 22% volume; 60 ml. perfume; 250 ml. toilet water; plus any other duty-free goods (including gifts) to the value of €15 ($13). There is no limit on the importation of tax-paid goods purchased within the European Union, provided they are for personal use. There are no currency regulations. Returning to the United States, you will be required to complete a customs declaration. You are allowed $400 worth of personal goods; keep sales slips and have them ready for inspection.

NO

No unlicensed drugs, weapons, ammunition, obscene material, pets or other animals, counterfeit money or copied goods, meat or poultry.

MONEY

Italy's currency is the euro (€), a currency shared by most other European Union countries. The euro is divided into 100 cents (¢). The denominations of euro bills are 5, 10, 20, 50, 100, 200 and 500. There are coins of 1, 2, 5, 10, 20 and 50¢ and €1 and €2. Exchange dollars or traveler's checks *(assegni touristici)* at a bank *(banca)* or exchange office *(ufficio di cambio)*. Hotels may exchange traveler's checks, but stores do not. ATMs *(sportello automatico)* are fairly common and accept major credit cards.
Exchange rate at press time: $1 = €0.82

TIPS AND GRATUITIES

Restaurants (where service is not included)	10%–15%
Cafés/bars	20¢
Taxis	15%
Porters	€1
Chambermaids	€2 weekly
Restrooms	10¢ minimum
Cloakroom attendants	50¢

COMMUNICATIONS

POST OFFICES

Buy stamps *(francobolli)* at a post office *(ufficio postale)* or at a tobacconist *(tabaccaio)*. Mailboxes often have two

slots, one for local mail *(città)*, the other for out-of-town mail *(altre destinazione)*. *Posta priorità* is a more expensive post service; or send mail *(espresso)* in the blue boxes or registered *(raccomandata)* .

TELEPHONES

Pay phones are usually found in bars and other public places. Prepaid cards *(schede telefoniche)* for card-operated phones are available from tobacconists, bars, post offices, newsstands, railroad stations and

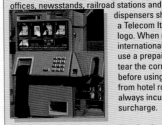

dispensers showing a Telecom Italia (TI) logo. When making international calls use a prepaid card; tear the corner off before using it. Calls from hotel rooms always incur a surcharge.

Phoning inside Italy
All telephone numbers in Italy include an area code that must always be dialed. To call the operator dial 10.

Phoning Italy from abroad
The country code for Italy is 39. Note that Italian numbers in this book do not include the country code; you will need to prefix this number if you are phoning from another country. To call Italy from the United States or Canada dial the prefix 011 39. Include the first zero of the regional code. There is no standard number of digits in Italian numbers. Example: 01 122 3344 becomes 011 39 01 122 3344

Phoning from Italy
To phone the United States or Canada from Italy, prefix the area code and number with 001. Example: (111) 222–3333 becomes 001 111 222–3333.
To call international information dial 170.

EMERGENCY NUMBERS

Police *(policia)* 113 (local), 112 (national)
Fire service *(pompieri)* 115
Ambulance *(ambulanza)* 118
Emergency calls are free from phone booths.

Italy – Essential Information

HOURS OF OPERATION

- Stores Mon.–Sat.
- Museums/monuments
- Offices Mon.–Fri.
- Architectural sites
- Banks Mon.–Fri.
- Churches/pharmacies
- Post offices Mon.–Fri.

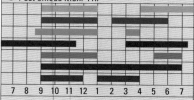

7   8   9   10   11   12   1   2   3   4   5   6   7

Department stores, some grocery stores and stores in tourist areas may not close at lunchtime, and sometimes stay open until later in the evening. Some stores close on Monday morning and may close on Saturday afternoon in summer; most stores close on Sunday.

Some banks close at 2 and do not reopen later in the afternoon.

Many museums are open into the early evening (usually 5–7); others are open all day, and a few stay open late into the evening. Many museums close early on Sunday (around 1), and most are closed Monday.

Post office times may vary slightly, and they may be open Sat. 8:30–noon.

NATIONAL HOLIDAYS

Banks, businesses, and most stores and museums close on these days. Most cities, towns and villages celebrate their patron saint's day, but generally most establishments remain open.

Jan. 1	**New Year's Day**
Jan. 6	**Epiphany**
Mar./Apr.	**Easter Monday**
Apr. 25	**Liberation Day 1945**
May 1	**Labor Day**
Aug. 15	**Assumption of the Virgin**
Nov. 1	**All Saints' Day**
Dec. 8	**Immaculate Conception**
Dec. 25	**Christmas Day**
Dec. 26	**St. Stephen's Day**

RESTROOMS

Finding a restroom *(gabinetto/bagno)* can be difficult away from airports, rail and bus stations, highway service areas and museums. Leave a small tip (about 10¢) for the attendant. If using the facilities in a bar you will be expected to buy a drink. Some bars have separate restrooms for men *(signori)* and women *(signore)*.

HEALTH ADVICE

MEDICAL SERVICES
Private medical insurance is strongly recommended. Visitors from non-European Union countries can receive treatment in a hospital accident and emergency room, but you will be charged if you are admitted to a bed. A general practitioner *(medico)* can deal with less urgent cases, but also will charge.

DENTAL SERVICES
Emergency dental treatment is available from English-speaking dentists listed in the Yellow Pages *(pagine gialle)*. A fee will be charged, so check that you are covered for treatment on your private medical insurance.

SUN ADVICE
In summer, particularly in July and August, it can be oppressively hot and humid in cities. On sunny days cover your head as well as your shoulders and use a sunscreen. Cathedrals and other stone buildings can be refreshingly cool. Take frequent breaks in the shade and drink plenty of fluids.

DRUGS
A pharmacy *(farmacia)* displays a green cross symbol and has staff who can provide prescription medicines and offer advice on minor ailments. Information about the address of the nearest 24-hour facility is normally posted at every pharmacy.

SAFE WATER
In isolated rural areas it is not advisable to drink tap water. However, across most of the country tap water is perfectly safe, although most Italians prefer to drink bottled mineral water *(acqua minerale)*, which is inexpensive and widely available.

PERSONAL SAFETY

Keep valuables (passport, money, checks, credit cards) hidden when you're on the move, and hold bags and cameras across your front – never hung over one shoulder, where they can be easily grabbed. Put money in different places so if one bag is lost you have another source of funds. Tourist attractions and public transportation are prime territory for pickpockets. Avoid lingering

alone after dark, particularly in parks or around railway stations. Contact a police officer if anyone becomes aggressive; police on city streets throughout Italy are usually very approachable and often speak English.

NATIONAL TRANSPORTATION

AIR (aeroplano)
Alitalia and several smaller national carriers, notably Meridiana, offer frequent service between cities and islands. Fares are high, and you will often find it cheaper and more convenient to travel by rail. Students and passengers between 12 and 25 qualify for 25 percent discounts on certain Alitalia flights, and there are 30 percent reductions available on some night flights, as well as 50 percent savings for family groups.

TRAIN (treno)
Italian State Railways, known as Trenitalia, but often referred by its old name, Ferrovie dello Stato, or FS, provides an efficient range of services. Regionale, Diretto and Espresso trains are slow for long journeys; InterCity trains, which do not make stops at each station (stazione), cost more but are faster; the Eurostar is the fastest and most expensive. One-way (andata) or round-trip (andata e ritorno) tickets (biglietti) are available in first (prima) or second (seconda) class. Fares, calculated on a kilometer basis, are some of the cheapest in Europe. Three-day, round-trip tickets are discounted 15 percent on distances up to 250 km (50 km for a 1-day, round-trip ticket). Tickets are valid for 1 day from the day of issue for distances up to 250 km, plus an extra day of validity for each additional 200 km up to a maximum of 6 days. The validity period takes effect from the moment you punch your ticket on the platform machines. Tickets must be used within 2 months of purchase. Stations usually have separate ticket windows for reservations and sleepers (cucetta). Reservations are worth considering for long journeys in summer, when trains can be crowded. The Italy Railcard is a travel-at-will card available for 8-, 15-, 21- and 30-day periods (both first and second class). If you intend to use trains regularly buy the Pozzorario, a biannual timetable that is available in bookstores and at station kiosks.

BUS (autobus)
There is no national bus company, but major cities have their own company for short-, medium- and some long-distance bus travel. International Eurolines run from the main Italian cities; ☎ 055 357 110; www.eurolines.com. Ask about services at tourist offices or visit the local bus terminal (autostazione). Tickets must usually be bought beforehand from tabacchi (tobacconists) or the bus terminal.

FERRY (traghetto)
Genoa and Naples are the main Mediterranean ports, with regular service to Sicily and Sardinia. Naples also has a ferry to Capri and other islands. Many services are reduced off-season, and some are cut. Car ferry bookings for summer travel to Sardinia and Elba should be made serveral months in advance.

PHOTOGRAPHY

The regions of Italy are fascinatingly diverse, each with unique geographical traits, its own cultural identity and a strong sense of individualism. With such diversity the possibility of subject matter is almost endless. From fishing ports off the coast and the wine-growing regions of Tuscany to the peaks of the Apennines and sandy beach resorts, you'll find plenty at which to direct your lens at. If you're interested in architecture there will be much to interest you. In the summer months, most regions will have a good amount of sun and 100asa film should suffice. If you intend to take a few interiors and are cautious about the weather, then pack some 200asa. Film (pellicola) and batteries (batteria) can be easily found, and if you're visiting a particular tourist attraction there will normally be a kiosk selling a selection of brands. There are developing and printing facilities in most large towns, but these are generally expensive. Don't be concerned about your film and camera going through security equipment at the airport; it is quite safe for film rated up to 1600asa.

MEDIA

Italy's national newspapers (giornali) include the authoritative Milan-based Corriere della Sera, the Turin-based La Stampa and the Rome-based La Repubblica. The biggest-selling papers are sports papers. In larger cities, American newspapers (usually previous-day editions) and magazines are available; the most common are USA Today, the international edition of the New York Times and Time magazine. They can be purchased at airports and central train stations, as well as at newsstands and tobacconists. Italian radio and television are deregulated and offer a vast range of national and local stations. Standards are low, with local networks geared mainly to advertising, pop music and old films. National stations are better, dividing equally between the three channels of the state RAI network and the those founded by Silvio Berlusconi (Canale 5, Rete 4 and Italia Uno). On the radio you can pick up Voice of America, Radio Canada or BBC broadcasts, and larger hotels often have satellite or cable connections that broadcast BBC channels, the British Sky network or CNN.

ELECTRICITY

Italy has a 220-volt power supply (in some areas, 125 volts). Electrical sockets take plugs with two round pins, or sometimes three pins in a vertical row. American appliances will need a plug adapter and will require a transformer if they do not have a dual-voltage facility.

Italy – Essential Information

DRIVING REGULATIONS

DRIVE ON THE RIGHT
Driving is on the right, and you should yield at intersections to vehicles approaching from your right.

SEAT BELTS
Must be worn in front seats at all times and in the rear seats where fitted.

MINIMUM AGE
The minimum age for driving a car in Italy is 18 (may be higher for some car rental firms).

BLOOD ALCOHOL
The legal blood alcohol limit is 0.08%. Random breath tests are carried out frequently, especially late at night.

TOLLS
You will be issued a ticket on entering nearly every limited-access highway *(autostrada)*; pay on leaving. You can buy prepaid cards at tollbooths, service areas, tourist offices and tobacconists.

ADDITIONAL INFORMATION

An International Driving Permit (IDP) is recommended when driving in Italy. It is a document containing your photograph and confirming that you hold a valid driver's license in your own country. It has a standard translation in several languages and is a useful document to carry; it can speed up formalities if you are involved in an accident.

A Green Card is advised if you are driving a private vehicle overseas to prove that you have liability insurance. For additional information contact your automobile insurer.

Dimmed headlights are required by law when passing through tunnels, even if they are well lit.

SPEED LIMITS

REGULATIONS
Police can demand up to a quarter of an imposed fine to be paid on the spot.

Limited-access highways *(autostrada)*
130 k.p.h. (80 m.p.h.).

Main roads
110 k.p.h. (68 m.p.h.)

Urban areas
50 k.p.h. (31 m.p.h.)

CAR RENTAL

CAR RENTAL
The leading rental firms have offices at airports, railroad stations and ferry terminals. Hertz offers discounted rates for AAA members. For reservations:

	UNITED STATES	ITALY
Avis	(800) 722-5909	02 7541 9761
Budget	(800) 654-3131	(0800) 472-3325
Hertz	(800) 654-3080	(0800) 654-3001

To rent a car you will need a valid U.S. driver's license and preferably an International Driving Permit, and you will probably be asked to show your passport. Depending on which rental company you use, you may be asked for an additional credit card or further proof of identity for renting premium or luxury cars. Most car rental companies will not rent to an individual under 21. If you intend to drive across national borders tell the company, as this will affect both the rate and the type of insurance documentation required.

European cars are generally small, have manual transmissions and rarely offer air-conditioning. Rates vary, but a AAA travel agent should be able to give an accurate estimate. Be sure to inquire about local taxes and find out what insurance coverage is included, and check whether you need a collision damage waiver. AAA Travel Agencies can reserve a car for you before you leave, provide prepayment arrangements, or reserve a car for you for specified dates and destinations. Rates are lower if reservations are made in the United States prior to departure, and guaranteed in U.S. dollars if you prepay.

FUEL

Gas in Italy is among the most expensive in Europe. It is unleaded *(senza piombo)* and sold in liters. Diesel *(gasolio)* is cheaper. Outside urban areas, stations are open daily 7–12:30 and 3–7:30. Gas stations on highways are open 24 hours. Credit cards are not widely accepted away from highways. Self-service and 24-hour pumps are becoming increasingly common.

PARKING

Parking is often difficult in towns: Parking lots *(parcheggi)* are invariably full, and most historic centers are partially or fully closed to traffic. Check the signs in the vicinity of your car: Make certain there are no restrictions, that you pay for and display a parking sticker if necessary, and check closing times if you use a multistory parking garage. Cars may be towed if illegally parked; contact the local offices of the *Vigili Urbani* to reclaim your vehicle.

AAA

AAA AFFILIATED MOTORING CLUB

Automobile Club D'Italia (ACI)
Via Marsala 8, 00185 Rome
☎ 06 49 981 or 06 803 116 (24 hour emegency help line). If you break down while driving, phone 116 or 803000 from a fixed phone (towing service).

Not all automobile clubs offer full services to AAA members.

BREAKDOWNS/ACCIDENTS

There are emergency phones at regular intervals on all highways. If you are involved in an accident, ☎ 118 for emergency medical help, 112 or 113 for police help.

Most car rental firms provide their own free rescue service; if your car is rented, follow the instructions given in the documentation. Use of a car repair service other than those authorized by the rental company may violate your rental agreement.

ROAD SIGNS

Driving in busy Italian cities can be a daunting prospect if you're not used to the signs, driving habits and local regulations. If you are renting a car, be sure to get as much information from the rental company as possible. They will usually provide a chart of common road signs and an area road map. Most road signs in Italy conform to the usual international standards; below is a glossary of terms which may not be familiar to the foreign traveler:

entrada	entrance
incrocio	crossroads
lavori in corso	roadwork ahead
passaggio a livello	level crossing
rallentare	slow down
senso vietato	no entry
sosta vietata	no parking
svolta	curve
uscita	exit

Traffic merges from right

Crossroads

ROAD SIGNS (continued)

Other danger

Steep hill downwards

No passing

No entry for vehicular traffic

Divided highway ends

Vehicles may pass on either side to reach same destination

Ahead only

Keep right

Double curve, first to the right

Two-way traffic straight ahead

Italy – Essential Information

SPEECH

Italian pronunciation is consistent with spelling, and vowels are always pronounced. The letter *h* is always silent, but can modify the sound of letters *c* and *g*. As a general rule, accentuate the next-to-last syllable.

c is hard before a, o, u, h	*medico; Chianti*
c is soft before i or e	*ciao* [chow]
g is hard before a, o, u, h	*Gucci, Lamborghini*
g is soft before i or e	*gelati* [jel-ah-tee]
gl as in Amelia	*figlia* [fee-lyah]
gn as in union	*gnocchi* [nyee-ok-kee]
sc before i or e is soft	*prosciutto* [pro-shoot-toh]

Where two consonants appear together, each belongs to a different syllable.

HOTEL

the hotel	*l'albergo*
I have a reservation	*ho prenotato*
a room	*camera*
for one/	*per una/*
two nights	*due notte/-i*
one/	*una/*
two people	*due persone*
how much does it cost?	*quanto costa?*
key	*una chiave*
shower	*una doccia*
with in-room bathroom	*con bagno*
room service	*il servizio in camera*
porter	*il facchino*

AIRPORT

airport	*aeroporto*
airplane	*aeroplana*
arrivals	*arrivi*
departures	*partenze*
check-in	*accettazione*
information	*informazione*
ticket	*biglietto*
flight	*volo*
baggage	*bagagli*
passport	*passaporto*
window seat	*vicino al finestrino*
first class	*prima classe*
economy class	*classe turistica*
international	*internazionale*

MEETING PEOPLE

good morning	*buon giorno*
excuse me	*scusi*
do you speak English?	*parla inglese?*
yes, no	*si/no*
sorry	*scusami*
please	*per favore*
thank you	*grazie*
your welcome	*prego*
I am American	*sono Americano/-a*
what is your name	*come si chiama*
my name is...	*mi chiamo...*
I don't understand	*non capisco*
pleased to meet you	*piacere di conoscerLa*
how are you?	*com'è va*
okay	*va bene*
goodbye	*arrivederci*
goodnight	*buona notte*
see you later	*a presto*
have a good trip	*buon viaggio*

EATING OUT

a table for two	*un tavolo per due*
we've reserved	*abbiamo prenotato*
could we see the menu?	*ci porta il menù*
fixed-price menu	*il menù a prezzo fisso*
first course	*l'antipasto*
main course	*il secondo*
cheese	*formaggio*
dessert	*i dolce*
waiter/ waitress	*cameriere/ cameriera*
wine	*il vino*
mineral water	*acqua minerale*
what's this? (on menu)	*cosa è questo*
I am a vegetarian	*sono vegetariano/a*
bread	*il pane*
beef	*il manzo*
chicken	*il pollo*
ham	*prosciutto*
lamb	*l'agnello*
pork	*il maiale*
seafood	*i frutti di mare*
mussels	*le cozze*
fish	*il pesce*
eggs	*uove*
salad	*insalata*
vegetables	*verdure*
soup	*minestra*
liqueur	*digestivo*
coffee	*il caffè*
hot	*caldo*
cold	*freddo*
good	*buono*
bad	*non è buono*
restroom	*bagno/toiletta*
the check	*il conto*
cover charge	*coperto*

DIRECTIONS

where is...?	dov'è
turn left/right	a sinistra/destra
straight ahead	sempre diritto
how far is it?	quanto è distante?
near here	qui vicino
far	lontano
facing	di fronte a
opposite/ in front of	davanti a
behind	(in) dietro

POST OFFICE

post office	l'ufficio postale
stamp	francobollo
airmail	posta aerea
letter	léttera
postcard	cartolina
package	pacchetto
registered letter	léttera raccomandata
mailbox	bucca delle lettere
address	indirizzo

TELEPHONE CALLS

phone booth	telefono pubblico
phone card	scheda telefonica
operator	il/la centralinista
international access code	il prefisso internazionale
my number is...	il mio numero...

SHOPPING

baker	panificio
delicatessen	salumeria
fish merchant	pescheria
market	mercato
grocery store	supermercato
bookstore	la libreria
fruit and vegetable	frutta e verdura
butcher	macelleria
do you have?	avete?
how much?	quanto costa
store assistant	commessa/o

PHARMACY

pharmacy	la farmacia
diarrhea tablets	astringente
bandage	fascia
tampons	i tamponi
razor blades	le lamette
suntan lotion	olio solare
aspirin	aspirina

EMERGENCIES

police	la polizia
ambulance	un' ambulanza
fire department	i pompieri
doctor	un medico
accident	incidente (m)
first aid	pronto soccorso
where is the nearest hospital?	dov'è l'ospedale più vicino?
emergency number	numero d'emergenza
stop thief!	al ladro!
help!	aiuto!

TRANSPORTATION

railroad station	stazione
subway	metropolitana
train	treno
platform	binario
ticket	biglietto
single or two-way	andata o andata e itorno
bus station	la stazione degli autobus
bus	autobus(m)
bus stop	fermata dell' autobus
timetable	orario
non-smoking	vietato fumare
taxi	il taxi

MONEY

credit card	carta di credito
traveler's checks	un traveller cheque
exchange rate	il cambio
bank	banca

NUMBERS

18

1, 2, 3	uno, due, tre
4, 5, 6	quattro, cinque, sei
7, 8, 9	sette, otto, nove
10, 11, 12	dieci, undici, dodici
13, 14	tredici, quattordici
15, 16	quindici, sedici
17, 18	diciassette, diciotto
19, 20	diciannove, venti
30, 40	trenta, quaranta
50, 60	cinquanta, sessanta
70, 80	settanta, ottanta
90, 100	novanta, cento
500	cinquecento
1000	mille
2000	duemila
10,000	diecimila

Index

Acknowledgments

The Automobile Association would like to thank the following photographers and libraries for their assistance in the preparation of this title.

JAMES DAVIS TRAVEL PHOTOGRAPHY 75, 157, 192; EYE UBIQUITOUS 42, 43; HULTON GETTY PICTURE COLLECTION 96/97, INTERNATIONAL PHOTOBANK 67, 179; 97; PICTURES COLOUR LIBRARY 52, 73, 82; REX FEATURES 117; SPECTRUM COLOUR LIBRARY 44, 47, 53a, 144, 154, 162, 167, 182, 184, 191; TOPHAM PICTUREPOINT 189a, 189b; WORLD PICTURES 53b, 72b 74, 76, 77, 78, 81, 148/149, 156; www.euro.ecb.int/ (euro notes) 215.

The remaining photographs are held in the Association's own library (AA PHOTOLIBRARY) and were taken by Clive Sawyer with the exception of the following:

AA Photolibrary 196; Pete Bennett 20, 48; Eric Meacher 54, 55; Jim Holmes 128, 132a, 134, 135, 215a; Max Jourdan 153, 155a, 155b; Dario Miterdiri 3, 9; Ken Paterson 10a, 14/15, 16/17, 18/19, 31, 84, 86, 89, 93, 98, 102/103, 103, 104, 106, 107, 112, 113, 114, 115, 116, 139, 141b; Barrie Smith 215b; Anthony Souter 13, 26, 51, 60/61, 100, 132b, 140, 141aa, 142, 159b, 166; Peter Wilson 118, 121